PENSHURST

Penshurst Place

TONBRIDGE KENT

the home of Lord De L'Isle VC KG

PENSHURST

The Semiotics of Place and the Poetics of History

Don E. Wayne

The University of Wisconsin Press

Published in 1984 in the United States of America by

The University of Wisconsin Press
114 North Murray Street
Madison, Wisconsin 53715

Published in Great Britain by
Methuen & Co., Ltd

First printing

Printed in the United States of America

For LC CIP information see the colophon

ISNB 0-299-09770-6

Publication of this book was made possible in part by a grant from
the University of California, San Diego.

Frontispiece: *Cover of the current guidebook, showing the north porch of the Great Hall and the perspective of arches from the main entrance to the King's Tower. Reproduced by permission of Viscount De L'Isle, V.C., K.G.*

For my father
Bill Wayne

and for Carla, David, and Benjamin

CONTENTS

ILLUSTRATIONS

PREFACE

IT IS a truism in the criticism of the arts that form and content are inseparable from one another. But to comprehend the relation between what these terms stand for in a given instance is a long and arduous process, especially if one tries to conceive the relationship in terms of a dialectic of social, psychological, and historical factors. In many respects, the present study has itself been a search for form, for a vehicle of expression that would help me and, I hope, my reader to a fuller comprehension of the relationship between form and content in cultural artifacts like those examined here. If this search has been at all productive, much of the credit belongs to the teachers, colleagues, students, and friends who assisted me along the way. My earliest thoughts regarding comparative study of the arts were stimulated by long discussions with Don Aanavi and Carla Wayne. Elizabeth Sewell taught me to think seriously about poetic language as a mode of cognition. Robert C. Elliott presided over the birth of this project and was a demanding, yet generous, reader of the manuscript in its early stage. Fredric Jameson and Louis Marin read and commented on early drafts, and provided me with the theoretical foundation of my work. Aaron Cicourel helped me, in conversation and in seminars we taught together, to work through some of the problems of method. Michel de Certeau and Roy Harvey Pearce offered criticism, advice, and encouragement that sustained me through the most difficult periods. Victor Laruccia has shared in this study from the beginning and has helped me to close many gaps in the argument. In the early stages of research and writing, I benefited from discussions with Carol Becker, Richard Coe, Sandra Drake, Michael Oborne, Saul Steier, and Frank Whigham; more recently, I have profited from comments on the manuscript in conversations with Michael Davidson, Page du Bois, Susan Kirkpatrick, Louis Montrose, William Tay, Richard Terdiman, and Donald Wesling. I thank my students for being unrelenting in challenging me to clarify and to justify many points that were presented in the classroom prior to being argued here. I am especially grateful to those, some of whom remain anonymous, who provided detailed commentary on the manuscript at various stages and whose engaged, sympathetic, yet critical reading improved my judgment and made revision a process of further exploration and discovery: they include Jonas Barish, Harry Berger, Jr., Stephen Greenblatt, Annabel M. Patterson, and Andrew Wright. The errors and inadequacies that remain are, of course, my own.

A portion of Chapter 6 has appeared previously under the title "Mediation and Contestation: English Classicism from Sidney to Jonson," *Criticism* 25 (Copyright © 1983 by Wayne State University Press); my thanks to the editor, Leonard Tennenhouse, for permission to reprint this material in modified form here. Permission to reproduce the illustrations is acknowledged in the legends accompanying the plates. I am particularly obliged to the Viscount De L'Isle for his kindness in providing me with an excellent transparency of the painting at Penshurst of Barbara Gamage and her children.

The research and publication of this book was facilitated by grants from the University of California, San Diego. For their generous support I thank the Academic Senate Committee on Research and the Dean of Graduate Studies, Richard Attiyeh. Part of my early research was accomplished with the aid of a summer fellowship from the William Andrews Clark Memorial Library. I am glad to express my appreciation to the able and patient staffs of the libraries of the University of California, the Clark Library, the Henry E. Huntington Library, and, in England, the British Library, the Kent County Archive, and the National Monuments Record. I am grateful to the Viscount De L'Isle's staff at Penshurst Place for their helpful replies to my queries. Thanks are also due to those who assisted me with the preparation of the manuscript: to Teri Lamothe, an intelligent and impeccable typist; to Geoffrey Walton and David Wayne, who helped with the proofreading and with the illustrations; and to Susan Tarcov, who made a number of invaluable suggestions while taking the book through the editorial stage. I owe a special word of thanks to Allen Fitchen, Director of the University of Wisconsin Press, for his commitment to the project.

My most deeply felt acknowledgment is made in the dedication, to those with whom I have learned to think both critically and affirmatively about the family and the home.

To Penshurst

Thou art not, PENSHURST, built to envious show,
Of touch, or marble; nor canst boast a row
Of polish'd pillars, or a roofe of gold:
Thou hast no lantherne, whereof tales are told;
Or stayre, or courts; but stand'st an ancient pile,
And these grudg'd at, art reverenc'd the while.
Thou joy'st in better markes, of soyle, of ayre,
Of wood, of water: therein thou art faire.
Thou hast thy walkes for health, as well as sport:
Thy Mount, to which the Dryads doe resort,
Where PAN, and BACCHUS their high feasts have made,
Beneath the broad beech, and the chest-nut shade;
That taller tree, which of a nut was set,
At his great birth, where all the Muses met.
There, in the writhed barke, are cut the names
Of many a SYLVANE, taken with his flames.
And thence, the ruddy Satyres oft provoke
The lighter Faunes, to reach thy Ladies oke.
Thy copp's, too, nam'd of GAMAGE, thou hast there,
That never failes to serve thee season'd deere,
When thou would'st feast, or exercise thy friends.
The lower land, that to the river bends,
Thy sheepe, thy bullocks, kine, and calves doe feed:
The middle grounds thy mares, and horses breed.
Each banke doth yeeld thee coneyes; and the topps
Fertile of wood, ASHORE, and SYDNEY's copp's,
To crowne thy open table, doth provide
The purpled pheasant, with the speckled side:
The painted partrich lyes in every field,
And, for thy messe, is willing to be kill'd.
And if the high-swolne Medway faile thy dish,
Thou hast thy ponds, that pay thee tribute fish,
Fat, aged carps, that runne into thy net.
And pikes, now weary their owne kinde to eat,
As loth, the second draught, or cast to stay,
Officiously, at first, themselves betray.

Bright eeles, that emulate them, and leape on land,
  Before the fisher, or into his hand.
Then hath thy orchard fruit, thy garden flowers,
  Fresh as the ayre, and new as are the houres.
The earely cherry, with the later plum,
  Fig, grape, and quince, each in his time doth come:
The blushing apricot, and woolly peach
  Hang on thy walls, that every child may reach.
And though thy walls be of the countrey stone,
  They'are rear'd with no mans ruine, no mans grone,
There's none, that dwell about them, wish them downe;
  But all come in, the farmer, and the clowne:
And no one empty-handed, to salute
  Thy lord, and lady, though they have no sute.
Some bring a capon, some a rurall cake,
  Some nuts, some apples; some that thinke they make
The better cheeses, bring 'hem; or else send
  By their ripe daughters, whom they would commend
This way to husbands; and whose baskets beare
  An embleme of themselves, in plum, or peare.
But what can this (more then expresse their love)
  Adde to thy free provisions, farre above
The neede of such? whose liberall boord doth flow,
  With all, that hospitalitie doth know!
Where comes no guest, but is allow'd to eate,
  Without his feare, and of thy lords owne meate:
Where the same beere, and bread, and selfe-same wine,
  That is his Lordships, shall be also mine.
And I not faine to sit (as some, this day,
  At great mens tables) and yet dine away.
Here no man tells my cups; nor, standing by,
  A waiter, doth my gluttony envy:
But gives me what I call, and lets me eate,
  He knowes, below, he shall finde plentie of meate,
Thy tables hoord not up for the next day,
  Nor, when I take my lodging, need I pray
For fire, or lights, or livorie: all is there;
  As if thou, then, wert mine, or I raign'd here:
There's nothing I can wish, for which I stay.
  That found King JAMES, when hunting late, this way,
With his brave sonne, the Prince, they saw thy fires
  Shine bright on every harth as the desires

Of thy Penates had beene set on flame,
To entertayne them; or the countrey came,
With all their zeale, to warme their welcome here.
What (great, I will not say, but) sodayne cheare
Did'st thou, then, make 'hem! and what praise was heap'd
On thy good lady, then! who, therein, reap'd
The just reward of her high huswifery;
To have her linnen, plate, and all things nigh,
When shee was farre: and not a roome, but drest,
As if it had expected such a guest!
These, PENSHURST, are thy praise, and yet not all.
Thy lady's noble, fruitfull, chaste withall.
His children thy great lord may call his owne:
A fortune, in this age, but rarely knowne.
They are, and have beene taught religion: Thence
Their gentler spirits have suck'd innocence.
Each morne, and even, they are taught to pray,
With the whole houshold, and may, every day,
Reade, in their vertuous parents noble parts,
The mysteries of manners, armes, and arts.
Now, PENSHURST, they that will proportion thee
With other edifices, when they see
Those proud, ambitious heaps, and nothing else,
May say, their lords have built, but thy lord dwells.

PENSHURST

CHAPTER 1

Introduction: Transformations of House and Home

For a man's house is his castle,
et domus sua cuique tutissimum refugium.

—Sir Edward Coke,
Third Institute (1644)

First we shape our buildings,
then they shape us . . .

—Winston Churchill

Pragmatic and Historical Foundations of Culture

THE NAME Penshurst carries a double set of connotations. First, it designates a famous English house, seat of a great English family, the Sidneys, paramount among whom stands the legendary figure of the Elizabethan soldier-poet Sir Philip. But the name also calls to mind a famous English poem which initiated the genre of country-house poetry in the seventeenth century, and its author, another great English poet, Ben Jonson. While these artifacts—the house and the poem—are in entirely different media, and while each amounts to a complete system of representation in its own right, there is a convergence of their respective semantic fields that makes them especially valuable subjects for comparative study.[1] This book is about the relationship between the two sign systems connoted by the name "Penshurst," about the sixteenth- and seventeenth-century contexts—social, moral, intellectual, and psychological—that produced them, about the ideologies that figure symbolically in their respective structures, and about the continuity of certain aspects of these ideologies in our own time.

The book is also about the ambiguities and contradictions that help to characterize such sign systems as works of art. Lévi-Strauss tells us that the resolution of contradictions in a social structure is an apparent effect of myth: "The purpose of myth is to provide a logical model capable of overcoming a contradiction (an impossible achievement if, as it happens, the contradiction is real)."[2] Unless we assume that modern culture, with its emphasis on historical, philosophical, and scientific modes of thought, has dispensed with myth altogether—a highly problematic assumption—we should have no difficulty recognizing the applicability of Lévi-Strauss's assertion to the study of narrative, iconic, and architectural representation in Western art.

At the surface, a work of art in our cultural tradition is an apparent synthesis of diverse and often contradictory elements; traditionally this was understood under the topos of *concordia discors*, and more recently, with regard to poetry, it has been discussed by the New Critics in terms of "tensions," "ambiguity," and "irony." To the extent that we can think of such tensions as embedded "in" the work's structure, they function as constraints on the complex emotive and cognitive activity through which we are guided in reading it.[3] Most twentieth-century formalist theorists have tended to view these constraints as strictly "intrinsic" properties of the work of art. So, for example, while the New Critics insisted on the inseparability of the work's form from its content and its context, their conceptions of content and context were restricted to the linguistic phenomena of the individual work in itself. Their attitude was motivated by an understandable distrust of impressionistic "extrinsic" esthetics of the past. In recent years, however, a growing body of theory and empirical evidence from several disciplines has made it possible to challenge the more restrictive formalist view. If, for example, we apply the Lévi-Straussian conception of myth to the study of our own cultural objects, we can argue that the apparent reconciliation of diverse and discordant elements which we traditionally value in the work of art has a practical social function. It allows us to overcome, psychologically, conflicts and contradictions that our sense of history and, often, our personal experience tell us cannot be overcome in the world as we know it. From this perspective, "tension," "ambiguity," and "irony" in the internal structure of a particular work or of a style are viewed as symptoms of deeper conflicts in culture and society. To look for social and psychological conflicts that may underlie the ensemble of formal relationships constituting the art object does not mean abandoning the esthetic principle of the unity of form and content. On the contrary, it amounts to extending the logic of that principle further by pointing up the fallacy of distinctions between "intrinsic" and "extrinsic" criticism, and by maintaining instead that form is the vehicle of a historical content which is itself both social and psychological in nature.

Given the intensification of change and development in Western societies during the later Middle Ages, a process further accelerated in the Reformation by the dissolution of a unified, authoritative system of knowledge and belief, it is not surprising that secular art should have begun to assume the function of helping to stabilize an existing social construction of reality. At the same time, the very necessity of accommodating an increasing tempo of social and technological change has given to art another function, that of marking actual or potential disjunctions and discontinuities in the order of things as represented by a dominant ideology.[4] The latter function can be understood as a critical activity within the esthetic realm, so long as we recognize that the criticism involved here is often implied rather than stated and is not necessarily attributable to a conscious intention on the part of the artist. It can also be understood as the expression of a utopian desire for alternatives to certain aspects of the existing order, and as the manifestation within the limits of a given cultural and historical frame of the potential form that such alternatives might take.[5]

There has been, I would claim, an overriding tension within Western art since the early modern period between these two sorts of objectives, ideological and utopian. That Renaissance humanists were in some degree aware of such a tension is evident from their abiding concern with the problem of truth in works of fiction, a theme that is handled with supreme irony in Thomas More's *Utopia*, and with dialectical ingenuity in Philip Sidney's *Apology for Poetry*.[6] The psychological consequences of the increasingly ambiguous status of representational codes are dramatized in Shakespeare's *Hamlet*, where the young prince's utterance "I have that within which passes show" sounds a theme that will resonate in tragic, pathetic, or absurd tones through Western literature down to our own time. Hamlet's "that" remains, finally, an absence around which the play's action (or lack of it) is structured and into which succeeding generations have poured their respective conceptions of the human condition. To say this is not to admit to a relativistic notion of literary and historical interpretation; it is only to acknowledge that the play is an allegory and its main character a historically specific archetype by which modern relativism recognizes itself imaginatively and ideologically. *Hamlet* is a constitutive myth of our culture, both in its insistence that authenticity of being lies at the interior of the individual and in the tragic verdict it offers as to the possibility of making that authentic identity known.

Undoubtedly, there are literary antecedents to the crisis of representation that appears in a highly focused form as Hamlet's "problem." My concern here is not to designate an origin, but to identify an ideological conflict, experienced psychologically as a division within the self, which moves into the foreground of European culture at the time of the Reformation and the emergence of modern, capitalist societies. Since that time, esthetic strategies have often been characterized by multiple, even contradictory objectives which resist all unitary modes of interpretation. This is one reason why the type of ideological criticism bent exclusively on "demystification" is as limited in interpretive power as the complacent, idealizing approaches to culture which it repudiates. While the following pages do involve ideological analysis and institutional criticism, I am also concerned with the question of how a cultural artifact can perform an ideological function and yet project changes in the ideology it serves. In the concluding chapter of this study, I have tried to demonstrate that even an art that is overtly ideological in purpose carries with it a potential for change.

The Sidney house at Penshurst and the poem which Ben Jonson addressed to it provide exemplary manifestations of such esthetic and psychological tension grounded in ideological conflict. There is, for example, a general contradiction in the Sidneys' architectural scheme between a mythic and a historical representation of their own relation to the past, between the representation of continuity and the need to rationalize discontinuity. There is the conflict in the poem between the traditional, hierarchical conception of social order based on hereditary rank, and a new doctrine, still hierarchical but founded on a conception of natural order epitomized in the patriarchal family and the home. And there are various forms of a conflict between desire and obligation: in the case of the Sidneys, the wish to be represented as both powerful and just; in the case of Jonson, the obligation to write an encomium to his patron and the desire for a type of recognition that would not depend on such an obligatory function.

Admittedly, any effort to discover and to elucidate the conflicts that may underlie works of this kind is bound to encounter difficulty. This is so not only because information concerning the age and the particular people involved is limited, but because the manner in which historical content is mediated by works of art is so complex. Still, while acknowledging such limitations, we can begin to develop methods for approaching this kind of problem with the eventual aim of constructing a more adequate theory of the origins of modern culture than we now have. With this in mind, I offer some preliminary remarks concerning my approach to the analysis and interpretation of the symbolic orders associated with the name "Penshurst."

Questions of Method

Methodologically, there are two aspects to the present study that may distinguish it from other approaches. First, I have attempted to draw together formal and historical methods of analysis and interpretation into what might be called a *historical semiotics*. Essential to this orientation is the effort to integrate what are ordinarily distinguished as "practical" and "theoretical" modes of criticism. The set of poetic and architectural "texts" is deliberately and necessarily restricted in order to permit an extended, close analysis that would not be possible if an effort were made to survey a style or genre (even so limited a genre as the country–house poem). A number of excellent surveys of this kind already exist, and I have been fortunate in being able to draw on them in connection with the particular works examined here.[7] I am convinced, however, that generalizations about cultural artifacts, especially generalizations about the relationship between changes in style or genre and developments in other cultural and social domains, need to be grounded in the close and sustained analysis of specific representative works.

The second prominent feature of the method I have employed is its comparative nature. Although our ability to comprehend what Jonson's poem and the house at Penshurst meant in the early seventeenth century is extremely limited, comparative study can extend these limits by establishing a larger, more complex, and ultimately more convincing set of coordinates from which to plot the possible contemporary meanings of the works in question. If different modalities of representation and signification addressing themselves to different modes of perception and cognition reveal certain sets of relations in common, these common elements may constitute a pattern of repetition that is meaningful, though not necessarily apparent when the forms are studied separately. (These principles find their most outstanding vindication in Panofsky's classic *Gothic Architecture and Scholasticism* [1951].)[8] In the present study the common ground of comparison is multifaceted. Not only did Jonson compose a poem that reproduces certain aspects of the architectural and topographical scheme at Penshurst. He also makes interesting and revealing use of architectural metaphors in his theoretical pronouncements on writing. And although he is a classicist, whereas the Sidneys' country estate remains essentially medieval in design, the manner in which Jonson employs architecture as a model for composition in the "plain style" suggests something closer to the idea of nature embodied in the "ancient pile" at Penshurst than to the Palladian symmetry introduced in England during Jonson's lifetime.

While comparative study serves to identify common elements, it may also lead us to a more precise and detailed account of the significant differences between the two orders of representation at Penshurst. This, in turn, will enable us to prepare a fuller explanation of each system in its context. Finally, comparative analysis may help us to understand our own relationship to these works by revealing what they share as constituents of that broader cultural and ideological sign system which we are accustomed to call "tradition." For despite the fact that the country house is a dead institution[9] and the country-house poem an archaic literary genre, I believe the "tradition" they helped to establish is, given certain transformations, very much alive. I shall argue that the values and imagery connected with that tradition are still a vital part of the self-image of actual or prospective twentieth-century householders.

The tradition of which I speak has been a remarkably tenacious one in Anglo-American societies. It concerns the significant associations bound up with our images of *house* and *home*, images which we tend to take for granted as the indices of immutable truths or universal conditions but which have, nonetheless, their own history. The effacement of that history over the generations in which these images have become normative within our culture gives them the appearance of being natural rather than cultural phenomena. As such, they have become an important part of what social researchers call the "background expectancies" shared by the members of a society, those spontaneously acknowledged yet unnoticed "sanctioned properties of common discourse" according to which members routinely understand each other and organize their activities.[10] This naturalization of historically and culturally determined ways of seeing, thinking, speaking, and behaving in the world is what I take to be the essence of any ideology.[11]

Concerning Old Buildings

In certain respects architecture provides a more immediate access to ideology and to the social origins of a tradition than literature. Indeed, I have found that, generally speaking, questions concerning ideology are more commonly addressed in the field of architectural history than in literary criticism. This is undoubtedly because the relationship between architectural form and social function is relatively tangible. The representation of order and of power can be more easily overlooked in discussing the poetry of a society than in a consideration of its buildings. But form in architecture is inseparable from the specific social activity (functional or symbolic) which is its purpose. Paul Frankl, an important architectural historian and theorist earlier in this century, described architectural monuments as "molded theaters of human activity." Activity and purpose are the central categories in Frankl's account of the interpretive sequence through which we apprehend architectural forms:

> The visual impression, the *image* produced by differences of light and color, is primary in our perception of a building. We empirically reinterpret this image into a conception of *corporeality*, and this defines the form of the *space within*, whether we read it from outside or stand in the interior. But optical appearance, corporeality, and space do not alone make a building. Distinctions between church, palace, villa, and city hall are based upon specific, typical forms, which crystallize for specific purposes.[12]

Because activity and purpose are clearly the focus of our perception in interpreting buildings, any critical reading of an architectural form will require knowledge of the social, political, and technological contexts in which the building was erected. And, to the extent that the building's purpose was symbolic as well as functional, its interpretation will require attention to the matter of ideology. When a building ceases to have a purpose for us, the reconstruction of its content, its meaning, necessitates historical study: "Many people can surrender themselves to . . . sentimental moods in a well-preserved medieval castle, but only the few who have a vivid conception of the weapons and the conduct of war in that period will *understand* it." Although Frankl does not consider the matter of ideology directly, he does acknowledge the symbolic and ritual aspects of architectural space. So, in remarking on an eighteenth-century palace, he emphasizes the significance of festivals in the life of the patron "and the predominance of artistically decorated state rooms over work spaces."[13]

There is one respect in which Frankl's principles require qualification, however, especially where the architecture of the English country house is concerned. He lays stress on the "purposive intention" that is the "essence" of a building *at the time of its creation.*[14] But the fact that the original purpose for which a building was conceived is obsolete does not necessarily mean that people have ceased to interact with it. It is possible for *purpose* to be redefined, though of course redefinition will be limited by the particular form of the "molded space" in question. Frankl insisted that "a building dies as soon as the life within it has vanished, even if we know the customs of the people who once belonged to it." Yet he also admitted that "a trace of this vanished life remains behind in a building to the extent that the purpose is incarnated in the form of the space." What he neglected to mention or failed to recognize is that new purposes can interact with the original one. Penshurst provides an interesting historical case in point. Even the sixteenth-and seventeenth-century owners of Penshurst could not have understood the "purposive intention" of the original fourteenth-century baronial hall without calling upon some sense of history. Their additions to the house, while consistent with the original style, involved a redefinition of the *purpose* of the central hall. Moreover, while it is generally true that the purpose determining the form of a medieval castle was primarily military, in England, already during the sixteenth century, that purpose became symbolic as well when existing crenellated walls or imitations of them were incorporated into "sham castles."[15]

The point is especially important in considering the country house today. Most of the architectural historians I have consulted in writing this book—including Mark Girouard, Gérard Labrot, Eric Mercer, Sir Nikolaus Pevsner, and Sir John Summerson—have a historical perspective that involves some concern with the ideological aspect of a building's purpose. But there is another, less critical type of language in which architecture is discussed, particularly domestic architecture. It is the discourse we often encounter in the guidebooks, the magazine articles, the coffee table pictorial surveys, and, with varying degrees of subtlety and refinement, in descriptive essays of a rather personal nature written by the modern-day direct heirs of the tradition that was built into the "stately homes."[16] In such accounts of the architecture of the past, an idealization occurs that is symbolically, if not functionally, purposive in the present. This modern-day purpose draws on, and yet redefines, whatever "purposive intention" may be embodied in the designs of the buildings themselves.

On the surface, the purpose for which the great country houses were built is now obsolete. Yet a house of this type, which was once the theater for the enactment of a certain concept of "home," may retain a vestige of that purpose even if, as in most cases, the home has been transformed into a museum. For one thing, it remains a building and there is still an activity involved in the way visitors apprehend it. To be sure, this latter-day activity is governed by other purposes as well. There are different "rules" to be observed in passing through the house. Doors, passageways, vestibules which formerly guided inhabitants and guests through the various rooms according to their respective utilitarian and symbolic functions may now be closed or roped off; the modern visitor's itinerary will more likely be controlled by the linear sequence of exhibits arranged for his or her appreciation. Still, an activity and an interaction with the house are necessary if we are to perceive it, let alone understand it. Moreover, this is not just any kind of museum; it is a museified "home." While the particular kind of molded space that was the "country house" may be obsolete, its *image* for the modern visitor will include an identification of certain activities with this space—hospitality on a grand scale, domestic and conjugal relationships—even if he cannot directly experience the house in this way. If he is not already prepared to make that identification when he arrives at the house, the guidebook will undoubtedly help him imagine the scene. And finally, even if one has never visited the house but has access to it only through pictures and descriptions in magazines like *Country Life*, an image of the original purpose will be assimilated into a more general image of what a house and a home is for us.[17] What else is the operative principle behind modern advertisements like those appearing in *Better Homes and Gardens* and *House Beautiful* (Figs. 1 and 2; and see Appendix B) than a play on this type of imaginary identification?

No doubt this identification is the expression of a need to validate, by the appeal to an outmoded but still powerful image of nobility, grace, and status, our own most recent domestic activities and rituals. Perhaps, too, our readiness to respond to such imagery is a symptom of the limited capacity of present-day institutions to provide us with a stable sense of community and continuity. The kind of language that elicits this sort of identification evokes a peculiarly synchronic version of history. It is as though the past were like the furnishings of the houses themselves, placed on display in full view of the spectator. As a phrase from a pamphlet guide to

Figure 1. *Advertisement,* Better Homes and Gardens, *May 1975. Courtesy of Charmglow Products.*

Figure 2. *Advertisement*, House Beautiful, *September 1973. Reproduced by permission of* Genstar/Flintkote.

Penshurst Place puts it: "Thus passing from room to room, we advance through the centuries . . . ."[18] The sense is of an effortless passage in which we are witness to a history where nothing *essential* has changed.

Such versions of the past are more mythic than historical to the extent that they confound diachrony with synchrony, rendering as static and constant a process that has been dynamic and variable. Of course, old buildings and the furnishings and artifacts they contain do provide tangible evidence of the continuity between past and present. This is certainly part of the excitement of a visit to a place like Penshurst. But what we are offered as tradition and heritage in the guidebook rhetoric is often only an innocuous residue of history, what remains after the contaminating effects of social conflict, uprootedness, and change have been cleaned away. I am not proposing here a simple dichotomy between true and false versions of the past. But I do think we need to maintain an analytic distinction between historical and mythic representation in studying artifacts produced in Western societies since the Renaissance.[19] The historical is in one sense more accurate than the mythic; but the latter is grounded in a desire for stability and continuity that is experientially no less real than the discontinuities which provoke that desire and which are themselves registered by the historical mode. What is lacking in the sentimental versions of tradition and culture that I have criticized is a sense of the ironic relationship that obtains within our own mythology between mythic and historical ways of interpreting the past. The house at Penshurst and Jonson's poem addressed to it exemplify this ironic facet of our culture precisely because in their respective designs we can detect a self-conscious tension between mythic and historical representation, and, perhaps too, a frustration at the difficulty of reconciling the two modes.

"To Penshurst": The Encoding of Tradition

Up to this point, I have focused these introductory remarks on architecture because, as I indicated earlier, the social determinants of form and function are more immediately evident in this domain than in the fields of literature and literary criticism. Turning now to the literary genre associated with the English country house, I want to sketch out the ways in which my interpretation of "To Penshurst" will differ from traditional readings of the poem.

A central component of the ideology adumbrated in the country-house poem can be encapsulated in Coke's dictum: "A man's house is his castle." The sentence might well serve as an alternate subtitle for this book, for the associations that resonate from it are largely what the book is about. And since we in America have inherited some of these associations, I believe that what is unfolded here may be of relevance for the critical understanding of our own culture and its sources. While the country-house poem and the type of dwelling it surveys are native English phenomena, there are certain wide-reaching and long-lasting aspects to the ideology or, more precisely, the conflict of ideologies adumbrated in this seventeenth-century literary form. The genre represents a stage in the emergence of a national culture closely identified with the land of England and with the values associated with land tenure. In it the pastoral conventions of Elizabeth's reign are transformed into a more domestic, historical, and a relatively naturalistic mode. It is a type of "nature poetry" better fitted than its courtly antecedents to serve as the cultural accompaniment to a developing agrarian capitalism. But beyond this specific and immediate historical context or occasion, there are aspects to the country-house poem which constitute in a real sense the elements of a living tradition. Jonson's "To Penshurst" marks the beginning of this tradition. The poem can be distinguished from anything that precedes it in English literature by the manner in which it achieves an image of what we have come to associate with the term "home." In its ideological aspect, which is by no means its only aspect, "To Penshurst" was part of the slow process whereby new values and traditions were encoded in Anglo-American culture at the inception of the modern epoch.

My views in this regard diverge from generally accepted readings of the poem, though they are close in certain respects to the discussion of "To Penshurst" and of the country-house genre in Raymond Williams's *The Country and the City*. Williams has described eloquently the more sinister aspects of this transformation of pastoral from an anachronistic form evoking shepherds and nymphs in a perpetual, idealized, romantic setting to one with a more specific, historical referent, i.e., real property. He points out that while such poems as "To Penshurst" entail a nostalgic idealization of precapitalist economic and social relations, they also make oblique reference to the requisites of an emerging capitalist agriculture: "There is more than a hint, in the whole tone of this hospitable eating and drinking, of that easy, insatiable exploitation of the land and its creatures—a prolonged delight in an organised and corporative production and consumption—which is the basis of many early phases of intensive agriculture."[20]

However, Williams's ideological critique of "To Penshurst" and of the ensuing country-house tradition in English poetry is characterized by a weight of moral indignation that is not really adequately supported by a thorough, close analysis of the texts. This is, of course, partly because the scope of his book is too broad to permit a close reading of any individual text. Nevertheless, the result is a flattening of the complexity to which Williams himself refers in writing of "To Penshurst."[21] While he allows a certain aspect of the poem to appear which had previously been taboo in the critical tradition, his own discussion of "To Penshurst" does not adequately explain the conflict and ambiguity concealed beneath the polished surface of Jonson's verse. Moreover, as George Parfitt has remarked, Williams seems "to berate the seventeenth century for not being able to think like the nineteen and twentieth."[22] Anachronism is one of the dangers of any criticism that is fundamentally a moral polemic (whether of the right or the left). Despite these limitations, Williams's treatment of the country-house poem constitutes a major turning point in the criticism devoted to the genre (just as his book, taken overall, represents a significant shift in British literary criticism generally). His commentary provides an important corrective to the other type of moral criticism, certainly in its own way anachronistic, which has prevailed in discussions of "To Penshurst."

While most critics have recognized that "To Penshurst" is not built entirely on the social and moral code of an older, feudal order, they have been reluctant to acknowledge the presence in the poem of a content that is *antithetical* to feudal and aristocratic values. For example, Geoffrey Walton points out that contemporary moralists were disturbed by the decline of the tradition of "house-keeping" associated with the hall of the English manor house and that Jonson was reflecting on the demise of such hospitality. But he also insists that because "we know from the plays what he [Jonson] thought of the projectors and of other pioneers of nascent capitalism," we can be sure that "he held older ideals of social justice and responsibility," and that these older values are what we find espoused in "To Penshurst."[23]

Yet surely "nascent capitalism" (and the ideologies accompanying it) was a more complicated phenomenon than that. In the first place, we know that the "pioneers of nascent capitalism" included aristocratic families like the Sidneys, and that, in particular, the more daring ventures in shipping and the early efforts to develop mining and industrial enterprises were led not by London merchants or by a rising gentry but by members of the aristocracy.[24] It is not unlikely therefore that some of the values and behavior patterns which we identify as "capitalist" would already begin to emerge in the culture produced by and for this portion of the aristocracy, a point which I hope this study will help to demonstrate. Furthermore, Jonson's own "ideals" as they emerge in poems like "To Penshurst" are not as simply old-fashioned as Walton suggests. He may indeed have looked with contempt on the projectors and even, perhaps, on the ordinary tradesmen of the Jacobean middle classes. But this was partly a way of distinguishing himself, on the basis of his personal accomplishments as a poet and scholar, from his early connection with the trade of bricklaying.[25] Such disavowal was a gesture characteristic of those early professional writers in the seventeenth and eighteenth centuries who depended on aristocratic patronage for their livings and their social status. Given this situation, it may be ironic but it is hardly paradoxical that the writer should identify so completely with the hand which not only fed him, but "consecrated his genius."[26] The only freedom from a rigidly hierarchical social structure attainable for him depended on the willing subjection of his power as a writer to the legitimation of the existing hierarchy. Yet in serving that function in exchange for the recognition and consecration of his genius, the writer became an embodiment of a new ideology, one that asserted the possibility of individual transcendence. If we recognize that this ideology of the individual as exemplified in the successful author would most likely and logically be accompanied by that author's denial of his own class origins, we should have little difficulty in reconciling Ben Jonson's antipathy for merchant capitalism with his own middle-class aspirations.

If Jonson did hold "older ideals of social justice and responsibility," which he attributed to the Sidneys of Penshurst, as Walton assumes and as most critics would agree, then it is important to add that these old ideals and the words used to signify them had a new content. This qualification is particularly crucial for an understanding of seventeenth-century English ideas and institutions, a point emphasized by Christopher Hill who cautions historians against the illusion "that institutions which retain the same name remain the same institutions—whether monarchy, Parliament, common law or universities."[27]

The illusion is one shared by literary critics who view Jonson's conservatism in portraying a benevolent, gracious society at Penshurst as a throwback to classical antiquity or "to the better features of the medieval social order and to the half-religious ideal of Courtesy."[28] Even Raymond Williams views the "idea of rural society" embodied in the house of Jonson's poem as an idea set "against the pressures of a new age."[29] While this is certainly the case, I would argue that it is so only in part, that what makes the poem complex is the presence of those "pressures" in the idea itself; that is, there are qualities associated with the house and its landscape which do *not* stand in opposition to the new capitalist age, but form instead the very rudiments of an essential aspect of its ideology. Jonson's conscious aim may have been to celebrate a retrospective ideal of feudal obligation and responsibility, "the half-religious ideal of Courtesy" (Walton), and perhaps, also, the religious ideal of Charity (Williams). But consciously or otherwise, he also celebrated certain values in "To Penshurst" which are more indicative of the rise of capitalism than the recrudescence of feudalism in early-seventeenth-century England. That is why, rather than viewing "To Penshurst" simply as a nostalgic evocation of an old-fashioned tradition of hospitality, I have attempted an interpretation that describes the emergence or the encoding in this poem of a new tradition. It might seem something of an oxymoron to speak of a "new tradition." But traditions do have beginnings. It is often the case, however, as Hill reminds us, that what is new is represented and even thought of by those who espouse it as something reclaimed from an earlier tradition.

"To Penshurst": The Decoding of Tradition

Many of those who have written about "To Penshurst" frame their conclusions in that very "tradition" which the poem helped to establish. They are therefore unable to ask the questions that need to be asked if the poem is to achieve its potential for going beyond its nominal ideological limits. If a poem such as this—clearly intended as an ideological statement and written in an age when authors did not consciously place themselves in opposition to the values of the class which formed their readership—is a great literary text, it is not because of the ideology it can be said to assert, or even because of the way in which it achieves that assertion. Rather, it is a great poem because of a certain complexity of structure and of feeling (though feeling is not the word we ordinarily associate with such poetry). I maintain that this complexity is the result, at least in part, of a project that simultaneously asserts an ideology and places it in question. The conflict here, and its tenuous resolution as worked out through the poem, are the outcome of a complex strategy for rationalization. What is rationalized is the author's intuitive grasp of a contradiction in his poem's ideological purpose, an intuition arrived at in the very process of realizing that purpose.

I have worked on the assumption that the trace of such an intuition can be verified through formal analysis combined with historical research. The intuition is not yet knowledge in the precise sense; it does not appear in the poem as information in the form of a statement. Rather, it is compounded of the writer's feelings, the semiconscous critical awareness of his situation in relation to the class he serves, and perhaps even the libidinal satisfaction of sensing his potential to transcend that situation through the potency of his art. The writer may have managed to get this into his poem in spite of the social function he was required to perform, and in spite of his own rationalizing effort to protect himself from failing to perform that function. What is personal or "private" in this is at the same time social and political in the sense that it is antithetical to the social order and the ideology which the poem was designed to uphold. In that sense, even an "occasional," "public" poem like "To Penshurst," which seems so bound to a particular society at a particular time and in a particular place, may hint at an understanding that is ahead of its time; even the most conservative poem of this sort may carry the intuition of an alternative to its own present. And by "alternative" I do not mean a retrospective nostalgia for an idealized version of a previous epoch. What I do mean is set forth in my concluding chapter.

I am arguing that poems like "To Penshurst" which are intentionally ideological cry out to the modern reader through their inherently contradictory structures to be confronted and called into question; I claim that a reading which analyzes such a poem's ideological strategy will be less reductionist and ultimately more interesting than one which mimics the poem by paraphrasing its ideological content. This argument is put forth not in the aim of abolishing the notion of "tradition," but rather in the hope of historicizing it. For taken in its ordinary usage, the term "tradition" is invoked most often in order to preserve a static image of culture. Such an image has the power of eliciting from us a strong emotional commitment because it fulfills, however temporarily, our desire to escape that palpable sense of discontinuity which has marked our social and personal experience for more than a century. But in order to have that power of imaginary reintegration the image must, presumably, correlate with some common experience in the lives of those to whom it appeals. Perhaps it is the sense of discontinuity itself, and the attendant uncertainty which is the residual effect of alienation and social fragmentation, that have provided the common grounding in our actual experience for that sense of continuity and community we feel in the face of the documents and monuments that are the repositories of the "tradition."

CHAPTER 2

The Mapping of an Ideological Domain

The stately Homes of England
How beautiful they stand!
Amidst their tall ancestral trees,
O'er all the pleasant land.

—Felicia Hemans, *The Homes of England* (*ante* 1835)

The glory of our civilisation largely arises from the fact that the families of so many aristocrats, squires, yeoman farmers and labourers have lived for so many generations in the same houses and on the same property. This continuity of English land tenure would scarcely have been possible but for the fact that the English Channel has protected us from foreign invasion and that we have never had a civil war which was fought on a class basis. Hence the long, traditional and evolving progress of the English story and the growth of those free Parliamentary institutions which won our wars and made our Empire and which, in the decline of the latter, are still, under a constitutional and hereditary monarchy, shining if imperfect examples of how free men and women should live at peace among themselves.

All the material included in this book has appeared before, or will appear shortly in a necessarily abbreviated form in *Woman's Illustrated*, to whose editor, Mr. R. J. O'Connell, I am indebted for his constant and comprehending support.

—Randolph S. Churchill, *Fifteen Famous English Homes* (London, 1954)

"Propriety" and the Country-House Poem

WE CAN trace back to antiquity a semantic differentiation comparable to that conveyed by the pair of terms "house" and "home" in English.[1] But in the seventeenth century Ben Jonson employs a variant of this distinction that bears a certain historical specificity. It marks an early stage in the formation of an ideology in which the nuclear, conjugal family is represented as the institutional foundation of morality and social order.[2]

An important facet of this emergent ideology is the central role of property in concepts of self and society. There is some linguistic evidence that in the sixteenth century, if not earlier, the self began to be thought of in territorial and possessive terms. A shift can be detected away from the idea of subjectivity as a quality shared by members of a community to a notion that located the subject *in* the individual.[3] A related phenomenon may be the elaboration, as traced by Walter J. Ong, of a spatial model of mind from Ramus to Descartes.[4] In England, by the middle of the seventeenth century, the latent proprietary connotations of the territorial or spatial conception of the self became overtly manifest in political theory. The individual's "person," as C. B. Macpherson has persuasively argued, was identified with private property.[5] And whereas the term "property" (or "propriety") had formerly signified a relationship, by the seventeenth century the relational concept was subordinated to the more reified notion of a thing.

In precapitalist English society property was understood as a *right*, that is, a right to revenue (in service, produce, or money) based on title to land. With the ascendancy of a market economy and its accompanying ideology, the distinction between the right and the thing became blurred: property became the thing itself.[6] Moreover, the "thing" in question was not limited to material wealth in land or money. The term "property" or "propriety" took on wider connotations. "Of things held in propriety," writes Hobbes, "those that are dearest to a man are his own life, and limbs; and in the next degree, (in most men), those that concern conjugall affection; and after them riches and means of living."[7] While Hobbes ranks the more obvious material forms of property, "riches and means of living," below other forms that have spiritual connotations, "life" and "conjugall affection," it is only after having already assumed the metaphor identifying the latter as property, itself understood as "things." Locke would later justify the institution of private property and its unequal distribution by deriving property in things from labor, but only after having defined labor as a thing, a form of property, a commodity equivalent to land and money: "Every Man has a *Property* in his own *Person*. This no Body has any Right to but himself. The *Labour* of his Body, and the *Work* of his Hands, we may say, are properly his . . . though the things of Nature are given in common, yet Man (by being Master of himself, and *Proprietor of his own Person*, and the actions or *Labour* of it) had still in himself *the great Foundation of Property*."[8]

A corollary of the proprietary concept of the individual is the idea of the family as an extension of the identity of the father, and, consequently, as an extension of his property (i.e., those "things," in Hobbes's revealing phrase, "that concern conjugall affection"). This entails, in turn, the creation of a new kind of space occupied by the family and called the *home*.

We can readily identify this ideology in the "bourgeois" literature of the eighteenth and nineteenth centuries; however, in England its earliest signs can be found in representations of the aristocracy during the prerevolutionary period. This was a "new" aristocracy in a double sense. Chronologically, its families had been elevated as part of the Tudor policy of eradicating potential opposition from the remnants of an older, feudal baronage that had largely destroyed itself in the Wars of the Roses. But the "new men" were also different in *kind* from their medieval predecessors. Although they continued to employ the imagery of the chivalric ideal, the members of this new aristocracy functioned primarily not as warriors, but as administrators of the governmental apparatus erected in the reign of Henry VIII.[9] In addition, they saw to the management of their own vast land holdings accumulated through the combined effect of the enclosures and the dissolution of the monasteries. They constituted an agrarian capitalist class with strong links to the trading community, and with investments in incipient mining and manufacturing enterprises and in the earliest colonialist ventures in the New World. Protestantism, with its emphasis on the domestic environment as the center of religious training and discipline, and on the doctrine of predestination (which although originating in Calvinism was held in common by most English Protestants),[10] enabled these aristocrats to view themselves as providential administrators of "Nature" in the form of land, household, and tenants. And by extension of this vision they could begin to imagine themselves the legitimate administrators of the English nation and of that newly "discovered" portion of "Nature" that lay untainted (or unredeemed, depending on the particular version of the argument) across the seas in America.[11]

In this way, by the end of the sixteenth century and long before the consolidation and triumph of a "bourgeois ideology" in England, images and values we tend to identify as middle class had already begun to appear in the transformation of the aristocracy's own self-image. The genre of the country-house poem emerged as part of this redefinition of traditional, feudal notions in terms which fit a new historical situation. Architecture and landscape, and subsequently the poetry in which these were celebrated, constitute stages in the preliminary "mapping," as it were, of an ideological domain, a laying out of a ground plan which gave form to attitudes and values that were not yet formulated in consciously systematic terms and which were most likely not yet clearly evident to the people who shared them and who behaved in accordance with them.

Jonson's "To Penshurst" is probably the first major poem in English literature to be directly concerned with this redefinition. It is not a poetic description of a house so much as it is an attempt to evoke the significant connotations of the term "home." In that respect, although the poetic genre inaugurated by "To Penshurst" is a native English phenomenon, what it stands for is an image that cuts across national and even class lines in important ways. The tensions in the poem arise partly out of the conflict between, on the one hand, an assertion of hierarchy in traditional and territorially restricted terms, and, on the other, the positing of an order in which hierarchy is rationalized in terms that transcend genealogical and national boundaries. The latter side of this opposition is grounded in a concept of Nature, a concept which is in a rudimentary sense sociological and anthropological, implying both an analysis of contemporary social structures and a model of their origins.

At the center of Jonson's concept of Nature are the images of the family and of the house as home. The house is still an aristocratic house, and the family still bears traces of the feudal extended household, including blood relations, servants, and members of the surrounding community under the protection of the *paterfamilias*. But there are other connotations as well. These include the equation of power and of personal identity with private property, the image of house and land as the visible domain of property and of identity, the notion of home and family as the legitimating spiritual nucleus of that material domain, and a corresponding view of history to which I shall return shortly. After more than three and a half centuries such notions have inevitably undergone alteration. But their essential features are still with us. And it is not too much of an exaggeration to say that the referent for a poem like "To Penshurst" is an archetype (and an origin) of the image which the twentieth-century mortgager of a cottage in Surrey, a *petit pavillon* on the outskirts of Paris, or a suburban tract house in Southern California is likely to have of himself, his family, his home.

This is not to say that "To Penshurst" exhibits liberal, egalitarian ideals. On the contrary, Jonson's concern in this poem was to build a doctrine as to what constitutes the nature and the responsibilities of rank. But the spiritual and ideological foundations of that doctrine are derived from a notion of what is meant by family and home. This spiritual foundation, which has its material counterpart in the "countrey stone" that distinguishes the buildings at Penshurst from other lords' houses, is asserted through an identification of a ruling-class family and its home not only with the land but with the families and homes of the subjects who inhabit that land. Jonson's strategy was to distinguish the Sidneys by means of this identification from other members of the Jacobean aristocracy. Thus, while the poem ostensibly expresses admiration for rank, the essential qualities that ultimately distinguish good rulers from bad ones are qualities vested in an institution that threatens to transcend the distinction between lord and commoner. This institution, not bound to a particular social class, is signified by the word *home* (or, indirectly in Jonson's poem, by the verb "dwells"—one builds a house, one dwells in a home). *Home* and *family* connote each other, the two terms being metonymically related in that one designates a space which encompasses the structure of social relations and the attendant values signified by the other. In the poem, *home* is enunciated as the essential and transhistorical center from which emanate all the important ideals and values upon which society is founded. It is also the place from which a new and different justification of hierarchical social relations and the authority and power to sustain such relations will be made.

But there is yet a further aspect to the ideological configuration that marks the appearance of the country-house poem. For while the genre is symptomatic of a changing historical situation, it is also an attempt to account for that change. Moreover, "To Penshurst" draws and elaborates on a historical account already adumbrated symbolically by the Sidneys in the ensemble of architecture and topography which is the subject of Jonson's poem. Behind the notions of Nature, home, and family, central to the ideology at Penshurst, lies a more inclusive function, that of providing a representation of history. But a curious inversion is evident here. While the quality with which the space of the Sidney estate is invested can unfold only through a temporal sequence—walking through the landscape and the house, reading through the poem—the image of history which both sign systems achieve is static and in a sense more spatial than temporal. In this respect, both the house and the poem exemplify the ambiguous way in which historical consciousness was introduced into modern Western culture. At the beginning of the modern epoch, poems like "To Penshurst" and the visual forms or environments they described contributed to the creation of images and to the construction of a narrative framework within which European societies made their experience of fundamental historical changes intelligible. Yet the narrative thereby constructed also served to occlude the basis of these changes. Its purpose was therefore double: to bring consciousness into a more coherent relationship with the experience of change and of contradiction in the realm of concrete social relations, and, at the same time, fulfilling the function of *myth* in Lévi-Strauss's sense, to provide a logical model capable of overcoming the contradiction.[12] In a sense, therefore, this study of a poem which is addressed to a house is not only about poetry and architecture. It is as much an examination of a particular kind of narrative structure through which a culture, caught between two epochs and not yet able to theorize the transformation it was undergoing, represented itself to itself.

The Strategy of Metonymy: Epistemological Aspects of Genre and Style

"A genre," Claudio Guillén has written, ". . . is a problem-solving model on the level of form." He goes on to point out that "although genres are chiefly persistent models, because they have been tested and found satisfactory, it has been generally known since the Enlightenment—since Vico, since Voltaire's *Essai sur la poésie épique*—that they evolve, or fade, or are replaced. . . . Thus, it seems important to reconsider the terms of generic theory from the point of view of *new* genres."[13] The fact that "To Penshurst" is the first of the country-house poems, and one of the first in the broader generic category of topographical poems in English, is significant. It suggests that Jonson felt it necessary to "discover" a form, a model that could adequately serve as the heuristic of a poetic inquiry into the ethical implications of the changes that marked the immediate social and historical context in which he was writing.[14] The model Jonson achieved is an interesting though curious combination of elements from older, classical genres with something that is distinctly new and different.[15] It is also curious in the way it both registers and denies the historical changes which were its occasion. There is a tension between these aims running through Jonson's poem, a tension evident in the form itself, that is, in a certain angularity and asymmetry of language and structure which work against the apparently serene and effortless flow of the verse.

In an excellent study of the country-house poem, Charles Molesworth notes that the poetic modes which characterize the method of this new genre are primarily those of allegory and metonymy. He adopts Kenneth Burke's description of metonymy as an attempt "to convey some incorporeal or intangible state in terms of the corporeal or tangible." Molesworth writes that the "strategy of metonymy" in such poems is a way of establishing the connection between value in the sense of property and value in its more spiritual sense. A man's estate is viewed as the "effect" of his virtue. The social value of real property is thus made to rest on the proper "use" of natural resources which depends, in turn, on the virtuous use by a great man of his God-given talent and potential.[16]

Molesworth follows Burke in focusing on the metonymic relation at the level of the *signified* (that is, in terms of the content of the relationship). The description of the corporeal estate as a *locus amoenus* validates the panegyric to the incorporeal virtue of the owner. But metonymy is also an important aspect of the genre at the level of form (that is, in terms of the form through which the "effect" of virtue is achieved). Of use here is Roman Jakobson's well-known discussion of the figures of metaphor and metonymy since, unlike Burke, Jakobson focuses chiefly on the linguistic plane of the *signifier*.

As part of a study of aphasic disorders Jakobson elaborates a distinction between two fundamental aspects of communication: the operations of selection and substitution involving a relation of *similarity*, and those of combination and contexture characterized by a relation of *contiguity*. He then writes of metaphor and metonymy as figures which express these two "poles" of communication respectively. Jakobson emphasizes that in most communication both processes will be operative, but adds that "under the influence of a cultural pattern, personality, and verbal style, preference is given to one of the two processes over the other."[17]

From the standpoint of literary studies, Jakobson's descriptions of metaphor and metonymy are quite limited when compared with the treatment of these figures in traditional rhetoric. Nevertheless, the specific features on which he focuses his discussion of metonymy are especially apropos for an analysis of the method of the country-house poem and of Jonsonian discourse in general. Contiguity and the building of a narrative context, which Jakobson associates mainly with prose, are the dominant features of a certain kind of seventeenth-century verse, like Jonson's, written in the "plain style." In such poetry, metaphor is deliberately abjured for the sake of notions of order, clarity of expression, and precision of thought, notions based on an implied, if not explicit, analytic and referential theory of language. Jonson's pronouncements on language in *Timber; or, Discoveries* confirm that he had something like a theory of this sort:

> Metaphors far-fetched hinder to be understood.
>
> The chiefe virtue of a style is perspicuitie, and nothing so vitious in it, as to need an Interpreter.[18]

His *English Grammar* contains a preface that is of some interest in the present context for the following:

> *Confusion* of Language, a *Curse*.
>
> Experience breedeth Art: Lacke of Experience, Chance.
>
> Experience, Observation, Sense, Induction, are the four Tryers of Arts. It is ridiculous to teach any thing for undoubted Truth, that Sense, and Experience, can confute. So *Zeno* disputing of *Quies*, was confuted by *Diogenes*, rising up and walking.
>
> In Grammar, not so much the Invention, as the Disposition is to be commended.[19]

There is evidence here of Jonson's affinities with Francis Bacon's program for the advancement of learning—the concern over "confusion of language" (Bacon's "Idols of the Marketplace"),[20] and the stress on "Experience, Observation, Sense, Induction." At the same time, the emphasis on "Disposition" over "Invention" is similar to that in the rationalist tradition from Ramus to Descartes. These early manifestations of modern scientific and philosophical inquiry share an orientation toward what Jakobson means by metonymy; contiguity and contexture are the dominant traits of a linguistic doctrine which emphasized the proper order of words based on an assumed correspondence between words, ideas, and things.[21]

There is a striking consistency to the preponderance of metonymy in Jonsonian discourse, which cuts across the boundary between verse and prose and which is evident even as a principle of his dramaturgy.[22] Linguistically, this is the result not only of Jonson's suspicion of the figure of metaphor but of his handling of syntax. Jonas Barish has shown that in the prose comedies Jonson rejected the artfully balanced syntax derived from the "Euphuistic" style of Lyly which survived in the prose of Shakespeare. Instead, Jonson developed a style in which "syntactic effects are equally studied, but with a different purpose: to dislocate symmetry and thus create the illusion of the absence of rhetoric."[23] Even in the relatively formal frame of his nondramatic verse, Jonson maintains his resistance to the use of conventional rhetorical device. He concentrates instead on the construction of a sequence and of a context, manipulating the reader's response primarily through careful control of syntax and by subtle variation of the caesura within a predominantly regular metrical pattern. The effect is that of evidence accumulating in support of the more general assumptions, feelings, attitudes, and values that are the ideational and emotional context.[24]

We must, of course, distinguish between the manner of Jonson's concentration on syntax and context in the satiric prose and in the poems. As Barish has shown, attention to detail and the dislocation of syntax in the prose comedies are devices for revealing what Jonson views as deformities of character, tactical devices in his general strategy for anatomizing social disorder. By contrast, in the poems of praise, control of syntax and the attention to detail are devices for building a sense of order and for achieving that quality of "urbanity" which is so often associated with Jonson's verse.

Yet in spite of these differences, there is more similarity between Jonson's method of composition in his prose satires and in his celebratory poems than is at first apparent. Jonson's attitude of mind could be called scientific, or at least protoscientific. I refer here to the empiricism for which he is celebrated and for which he was mocked by some contemporaries; and to a type of skepticism typical of his work—not the Pyrrhonian skepticism of Montaigne, but the methodological skepticism advocated by Bacon as a way "to establish progressive stages of certainty."[25] The anatomy of social disorder in Jonson's satires can be seen as his attempt to construct a "theory" of society (with the doctrine of characterization by "humors" constituting an early form of social psychology). It is a normative theory and draws on a tradition of moral philosophy. But it also involves principles of analysis and classification and a critical attitude that are not unlike Bacon's. The "humors" doctrine applied to the categorization of deformities of personality entails the same curious mixture of analytic and aphoristic method as Bacon's doctrine of the "Idols" (which is often cited as the prototype of modern theories of ideology).[26]

Unlike Bacon, however, Jonson does not appear to be very self-confident when it comes to delineating the norms on which the critical impulse in his work is presumably based. As Barish points out, in his plays "Jonson, like Swift, whets his irony not only against deviants from the norm, but against the norm itself. . . . The 'pure and neat . . . yet plaine and customary' language elsewhere recommended by Jonson . . . like other positive standards, evidently resists embodiment on the Jonsonian stage."[27] We may, of course, turn to the poems in seeking such an embodiment of the linguistic and moral norms that Jonson advocated. But there, too, I believe we will encounter difficulties.

"To Penshurst" would be one of the most likely places to look. It is perhaps the closest approximation we are likely to find in Jonson to an idea of Utopia. In its language the poem seems a consummate expression of the ideals recommended in *Timber; or, Discoveries*. One particularly striking passage from this collection of Jonson's pronouncements on style and language shows him employing the meticulous fitting together of stones in building as a simile of good writing:

> The congruent, and harmonious fitting of parts in a sentence, hath almost the fastning, and force of knitting, and connexion: As in stones well squar'd which will rise a great way without mortar.[28]

The notion that mortar is superfluous if the stones are precisely proportioned suggests a way of building (and writing) that produces a harmony of structure identified with a conception of what is natural. And the "ancient pile" at Penshurst seems to have provided Jonson with the perfect symbolic vehicle of the linguistic and moral ideals he associated with this conception of Nature.

It is not surprising, therefore, that one critic, Paul Cubeta, should identify "To Penshurst" as "a Jonsonian ideal." Cubeta asserts that Jonson succeeded here "in molding the ethical and the aesthetic into a harmony revealed in the structure of the verse."[29] But, minimally, a critical reading must ask: what is the "ethical," the "aesthetic," and the related "structure" of the poem? And I don't think that Cubeta's response, which is to take the "ethical" as a given and then to proceed to show how Jonson communicates this ethic, is an adequate reply to the question. Rather, like most of the criticism devoted to "To Penshurst," this amounts to little more than a rephrasing of the poem's central themes, and an acceptance at face value of the direct statement and orderly composition that characterize the poem on the surface. Only very recently have critics begun to address themselves to what Raymond Williams rightly terms "the complexity of 'To Penshurst.' "[30]

As I have already indicated, I believe the complexity results from tensions and contradictions in the poem. These are evident in the style itself. The "plain style" which Jonson adopted from late classical sources is characterized by an emphasis on brevity, disposition, and the mixture of rhetorical device with a concern for sensory detail. As Erich Auerbach has shown, the clear distinction maintained in antiquity between high and low styles gradually breaks down in late Roman times. A realism characterized by attention to sensory detail and traditionally restricted to the low style begins to invade the elevated discourse of Seneca and Tacitus. Eventually there is also a shift in Latin from hypotactic to paratactic structure which culminates, according to Auerbach, in the writing of the church fathers. Auerbach associates hypotaxis with a rhetorical concern in antiquity for temporal and causal relationships, a concern which is not, however, fundamentally historical: "On the contrary, the ethical and even the political concepts of antiquity (aristocracy, democracy, etc.) are fixed, aprioristic model concepts."[31] By contrast, parataxis entails a rejection of symmetry and of periodic structure for the sake of a fragmentary, discrete presentation which, though lacking the sense of continuity of the older style, is more historical in its mimetic specificity.[32]

A mixture of high and low styles and a preference for parataxis are characteristics of the anti-Ciceronian movement among writers of prose in the early seventeenth century. These principles are central to Jonson's *Discoveries*. The discussion of style there draws primarily on an epistolary rhetorical tradition; yet modern scholars have adduced evidence that Jonson did not intend his remarks on style to be restricted to the writing of letters.[33] Certainly there are significant differences between Jonson's stylistic practice in prose and in verse; and even within the latter, Jonson employs poetic language differently according to genre.[34] Nevertheless, there is a certain consistency running throughout his writing. It is a consistency based on the priority given to metonymy, on parataxis as opposed to hypotaxis in syntax, and above all, on a general asymmetry of structure at the level of the sentence and of the composition as a whole. Barish compares a passage from Bacon's *Advancement of Learning* with Jonson's adaptation of it in *Discoveries* as a way of pointing up the relative asymmetry of Jonson's prose. He prefaces the comparison by remarking that " 'asymmetrical' seems to define the shape of Jonson's prose so exactly that one is tempted to use it to describe the topography of his mind."[35] The evidence for this assertion in Barish's analysis of Jonson's prose is impressive. I would add that evidence can be found in the verse as well. The asymmetry of such an order-seeking poem as "To Penshurst" is striking; and it is no accident that the most symmetrical section of the poem is the opening which depicts elements of the ostentatious "prodigy" houses against which Jonson opposes the natural state of things at Penshurst.

Following Morris Croll, Barish identifies this asymmetry as "baroque" style. Yet he distinguishes Jonson from other baroque writers such as Donne, Browne, Milton, Burton, Montaigne, and Pascal, and in so doing draws a convincing portrait of the person who speaks through the Jonsonian style:

> where the other baroque writers explicitly dramatize their tensions, in Jonson the tensions remain buried. The other writers manage to relate their private disturbances to large cultural crises, theological, ecclesiastical, or political, but Jonson, by refusing to acknowledge his, can express them only in oblique and devious ways, which makes them less easy to isolate. . . .
>
> In Jonson, in short, we have a subjectivity as intense as

> Donne's masquerading as its opposite, a thin-skinned suspiciousness masking itself as a benign imperturbability, and an acute social insecurity clothing itself in the mantle of achieved status, in a fashion similar to that in which the social-climbing citizens of Jonson's own comedies clothe themselves in the jargon and gestures of a superior class in order to be accepted by it. And it is dissonances like these, no doubt, within Jonson himself, that lead him to adopt baroque style, with its broken rhythms and perilous balances, rather than the stabler rhetorics of Euphuism or Ciceronianism, with their implicit sense of integration into a harmonious, ordered cosmos.[36]

This attempt to describe an epistemological and psychological frame of mind on the basis of stylistic analysis is speculative, and Barish is the first to admit the fact.[37] But it is well-grounded speculation to anyone who has read much Jonson. And to the extent that it is plausible to relate Jonson's prose to his personality, the correlation ought to hold true for his poetry as well.

Now it seems to me that the harmony and order which critics have celebrated in speaking of Jonson's nonsatiric works, verse as well as prose, are largely illusory. The illusion depends on a context of shared assumptions which are rarely made explicit in the works themselves, though critical analysis may help to uncover them. If we look back at Jonson's comparison of the "connexion" of words in a sentence to the piling of stones without mortar, we realize that besides referring to paratactic structure the simile implies a refusal of the connotative dimensions of language. Yet the capacity of words to function denotatively depends on an existing context of assumptions and goals shared by the writer and his readership. The "mortar" which binds words in a sentence is not composed merely of grammatical connectives, nor even of strictly verbal phenomena; it is as much in the context, what Kenneth Burke calls the "verbal scene" in which the "verbal act" is performed. Metonymy can function as the chief device of Jonsonian rhetoric only by reference to an a priori communicational framework. In both Burke's and Jakobson's senses of the term, metonymy depends on a relation to the context of the communication. The immediate context of a metonymic operation (that is, what Jakobson means by "context") is a logical or causal relationship between terms. However, this relationship is clear and distinct only to the degree that it follows from a wider context of presuppositions or background expectancies. The latter, more inclusive context remains obscured, however, perhaps as a result of habit or because of the efficiency of the signifying process in the sequential activity of reading.

The obscuring of this wider context in the functional efficiency of the metonymic "connexion" of ideas is acknowledged, to a degree, by both Jakobson and Burke. Jakobson equates the principle of association by contiguity in metonymy and synecdoche with Freud's "displacement" and "condensation" respectively. Burke is more explicit about the possible distorting effects of the metonymic operation. For him, "metonymy" is synonymous with "reduction." Burke distinguishes, however, between metonymic reduction in "poetic realism" and in "scientific realism." He argues that unlike the behavioral scientist, the poet who uses a material effect to dramatize a certain incorporeal state does so with the understanding that the metonymic operation is a figurative or symbolic one:

> [The poet] is using metonymy as a *terminological* reduction whereas the scientific behaviorist offers his reduction as a "real" reduction. (However, he does not do this *qua* scientist, but only by reason of the materialist metaphysics, with its assumptions about substance and motive, that is implicit in his system.)[38]

Yet in Ben Jonson (and in other seventeenth-century writers) the distinction is not so fine. We might expect that at a time when the discourse of science was in its formative stage an ambiguous relationship should exist between the "poetic" and the "scientific." During the seventeenth century a number of protoscientific theories of language were proposed. The most important of these from a modern viewpoint was the rationalist theory of the sign developed by the linguists and logicians of Port Royal for whom the word was a transparent signifier through which the physical and moral universe could be apprehended. Jonson's image of the word as a perfectly squared stone that requires no mortar, a unit of meaning complete unto itself, is the equivalent, in what Burke terms "the materialist metaphysics," of the rationalist doctrines of the Cartesians. Both share the assumption of a preestablished harmony between words, ideas, and things. It is not clear in such seventeenth-century doctrines whether what is being asserted is the statement of a natural *datum* or whether it is the affirmation of a *norm*.[39] These observations suggest the need for some qualification of Burke's analysis of the relationship between "metonymy" and "reduction." They indicate the problem we are likely to encounter in attempting to apply his distinction between poetic and scientific "metonymy" to the period when the division between poetry and science was only beginning to take shape in Western thought. It is therefore difficult to separate the ethical assumptions of classicism in seventeenth-century poetry from the reductive epistemology of the scientific revolution in its early stage. To the extent that Jonson seeks to convince his readers of the clarity and certainty of his thought, to the extent, that is, that he represents the metonymic reduction as the equivalent of the "real," he leaves the realm of what Burke calls "poetic realism" and approaches what he means by "scientific realism."

As long as the reader shares the assumptions on which the reduction is based, a text by Jonson will have the appearance of order and clarity and the harmony of structure that critics have attributed to it. But such a text will lose its apparent clarity if the reader happens not to share these assumptions—and presumably fewer and fewer readers do, which is one reason why Jonson's noncomic writings have suffered a steady decline in popularity during the past two centuries. In such a case, the text may be relegated to the dust heap of works we may occasionally feel an obligation to read out of some sense of duty to our literary tradition but in which we find no immediate pleasure or relevance. Or it may be experienced in a new way that undermines the certainty and clarity of theme promised by the authoritative tone of the rhetoric. A poem in the plain style may not necessarily correspond to what Stanley Fish characterizes as a "self-consuming artifact," but it can, and in the case of "To Penshurst" I maintain that it does, expose the assumptions on which its own method is based.[40] A reader who is not predisposed to share these assumptions will most likely notice the points at which the strategy of metonymy breaks down in the course of reading the poem. Such a reader will not passively assist in the construction of a sequence which achieves the sense of solidity and integrity of the epistemological, the ethical, and the esthetic. Instead, he or she will pause at those strategic points in the poem's structure where ambiguity and uncertainty are revealed. And at such points, he or she will be brought into contact with Ben Jonson in spite of himself, that is, the *other* Ben Jonson who so desperately wished to hide from his readership behind the surface of a confident and coherent epideictic rhetoric. To me, this is the more interesting of the types of experience which a text like "To Penshurst" affords the reader. It may be discomfiting—for once we have recognized the tension and insecurity of the voice that appears to speak in such solid and urbane tones, its owner tends to become more like us and less like the aloof supersubject which a long tradition has decreed that the poet ought to be. It is the more interesting kind of experience precisely because of the chaos that threatens its surface order, because of the asymmetry of its structure and the gaps and inconsistencies in its logic. In this kind of reading, conceptual and linguistic tensions become the objectification in writing of a subjectivity in conflict; the social and historical contradictions which the poem attempts to resolve are instead exposed through the articulation of a subject's lived experience of these contradictions. The discourse of the poem ceases to be simply that of an institution and an ideology speaking through and for a detached subjectivity. It becomes, rather, the discourse of a subject who is forced to speak through conflicting institutions and ideologies.

Negative Description: Cockaigne, Utopia, Penshurst

Another significant feature of Jonson's rhetorical strategy in "To Penshurst" is his employment of negative descriptive phrases at key points in the poem. Raymond Williams has remarked on the procedure of "definition by negatives" that characterizes a number of the country-house poems.[41] I should like to elaborate on Williams's remarks here, though with somewhat different emphasis. Definition by negatives can be pointed to as a facet of all utopian literature, as is suggested by the very term *ou-topos*. If we are claiming that "To Penshurst" marks the beginning of a new genre in English, and if "negative definition" is an important feature of that new genre, then we need to analyze how such negatives may function in a distinctive way here. Among the possible antecedents of the country-house genre we can include the medieval legends of the Terrestrial Paradise. A native English version is the fourteenth-century poem *The Land of Cockaigne.*[42] It offers an interesting parallel and a basis for comparison with "To Penshurst" because of the way in which negatives are employed in the development of its theme.

The medieval poem is a comic, mythic commentary on a real condition of scarcity. It combines an outrageously funny catalogue of delights with a sequence of negative grammatical constructions which point up the absence of what is imagined by the anonymous poet. As Robert C. Elliott has suggested, the "negative emphasis" in the description of Cockaigne as a place where there is no strife, no pain, no death, evokes a quality of "longing." Elliott sees Cockaigne as containing elements of what will become Utopia in the literature of later generations. Behind the comedy of the interminable flow of oil, milk, honey, and wine, and behind all the sexual play, there is in these lines a reverie of desire for a place and an order of existence which, though mythical, are felt to be implicitly recoverable. The quality of longing is undercut by the self–satire in all the hyperbole; and yet, as Elliott argues, the "satire is easily overwhelmed in such express outpouring of desire."[43]

As in Cockaigne, Nature's providence seems to be infinite at the Penshurst of Jonson's poem. But Penshurst is not described in quite the same way as Cockaigne. One reason, of course, is that Penshurst is not a fantastic place but a real (though mythicized) one. Moreover, it is not characterized by luxury, self-indulgence, and idleness as is Cockaigne. Rather, Penshurst is represented as a place where everything that is natural and good is in abundance; this abundance is administered by a family which is, in turn, represented as the epitome of everything that is humanly natural and good.[44] And the abundance of Nature at Penshurst is consumed by all who dwell, or who are visitors, within its boundaries. Penshurst is a place where plenitude and prosperity are enjoyed by all, but in moderation. It is not a seat of sumptuous and ostentatious consumption. And it is not the scene of idle or frivolous behavior; on the contrary, everything on the estate is productive, vital, active in accordance with some implied design. Yet in all this activity there is no sense of the strain of labor. As in Cockaigne all that Nature provides at Penshurst is, in Jonson's words, "free provisions" (line 58).

The passages of "To Penshurst" which most closely resemble *The Land of Cockaigne* are those in which hyperbole is used to enforce the sense that everything of Nature gives freely of itself for the consumption of those who dwell there:

> Thy copp's, too, nam'd of Gamage, thou hast there,
> That never failes to serve thee season'd deere,
> When thou would'st feast, or exercise thy friends.
> . . . .
> Each banke doth yeeld thee coneyes; and the topps
> Fertile of Wood, Ashore, and Sydney's copp's,
> To crowne thy open table, doth provide
> The purpled pheasant, with the speckled side:
> The painted partrich lyes in every field,
> And, for thy messe, is willing to be kill'd.
> And if the high–swolne Medway faile thy dish,
> Thou hast thy ponds, that pay thee tribute fish,
> Fat, aged carps, that runne into thy net.
> And pikes, now weary their owne kinde to eat,
> As loth, the second draught, or cast to stay,
> Officiously, at first, themselves betray.
> Bright eeles that emulate them, and leape on land,
> Before the fisher, or into his hand.

A significant difference between this and the medieval poem is that here, Nature's providence is celebrated entirely in positive terms. There appears to be none of the longing associated with the negative constructions of *The Land of Cockaigne*.

Yet elsewhere in "To Penshurst," negative constructions are quite prominent. The poem opens with a series of negative comparisons which state that Penshurst is *not* like the more elaborate country houses built by wealthy Elizabethan and Jacobean landowners. And later, after the enumeration of natural abundance at Penshurst, there is a resumption of negative contructions that is striking. After thirty-seven affirmative, encomiastic lines in which we are brought from the outlying woods to the walls of the house, we are told suddenly that the latter "are rear'd with *no mans* ruine, *no mans* grone, / There's *none*, that dwell about them, wish them downe." In line 49 we read, "And *no one* empty-handed"; in line 50, "they have *no sute*"; in line 61, "Where comes *no guest*, but is allow'd to eate, / *Without* his feare"; in line 65, "And I *not faine* to sit"; in line 67, "Here *no man* tells my cups; *nor*, standing by, / A waiter, doth my gluttony envy"; in line 71, "Thy tables *hoord not* up for the next day, / *Nor*, when I take my lodging, need I pray / For fire"; in line 75, "There's *nothing* I can wish, for which I stay"; and so on. Thus, in "To Penshurst" the thirty-seven lines which most closely parallel the Cockaigne poem in so far as content is concerned are conspicuously lacking in the kind of negative construction which characterizes the form of the earlier poem. On the other hand, where negatives do occur in "To Penshurst," the lines have no equivalents in the Cockaigne poem, though the function of the negation seems to be similar in both cases. Instead of employing the negative to negate scarcity and to express a longing for sustenance, Jonson uses negatives first in connection with ostentation and later to negate what are understood as corruptive forms of social experience, i.e., exploitation, discrimination, and so on. In *The Land of Cockaigne* negatives suggest a longing which refers to something lacking in man's relation to Nature; in "To Penshurst," negatives suggest a longing and a lack in connection with man's relation to man.

In fact, sustenance is taken for granted in the Penshurst poem; the enumeration of abundance at Penshurst in positive rather than negative terms suggests an attempt to represent a less mythical place than Cockaigne. That is, the abundance at Penshurst, while exaggerated, is not felt to be quite as imaginary as that of Cockaigne. This is partly because, while the hyperbole in both poems serves a metaphorical function (evoking a magical Nature in both places), the tenor of that metaphor in the case of "To Penshurst" is meant to refer to an actual abundance.[45] It is because *The Land of Cockaigne* is a fantasy that it can incorporate a note of self-satire which relieves it of any responsibility for its extravagant catalogues; what is most serious in the poem is not the enumeration of an abundant Nature or even the externalization of desire in an ecstatic torrent of images, but the repetition of negative constructions which point to the absence of sustenance in the real world out of which the poem emerged. On the other hand, there is no satire in Jonson's poem; Jonson maintains a consistent seriousness of tone throughout "To Penshurst," because what his poem refers to is not intentionally fantastic. Here the positive representation of Nature's abundance is an assertion of the real possibility of sustenance in a place where Nature purportedly is governed according to her own laws. Again, however, it must be borne in mind that the use of negative constructions in passages that refer to social relations at Penshurst suggests that the poem is not as confident about relations among men as it is about the relationship between man and Nature.

It can be seen, then, that where negative constructions do occur in "To Penshurst," they generally function in the same way as in the Cockaigne poem; only the content of the negation and the longing it connotes are different. This difference may be an indication of a shift in focus which is historical and ideological. That is, in the fourteenth century all that is lacking is identified with the power of Fortune or Nature over men's lives, while social relations within a strict hierarchical order are largely taken for granted. Jonson's seventeenth-century poem is elaborated upon a principle of hierarchy also (the poem moves through the chain of being on the estate, from the natural elements earth, air, wood, water, to the presence of the king and to the abstract virtues associated with the Sidney family); but the delineation of hierarchy in the social sphere is ambiguous as compared with the hierarchy in Nature. The introduction of negative constructions precisely at points involving social and economic relations[46] suggests that it is in this domain that something is lacking. Instead of the longing for a mythical place where Nature is eternally bounteous, the longing in "To Penshurst" is for the recovery of a mythical past in which the relations of production on a manorial estate like Penshurst, and in the social order in general, are not exploitative. I do not mean to suggest that it is a necessarily intrinsic function of negative constructions to connote ambiguities, but rather that the ambiguity is connoted here according to a definite pattern marked by the presence or absence of negative constructions: they are absent when natural goods are being delineated; they are present when architectural features (lines 1–8) or when social and economic relations are being described. Thus, the pattern seems to be one of opposition between Nature and Culture, with the latter even being denied or excluded as a category within which anything can be asserted or affirmed about Penshurst. In other words, the pattern suggests a rule: regarding Penshurst, all affirmative statements refer to Nature, all negative statements refer to Culture. And this rule is a basic part of the code in which we are instructed on a first reading of the poem.

So, if there is a "longing" connoted by negatives in "To Penshurst," it is mainly the longing for a different ordering of social relationships. And these negatives, which assert the absence of exploitation and of discrimination on the basis of inherited rank, combined with the affirmative statements which assert the presence of natural abundance, make the representation of social order at Penshurst something of a Utopia. However, Penshurst is not Utopia; partly because the projection of an alternative social order is not sufficiently realized in the poem, but also because Penshurst is a real place. While the poem does constitute "a Jonsonian ideal," and while the Nature that is represented there is magical and the social relations idealized, Penshurst remains a topos with determinate geographical and historical coordinates; and it is for this reason that I believe it legitimate to analyze the poem in a way that treats the deliberately mythicized, magical Nature, which Jonson may have inherited from the Cockaigne tradition, as referring to real conditions on the estate and as an attempt to articulate an ideological norm. In other words, it is not sufficient to account for the exaggeration and distortion in "To Penshurst" on the grounds that this is a magical "ideal." The mythical elements in the early parts of the poem are designed to support the ethical and social norm of which the Sidney family is made the embodiment in the final fourteen lines. Thus, no matter how magical is the intended representation of abundance at Penshurst, we must understand the magical element as a function of a broader strategy in the poem. And we must weigh the overall image that that strategy is designed to enforce with the actual nature of manorial relations on a real country estate at the beginning of the seventeenth century.[47]

Yet in attempting to understand the ideological content of "To Penshurst," it is not sufficient to concentrate solely on what is stated there and then to compare that with the available historical data. This is the approach taken by Raymond Williams. His discussion of the poem is in the tradition of L. C. Knights's ethically based sociological criticism, though Williams is harsher in his judgment of Jonson than Knights.[48] As far as it goes, the approach tells us a good deal about the discrepancy between what is stated in Jonson's poem and the real conditions that obtained on estates like Penshurst in the seventeenth century. It locates the idealization and points to its ideological function. But it does not tell us very much about *how* the poem achieves the idealization at the expense of the reality. Nor does it account for Jonson's ability to distance himself sufficiently from the ideological function of his praise in order to betray that function in the very act of performing it. What is required is a detailed analysis of the poem, of its immediate referent, the estate at Penshurst Place, Kent, and of the historical contexts in which both were conceived.

CHAPTER 3

The Poem

Auream quisquis mediocritatem
diligit, tutus caret obsoleti
sordibus tecti, caret invidenda
sobrius aula.

—Horace, *Odes*

If a man would build a house, he would first appoint a place to build it in, which he would define within certaine bounds: So in the Constitution of a *Poeme*, the Action is aym'd at by the *Poet*, which answers Place in a building; and that Action hath his largenesse, compasse, and proportion. But, as a Court, or Kings Palace, requires other dimensions then a private house: So the *Epick* askes a magnitude, from other *Poëms*. Since, what is Place in the one, is Action in the other, the difference is in space. So that by this definition wee conclude the fable, to be the *imitation* of one perfect, and intire Action; as one perfect, and intire place is requir'd to a building. By perfect, wee understand that, to which nothing is wanting; as Place to the building, that is rais'd, and Action to the fable, that is form'd. It is perfect, perhaps, not for a Court, or Kings Palace, which requires a greater ground; but for the structure wee would raise.

—Ben Jonson, *Discoveries*

"TO PENSHURST" is composed of four basic sections: (1) lines 1–8; (2) lines 9–44; (3) lines 45–88; (4) lines 89–102. The first six lines of section 1 are concerned primarily with architecture. They are characterized by negative constructions that state what Penshurst is *not* architecturally, and by implication, ethically and ideologically. By contrast, the couplet that follows makes no reference to architecture; it epitomizes what Penshurst *is* by invoking the elements of Nature. Section 2 expands upon the concluding couplet of the previous section. The building itself is hardly referred to; instead, the surrounding estate, the natural environment, is described. Section 3 brings us inside the building, though there is still little in the way of architectural description. The relations of the Sidney family with its tenants, its peers, its king, and the poet, are depicted. Section 4 is an epilogue to the poem proper, which praises the members of the family, enumerating the virtues that give to the house that ethical essence that distinguishes it as a *home* in which a family and its lord-father dwell.

Lines 1–8

This breakdown of the poem into its thematic divisions reveals a basic asymmetry in its construction—four sections of eight, thirty-six, forty-four, and fourteen lines, respectively. Yet, while the poem as a whole may seem asymmetrical, the opening section manifests a certain symmetry that is in keeping with its theme. In addition to those ordering devices that characterize the poem throughout (rhymed couplets and a predominantly regular, though not inflexible, meter), there is a distinctive pattern of repetition in this first section that gives it more pronounced tension and uniformity of structure. In the first four lines, the initial words form a mirror (*abba*) pattern:

(a) Thou . . .
(b) Of . . .
(b) Of . . .
(a) Thou . . .

This sequence is repeated in compressed form in lines 7 and 8:

(a) *Thou* joy'st in better markes, // (b) *of* soyle, of ayre,
(b) *Of* wood, of water: // therein (a) *thou* art faire.

Despite elements that disturb this balance—most notably a variation in the stress pattern of line 6, to which I shall turn later in this discussion—the overall effect of the repetition in lines 1–8 is that of a more tightly knit structure than what we encounter in other sections of the poem.

This relatively closed structure, involving a conspicuous employment of poetic "parallelism" or "equivalence" in Roman Jakobson's terminology,[1] justifies closer attention to formal device in section 1 than will be necessary in discussing the remainder of the poem. However, I am interested less in a relentless Jakobsonian search for symmetries than in analyzing what I believe to be a dialectical relationship that operates at two levels in "To Penshurst": a dialectic of form (between closed and open, or symmetrical and asymmetrical structure); and a dialectic of content (exemplified in the theme of the opening lines).

A preliminary glance at the theme of section 1 will enable us to say something about the function of the structural parallelism employed there. As I have said, the first six lines of the poem deal primarily with negative comparisons. Penshurst is not one of the new houses, built by successful courtiers and Tudor administrators like the Cecils, men who were able to use their stature and power to amass vast wealth. Such "prodigy" houses combined elements of the native Gothic tradition with classical features borrowed from Italy: marble pillars, "lanthernes," elaborate staircases, and large courts around which the elevations were likely to be perfectly symmetrical as at Sutton Place and Longleat (Figs. 3 and 4; compare the asymmetry of the plan of Penshurst, Fig. 5). While these edifices are envied, "grudg'd at," Penshurst is "reverenc'd" as "an ancient pile." And while the appointments of the more ostentatious houses all represent the fashioning by *art* of certain substances—marble, touchstone, gold—which, in their natural state, would remain relatively useless and hidden in the earth, the "better markes" that mark Penshurst are of the most openly visible and useful elements of *Nature*—"soyle . . . ayre . . . wood . . . water," and the "countrey stone" referred to later in the poem. In these first eight lines, an opposition between Nature and Culture (manifested in decoration or ornament) is thus established, an opposition which will be developed thoughout the poem.[2]

Having noted this opposition, we can now observe that the *abba* pattern connecting lines 1–4 with lines 7–8 compels us to relate these two parts of section 1, to see the contrast between the "envious show" to which other houses are built, and the "better [i.e., natural] markes" of Penshurst. Our attention to this semantic

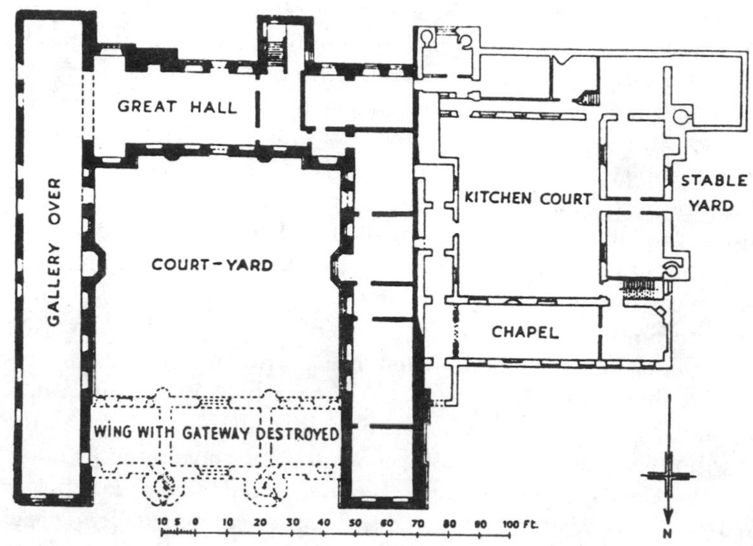

Figure 3. *Plan of Sutton Place, Surrey (1521–27). Symmetrical courtyard elevations, asymmetrical exterior elevations. From T. Garner and A. Stratton,* The Domestic Architecture of England during the Tudor Period *(London: B. T. Batsford, Ltd., 1929).*

opposition is enforced further by the positional equivalence of the phrases "Of touch, or marble," and "Of polish'd pillars," in lines 2–3, and "Of wood, of water," in line 8. Thus, superimposed upon the temporal order of these opening lines is a logical structure of parallelism and opposition that cuts across the sequence. We may represent this logic by the following rearrangement of the lines in question, bearing in mind that its structure becomes evident only retrospectively, that is, after the reader has progressed through the sequence in its proper order:

Culture 1 Thou art not, Penshurst, built to envious show
4 Thou hast no lantherne, whereof tales are told

Nature 7 Thou joy'st in better markes, of soyle, of ayre

Culture 2 Of touch, or marble; nor canst boast a row
3 Of polish'd pillars, or a roofe of gold

Nature 8 Of wood, of water: therein thou art faire

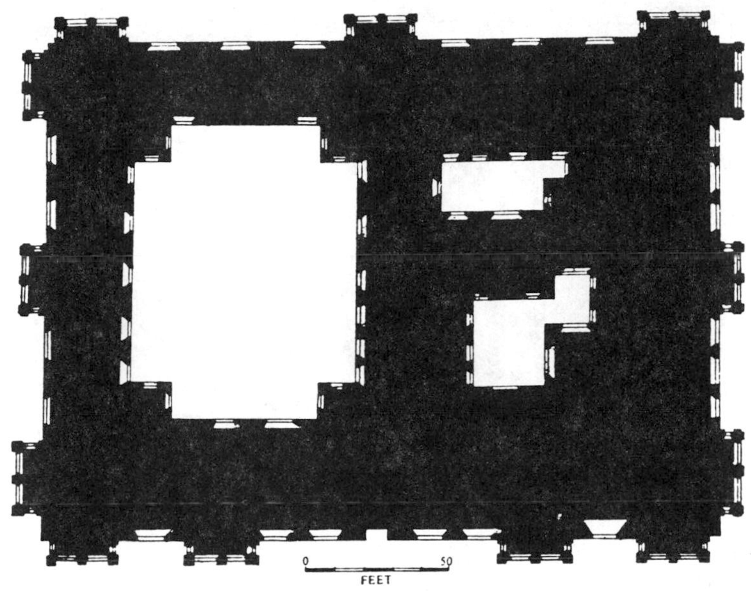

Figure 4. *Plan of Longleat, Wiltshire (1572–80). Symmetrical interior court and symmetrical exterior elevations. From Eric Mercer,* English Art, 1553–1625, *Vol. 7 of* The Oxford History of English Art *(Oxford: Clarendon Press, 1962).*

There are, moreover, other ways in which formal symmetry reinforces the sense of section 1. The importance of "gold" as the highest mark of "envious show" is emphasized by its appearance in the prominent position of a rhyme word at the end of line 3. By contrast, among the natural elements that mark Penshurst in line 7, similar positional prominence is given to "ayre." Gold has no immediate use value; it is valued only for its appearance, that is, as a visual sign of wealth and power. Air is the exact opposite of gold; it is without appearance, an invisible yet ubiquitous element in Nature that has the greatest use value in being absolutely essential to life. Thus, in his *Elements of Architecture* (1624), Sir Henry Wotton gives the choice of natural setting, "the Seate," as the primary concern in building a house; and as the first precept governing that choice, Wotton considers "the quality and temper of the *aire*."[3]

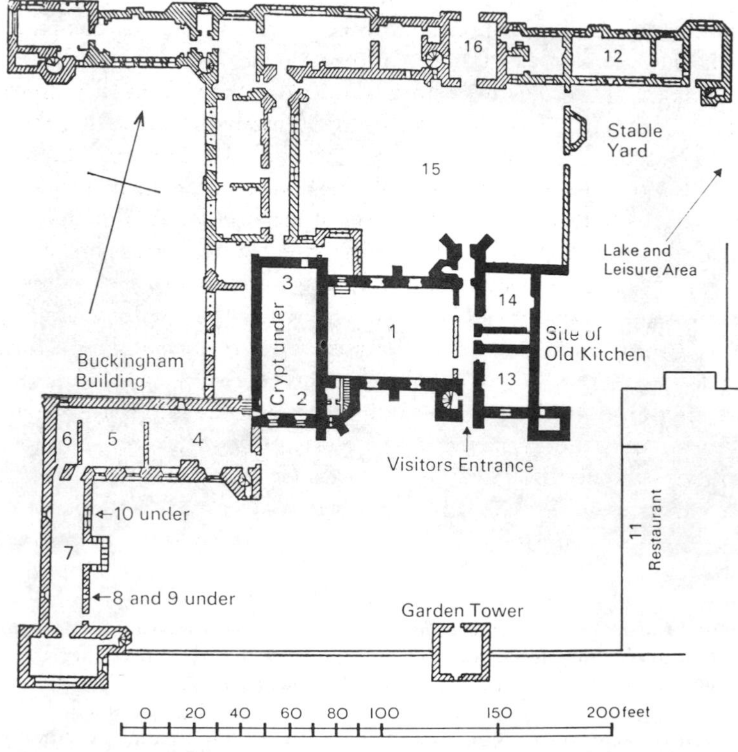

1 Baron's Hall (14th century)
2 Crypt
3 Solar, now State Dining Room
4 Queen Elizabeth's Room
5 Tapestry Room
6 Pages' Room
4, 5, 6: Buckingham Building (15th–16th centuries)
7 Long Gallery (early 17th century)
8 Panelled Room
9 Nether Gallery
10 The Old Kitchen Gift Shop
11 Restaurant
12 Toy Museum
13 Pantry
14 Buttery
15 Courtyard
16 King's Tower (16th century)

Figure 5. *Plan of Penshurst Place showing various stages of construction and the present disposition of rooms open to visitors. The darker areas demark the walls of the original fourteenth-century manor house. Reproduced by permission of Viscount De L'Isle, V.C., K.G.*

Another aspect of the opposition between Culture and Nature here is the fragmentation attributed to the former as compared with the unity of the latter. Culture in the form of *ornament* is composed of a series of materials valued either, as in the case of "gold," "touch," "marble," for the cost entailed in extracting them from Nature, or, as with "polish'd pillars," "lantherne," "stayre," and "courts," for their allegorical function as elements in a style or fashion. In both cases, the function of the ornament is to enforce, through what Angus Fletcher calls "the emotive pressure of the status symbol," a system of norms and a given social hierarchy.[4] Moreover, ornament can be combined with other types of allegory in a more elaborate system of architectural representation. Thus, for example, the "stayre" at Wimbledon (Fig. 6) is both ornament and monument. The representation of hierarchy and power in the "stayre" and the terracing there were probably adopted from a similar scheme designed by Vignola for the Farnese palace at Caprarola (Fig. 7). Gérard Labrot has written that in the case of Caprarola we cannot speak of the insertion of a building in a setting:

> [The] strategy of height, as it is manifested here, aims much less at the enjoyment of a panorama than at placing the master at a distance, high in the sky in the eyes of others. This is why it is impossible, here, to speak in terms of insertion in a site. . . . For the architect, the site has only one merit: to permit a structural arrangement [*aménagement*] which hides its natural character.
>
> . . . The succession in height of the different levels of ground in front of the palace, when set in the perspective of the street of the town, exalts the itinerary of access by detailing its stages and modulations, but at the same time, deprives it of all sincerity and transforms it in turn into a theatre.[5]

At Penshurst, on the other hand, it is precisely necessary to speak of "insertion in a site" because it is the house's "organic" relation with its environs and with those who dwell there that both the architecture and Jonson's poem assert. Penshurst *is* the creation of the illusion of "sincerity," of an open and direct participation in a community that extends beyond its walls, a denial of the closed theatricality that is characteristic of houses like the palace at Caprarola and the building modeled after it at Wimbledon.

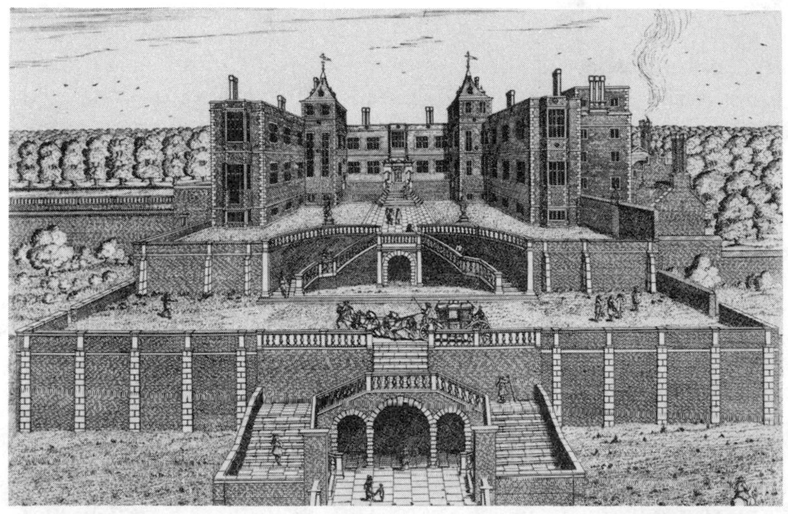

Figure 6. *Wimbledon House, Surrey (1588). Engraving by H. Winstanley. Reproduced by permission of the British Library.*

Figure 7. *Farnese Palace at Caprarola (ca. 1573), as engraved by Giuseppi Vasi in 1740. From Gérard Labrot,* Le palais Farnese de Caprarola: essai de lecture *(Paris: Klincksieck, 1970).*

In the poem, ornament (associated with Culture) is characterized as a set of alternative, discrete elements which are combined by accumulation; and this particulate and cumulative characteristic is formally reinforced by the frequent appearance of the coordinating conjunction *or*: "touch, *or* marble; [n]*or* . . . polish'd pillars, *or* a roofe of gold . . . lantherne . . . *or* stayre, *or* courts." The frequency of *or* here may also be designed to suggest the ephemeralness of such characteristics. By contrast, in lines 7 and 8, there are no coordinating conjunctions (only one connective repeated consistently, the preposition *of*); no alternatives (the elements of Nature are indeed elemental—they have no alternates nor can they be substituted for each other, and the connective *of* is an unambiguous *designatum* which relates each to the others as one function of a whole which is Nature); no fragmentation (nothing to suggest particularity—rather, the emphasis is on the universal, the universality of Nature's essential, irreducible elements "of soyle, of ayre, / Of wood, of water"). The relational unity of these four elements is impressed upon the reader by their appearance in an unbroken sequence, unlike the broken series of elements that were the marks of Culture in lines 2–5.

Finally, we may note that the alternative modes of "show" characterizing other houses suggest novelty, while the elements that mark Penshurst are "ancient" and eternal. Yet what is, perhaps, most striking about the comparison which we have been led to make by the time we have reached the eighth line of the poem is that Penshurst has not been described. We know nothing about its appearance save for the basic elements of its natural surroundings and whatever we can surmise from the resonances of "ancient pile" in line 5. In fact, we know more about the other houses with which Penshurst is compared.

The turning point of the comparison occurs in lines 5–6. This transitional couplet involves an ambiguity that disturbs the apparent unity and symmetry of the opening section. The alternative particulars describing the other houses overlap into the beginning of line 5 ("Or stayre, or courts . . ."). But the caesura which follows immediately marks a boundary between what has been stated thus far, and what will follow (Or stayre, or courts // but stand'st an ancient pile). Then, in line 6, the first hemistich briefly recapitulates the evaluation of the other houses' "envious show" (And these grudg'd at //), while the second hemistich (// art reverenc'd the while) resumes the development of the other side of the comparison. "Grudg'd at" is more than just a recapitulation, however. It would seem to point up, by reiteration, the special significance of the theme of envy which has already appeared as the central concept of line 1. This may also explain why "grudg'd at" is the only instance in the entire eight-line section where a trochee is substituted for an iamb in the second foot; that is to say, the metrical inversion serves to highlight the central significance of the concept of *envy* which is described as the main relation elicited by the other houses and their lords and which the poem attempts to define as unnatural and evil.

Another aspect to this recurrence of the theme of envy in the phrase "grudg'd at" is that the repetition is located at a critical turning point, in the vicinity of the boundary which divides the eight-line section into the realms of Culture and Nature. From a formalist point of view it might be appealing to argue that "grudg'd at" and the metrical inversion there mark the limit of the realm of Culture; that the caesura immediately following "grudg'd at" is the boundary between the two realms; and that therefore the concept of *envy* appears at the beginning (line 1) and at the end of the space occupied by Culture as its precise and symmetrical limits. Roughly speaking, this may be the case. But it is also rather too neat. There is at least one disjunctive element which intrudes on this symmetry and which violates the space occupied by Culture if we assume that "grudg'd at" marks one of its limits. I am referring to the words "ancient pile" which occur before "grudg'd at" and which pertain to Penshurst itself. Clearly, it is the poet's intention to distinguish between, even to oppose, Penshurst and the other houses, and therefore in some sense to exclude it from the realm of Culture as defined here. Hence, it would seem that the boundary between the two realms should be located at the caesura in line 5 rather than in line 6. Either the boundary is at the caesura in line 5, in which case the recapitulation in "grudg'd at" and the metrical inversion there would perhaps be only an indicator to alert the reader that a boundary had just been crossed, or "grudg'd at" is itself the mark of the boundary, in which case "stands't an ancient pile" can be understood only as lying on the Culture side of the line dividing Culture and Nature.

The latter reading might make sense since, as we have seen, "ancient pile" is the only reference to the house itself, and as a house it must certainly be a phenomenon of Culture. But by the same token, the poet wants to be able to say that the Penshurst house is *not* like other houses, that it is *not* of the realm of Culture to which they belong. Given his argument thus far, he has the option of accomplishing this distinction in one of two ways: he can argue that Penshurst is different from the other houses because it is more natural, or that it is different because there is more than one Culture. Jonson chooses the first option (the fact that he avoids the notion that there are two or more Cultures is interesting and significant in itself, and I shall return to this in a moment). The argument that Penshurst is not of the same realm as other houses because it is more natural requires the maintenance of a clear logical division between the two domains. But the placement of "ancient pile" ahead of "grudg'd at" is an inversion of the logical order in which the realms are described in the eight-line introductory section of the poem, and this implies (if, perhaps, unconsciously on Jonson's part) an ambiguous boundary between Nature and Culture.

In sum, there appears to be no clear boundary between the portion of these eight lines devoted to Culture and that describing Nature. Rather, there is an ambiguous, neutral territory from the caesura at line 5 to the caesura at line 6. This neutral sector, in which there is a logical and positional inversion of the sequence Culture-Nature, permits of alternative readings. But because an inversion has taken place, either of the alternatives must include a displacement: If we take the caesura at line 5 as the boundary, then the concept of envy, which has been designated a characteristic of the realm of Culture to which the other houses pertain, is displaced into the territory of Nature by its reappearance in line 6 ("grudg'd at") (alternative 1):

If we locate the boundary after "grudg'd at," then the house at Penshurst (the "ancient pile" of line 5) must be seen to occupy a different realm from all that is given as Penshurst's "better markes"; the house itself is displaced out of the realm of Nature (alternative 2):

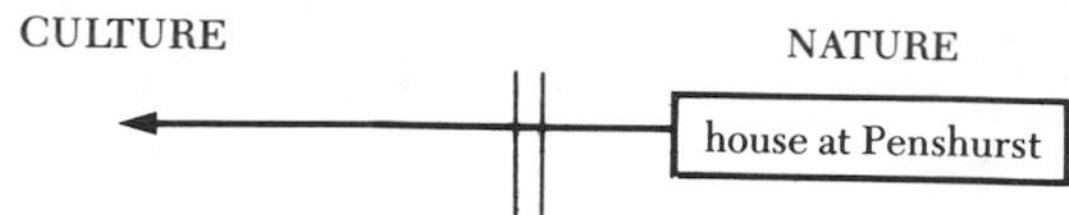

The dilemma involved in (1) is obvious and fairly simple. It entails a displacement into Nature of what is clearly unnatural by the standard established in line 1, i.e., envy. Here the process of displacement may be a sign of ideological ambiguity. It could, for example, be an indication that Jonson surmised the Sidneys' envy of other lords (and, at another level, it may betray Jonson's own envy of the Sidneys). This is not necessarily farfetched, since the poem can easily be read as a rationalization for the limited means of the Sidneys and for a house which, by the standards of the time, was less than a palace. If we read the opening negatives as instances of negation in the Freudian sense (*Verneinung*),[6] wherein a repressed image or thought is allowed to enter consciousness on condition that it is denied, then the displacement of envy ("grudg'd at") into the realm of Nature is further evidence of such an interpretation. Probably something of this sort is indeed operating in the poem. Yet even if that is the case, in this reading the term that is displaced (envy) within the logical and the ideological structure that distinguishes Nature from Culture in the opening section of the poem is not in itself ambiguous.

On the other hand, in (2) what is being displaced (the house at Penshurst) is not clearly of one realm or the other; thus, in this instance not only is the process of displacement a sign of ambiguity, but the very status of the house (the referent of the term "ancient pile") is ambiguous. The only other reference to the building itself comes in line 45 with the mention of walls of "countrey stone." As compared with "touch" and "marble," "countrey stone" seems to be of the realm of Nature. However, insofar as the eight-line introduction is concerned, the only direct reference to the house is "ancient pile"; the epithet "ancient" is an invocation of history in opposition to the novelty of the other houses, and it seems clear that the poem wants to appropriate history along with Nature as one of the "markes" of Penshurst. Yet the intent is to deny that history entails change and to deny that history is Culture. Instead, the association of "ancient pile" with the elements of Nature enumerated in lines 7 and 8 presents the paradox of history as *synchrony*, an unchanging, eternal phenomenon like Nature. Thus within the Nature/Culture opposition already established is inscribed a secondary opposition between synchrony (history) and diachrony (novelty, change). So it seems that even discounting the displacement diagramed above in (2), "ancient pile" is in itself an ambiguous term. It attaches value to the house at Penshurst by invoking history; and yet, its association with the absolute permanence and presence of Nature in this context denies the very historicity of history.

We can now, perhaps, begin to explain why Jonson chose not to argue that there is more than one Culture in distinguishing Penshurst from other country houses. To suggest that the house at Penshurst is not part of Nature on the estate but at the same time that it is not unnatural in the sense attributed to the other houses would be to imply alternative Cultures. And that would be to suggest a contradiction in ideology among factions of the Jacobean ruling class. Furthermore, to argue that Penshurst belongs to a different, older, better Culture than the newer houses might raise the uncomfortable question of how recently the present lord and lady of Penshurst had acquired title to this older, better Culture. To allow the specter of diachrony to appear in connection with Penshurst would be to call forth an aspect of history that the Sidney family would certainly prefer to have kept hidden: like most of the Tudor aristocracy, the Sidneys were *arrivistes*. From this point of view, the displacement of "ancient pile," which confuses the distinction between Culture and Nature, may be determined in part by the desire to distract attention from a more serious ambiguity, if not a contradiction, involving history. For, on the basis of the above analysis, it seems that the deliberate elaboration of an opposition between Culture and Nature in lines 1–8 is a mask to conceal the contradiction between a concept of history as synchronic (connoted by the epithets "ancient" in line 5 and "reverenc'd" in line 6) and an actual historical change which has brought the Sidneys to their present position of social status and power.

Despite these ambiguities, the repetition of the apostrophe to Penshurst at the beginning of line 7, and the shift to an affirmative mode—"Thou joy'st"—constitute a definite signal that a boundary has been crossed. And, of course, the clearest evidence that this is so, and that the Penshurst estate is of the domain of Nature, is the reference to Penshurst's "better markes." In these last two lines of the introductory section it is established that what marks Penshurst is Nature, and that what Penshurst marks is the limit of Nature.

Lines 9–44

Section 2 is a development of the theme that Nature "markes" Penshurst. It begins with another affirmative apostrophe: "Thou hast thy walkes for health, as well as sport." And the lines that follow describe, in effect, an informal walk around the estate. Appropriately, the structure is more open here than in section 1, though the style remains, in Wesley Trimpi's phrase, "relaxed without ever being loose."[7] Devices of balance and symmetry are still evident; but in one prominent instance, the parallel alliterative phrases at the beginnings of lines 28 and 29, it is significant that the parallelism does not serve to reinforce a closed couplet rhetoric but functions instead as a kind of enjambment that enables the thought to continue across the couplet form.

There are several interesting aspects to the cataloguing of Penshurst's "better markes" in section 2. To begin with, the house continues to be conspicuous by its absence. In the thirty-six lines the house is implied only three times; twice the reference is to the interior and, in both instances, specifically to the dining area ("open table" in line 27 and "thy messe" in line 30), that is, to the Great Hall which was the center of the original fourteenth-century structure and which continued to be the center of the household in the time when Jonson wrote his poem. The third reference occurs at the end of the section, at line 44 where Penshurst's "walls" are first mentioned. The emphasis on "table" and "messe" has obvious significance in that food consumption is a metaphor for all consumption of Nature's bounteous provision at Penshurst. The entire section catalogues Nature primarily as potential food. At the same time, this provision is dependent upon fertility, and that of course is another theme in these lines.

Most of the section represents the estate in terms of what are said to be its immediate natural attributes. But first there is a subsection (lines 9–18) in which the enumeration of abundance is less immediately natural, less synchronic, and, instead, in a diachronic mode that connects the topography of the estate with, respectively, a mythical and a historical past. Even the few topographical references to the estate that do appear in this subsection occur as signifiers of the domains of prehistory and history rather than as emblems of Nature ("Thy Mount, to which the Dryads doe resort"; "That taller tree, which of a nut was set, / At his [Sir Philip's] great birth . . . ," etc.). Yet this association of myth and history with Nature serves to dissolve diachrony and to assert the immediate and timeless presence of past, present, and future in which the Sidneys are in their rightful and immutable place.

The references to pagan deities ("Dryads," "Pan," "Bacchus," "Muses," etc.) and their "high feasts" evoke a Golden Age of prehistory,[8] while the subsequent reference to Sir Philip Sidney and to Barbara Gamage (the wife of Sir Robert Sidney) evoke history proper. The latter references by no means conflict with the attempt to repress diachrony discussed earlier, since the association with Golden Age images gives to these historical personages a mythical and ostensibly permanent status in their own right. Thus while the mode of description used by the poet is diachronic in lines 9–18, its function is to further enforce the notion that history is natural and synchronic. Here too, as in the remainder of the section, central images are the consumption of food (the feast of Bacchus), and fertility. The latter is evoked by the allusions to pagan rites and is specifically designated in each of the historical references: once in connection with Sir Philip's "great birth," and twice with relation to Barbara Gamage who, according to tradition, went into labor under an oak in the park (hence, in line 18, "thy Ladies oke").

In the remaining portion of section 2, the ambiguity in the division between Culture and Nature which was pointed to in section 1 is further in evidence. The itemization of natural abundance undergoes a gradual shift from the personification of the land which provides game and "feeds" and "breeds" domestic animals (lines 19–28), to the transformation of the animals themselves into active, willful, subjects beginning in line 29 ("The painted partrich lyes in every field, / And, for thy messe, is *willing* to be kill'd"). From here on, a further development takes place; the personification is intensified, and Nature is given more subtle human attributes. The ponds "pay . . . tribute fish." The fish, in turn, give themselves up of their own free will: "Fat, aged carps . . . runne into thy net"; "pikes [grow] weary their owne kinde to eat" and "officiously . . . themselves betray"; and "bright eeles . . . emulate" the pikes. Next, the imagery switches from fish to fruit and flowers:

> Then hath thy orchard fruit, thy garden flowers,
> Fresh as the ayre, and new as are the houres.
> The earely cherry, with the later plum,
> Fig, grape, and quince, each in his time doth come.
> (lines 39–42)

Here too, while the images are from Nature, an interesting and subtle transformation occurs in which human or cultural attributes are projected into Nature. The first sign of this shift is in the words "new as are the houres." We might expect an association of ripening fruit and blossoming flowers to be made with a change in *season*; but instead the connection is made specifically with *time*. It is linear, incremental, clock time rather than the cycle of seasons that is evoked here. This temporal connection is reinforced with "earely cherry" and "later plum" in line 41, and finally, in line 42, with the direct reference to "time." True, the order in which "each [fruit] in his time doth come" is intended as Nature's order; but it is human time that is measuring that order, and there is at least an ambiguity as to whether mathematical measurement is a natural phenomenon or whether it is a cultural phenomenon imposed on Nature. This emphasis on clock time over seasonal time is the surface sign of an emergent epistemological presupposition which is an element in Jonson's concept of value throughout the poem; it is the assumption that Nature is indeed a mathematical Nature, subject to precise quantitative analysis, an assumption which is prevalent at conscious and unconscious levels in much of the literature of the period as well as in other kinds of documents.[9]

Lines 43–44 are meant to provide further evidence of the ease with which provision is made by Nature on an estate governed in accordance with Nature's own laws:

> The blushing apricot, and woolly peach
> Hang on thy walls, that every child may reach.

But it is also in these lines that the outer walls of the house are first referred to; and the manner of the reference reinforces the ambiguity between Nature and Culture. Again, the ambiguity is located at a boundary; in the present instance, "walls" points to the architectural dividing line between what a house delimits (Culture) and what is outside (Nature). And, once again, the dividing line is unclear. The trees and their fruits which hang on the walls suggest that it would be difficult to distinguish between what is natural and what is not in the walls themselves. (This ambiguity is compounded if the fruit trees are interpreted as being espaliered, in which case it is a *cultivated* Nature that is being used to describe Culture as Nature.) The tendency in the previous lines for Nature to be personified, to be given attributes from the realm of Culture, is now inverted. Here, the sign of Culture ("walls" which denotes the house) is made ambiguous by the encroachment of Nature. This inversion becomes apparent, however, only with the reference to "walls" in line 44, since line 43 still contains the last of the series of personifications of Nature ("blushing apricot"). Thus, line 44 not only contains a reference to an architectural boundary ("walls"), but is itself the marker of a boundary in the poem where an inversion of the relationship between Nature and Culture takes place.

Lines 45–88

Why the ambiguity at this juncture? Perhaps a look at the following lines will tell us. We should remark, for example, the repetition (in precise positional equivalence) of the words "thy walls" in lines 44 and 45. Surely this is a signal to the reader to come to attention! But why here? The two lines are on either side of the division between section 2 and section 3 of the poem. Moreover, if we consider the final fourteen-line section as an epilogue which addresses itself solely to the moral attributes of the Sidney family and which is clearly distinct from the topographical presentation and evaluation of the preceding lines, it becomes evident that the two lines in which "thy walls" is repeated (lines 44–45) are at the exact center of the major portion of the poem (88 lines in all). Clearly some sort of logical boundary is being marked at the formal level of articulation by the symmetrical repetition of "thy walls."

At this central dividing line the mode of description undergoes a significant change. We have seen that from line 19 to line 44 there is a movement from the description of natural attributes on the estate to a personification or culturification of Nature. At line 44 we are shifted into a realm that must be understood, at least apparently and partially, as Culture, that is, the house. "Walls," in lines 44–45, is the first suggestion of this shift, and, of course, "walls" is both denotatively and connotatively the sign of a boundary: denotatively, in the sense that the walls of Penshurst literally separate the interior of the house, its court and its garden, from the open park and the woods outside; connotatively, in that the symmetrical repetition of the word at the exact center of the major part of the poem suggests a reading of "walls" as a metaphor for the logical division of the poem at this point.

But "walls" can also be understood in its connotative dimension as a metaphor for an ideological boundary which the poem is attempting to establish and yet to hide. The division marked by "walls" in lines 44–45 is the fulcrum of a delicately balanced paradox in which the ideological distinction between Nature and Culture, which was used earlier to oppose Penshurst to other estates, is now simultaneously asserted and denied as a distinction applicable to the Penshurst estate itself. The boundary at lines 44–45 appears to divide the description of the environment outside the walls of Penshurst (lines 9–44) from that within (lines 45–88). But as we have seen, the sign marking this division is ambiguous. The "walls" are described in such a way as to imply that they are part of the natural environment, inverting the previous orientation in which Nature took on the attributes of Culture (lines 19–36). It seems then that while we can speak of a division between exterior environment and interior environment at lines 44–45, it is difficult to describe that division as one between Nature and Culture. Of course, this is consistent with the ambiguity of the opposition established in the opening eight-line section, since the poem does not want to locate the house at Penshurst in the domain of Culture occupied by the other houses. Clearly, there is a difference between that part of the estate that lies outside the walls and the part contained within them. But, whereas in the opening section the poem described other houses and the materials of which they are constructed as a Culture antagonistic to what is natural, here the relation between the house and its exterior environment is seen to be nonantagonistic and in equilibrium. Thus, the important distinction that the poem seems to be trying to make about Penshurst is not that between Nature and Culture at all, but rather between one sort of Culture and another.

However, as we have already seen, to suggest the existence of opposing Cultures would be to come dangerously close to revealing contradictions within a ruling-class ideology, something that a common author seeking to maintain an all-too-precarious status in Jacobean society would do well to keep hidden. Instead, Jonson suggests that the houses which are opposed in "To Penshurst" need not be emblematic of opposing Cultures (or of an opposition within Culture). The house at Penshurst and the other houses are representations respectively of things that are natural (a house can be a house and still be part of Nature) and things that are unnatural. Instead of risking the identification of a conflict by asserting that the houses represent opposing forces, Jonson suggests that there is only that which is part of a neutral, continuous presence or plenum —Nature—and that which is not. In place of the opposition between two Cultures (and between factions of the ruling elite) which is his real theme, Jonson substitutes a simple binary difference: Nature/un-Nature. The identification of Penshurst with the plenitude of Nature thus serves to identify the other houses as deviant; and it is by this exclusion of the others as Other that the Penshurst poem, while maintaining the neutrality of its representation, succeeds with remarkable effect in providing an ideological weapon for one side of a social struggle which it yet manages to keep hidden.

In order to maintain a clear separation between Penshurst

(Nature) and other houses (un-Nature), it was necessary for Jonson to blur distinctions on the Penshurst estate itself. Jonson insists that Penshurst is entirely of Nature, and yet he persists in describing the internal territorial division of the estate through a logic that distinguished Culture from Nature. If there is a contradiction here, it is kept obscure by the ambiguity. The poem attempts to describe the difference between what the "walls" of Penshurst contain and what is outside; and yet, it retains a sense of the equivalence of everything within the wider bounds of the estate by means of an implicit rhetorical chiasmus. That is, through the device of personification in section 2, Nature at Penshurst is depicted as a *cultured Nature*, while at the juncture of lines 44–45 the process is inverted and, in section 3, the description of a *natural Culture* begins.

But while this strategy of inversion and equation explains the ambiguity at the boundary between Nature and Culture at Penshurst, it does not adequately account for the inconsistencies that appear on both sides of the equation. For example, with regard to the notion of a *cultured Nature* (section 2), we may recall the progression from "fat, aged carps" (scavengers) to the more voracious "pikes" which are said to have grown "weary their owne kinde to eat." It is obvious that Jonson selects a species of predators here and describes them as having renounced their basic nature in order to enhance, by a dramatic transformation, the representation of a benevolent Nature at Penshurst, a Nature in which there is no antagonism, no strain. Yet, under any conception of Nature that Jonson and his contemporaries might have adhered to, it is the very nature of pikes "their owne kinde to eat." Thus, it requires a logical contradiction—Nature is unnatural—to achieve the relation *cultured Nature*. On the other side of the equation, in connection with the idea of a *natural Culture*, we may note an interesting parallel that occurs at the beginning of section 3, where it is asserted that Penshurst's walls "are rear'd with no mans ruine, no mans grone." An association with the humanized pikes is perhaps intended here, since the central notion is that like the pikes, the Sidney family, who rank socially above the human equivalent of scavengers and who belong to a ruling class some of whose members are predatory, would not "their owne kinde . . . eat."[10]

The utterly fantastic (and logically contradictory) example of the "pikes" in the relation *cultured Nature* is thus a sort of *figural* preparation for the similar relation *natural Culture* at line 46, the notion, by no means fantastic though certainly utopian, that houses like Penshurst can be built and maintained without the exploitation of human labor. The purpose of the equation between *cultured Nature* and *natural Culture* in this instance seems to be to suggest that just as pikes will not eat their own kind at Penshurst, so the house is not built (and wealth is not accumulated) there at the expense of the labor of others. Indeed, here (at line 46) and through the rest of section 3, there is an implied negation of *labor* altogether and, therefore, the negation of a primary aspect of Culture. It could be argued that all the line implies is that no exploitation has gone into the rearing of these walls, and that the force and function of labor are not being suppressed. But the general sense of the section as a whole is that all the necessities and the comforts at Penshurst are provided without the expense of labor, as the reference to "free provisions" in line 58 seems to bear out. The house is represented in line 46 as a form of Culture that is not the production of labor, but rather somehow itself a provision of Nature. It is *natural Culture*. This notion is reinforced in line 47 ("There's none, that dwell about them [the walls], wish them downe"), which, given the context, could be rewritten: There's none that dwell in Nature (like the "Sylvane" referred to earlier and the "farmer, and the clowne" of the following line) who wish them down. The suggestion, begun here and developed in the lines that follow, is of a reciprocity between those who dwell in a part of Nature (*cultured Nature*) outside the walls of the house and those who dwell in a part of Nature (*natural Culture*) within. But it is not merely reciprocity that is being asserted here, it is also a relation of identity. For the reference to those "that dwell" on the manor outside the walls is echoed in the last line of the poem in which it is stated that where other lords "have built" (i.e., Culture), the lord of Penshurst "dwells" (i.e., in Nature).

This relation of identity between lord and farmer is only partial, however, since it is simultaneously denied by the very distinction lord/farmer. Despite its ambiguity, "walls" does mark a boundary (between an exterior and an interior environment) which enforces that social distinction. And the retention of a difference between lord and farmer requires a sign that is different; a lord's country house cannot be isomorphic with the rude dwelling of a tenant farmer. Yet if the latter is represented as signifying Nature, and Nature is being represented as a continuous and homogeneous plenum, then the lord's house must be something other than Nature. At the same time, a portion of the "Nature" signified by farmers' dwellings is expropriated and attached to the lord's house at Penshurst in order to distinguish it from other lords' houses. So, where earlier we noted the assertion and denial of a distinction between Penshurst and other houses in terms of the category of Culture (Penshurst is both the same as yet other than houses "built to envious show," i.e., it is and is not a form of Culture), here a similar double game is played with the category of Nature (Penshurst is both the same as yet other than the portion of the estate where farmers "dwell," i.e., it is and is not a form of Nature).

No doubt, some will argue that a distinction between the lord's house and the exterior environment where farmers "dwell" need not be interpreted as a break in continuity in the domain of Nature; after all, it will be pointed out, the poem makes use of a traditional conception of Nature as a hierarchically ordered domain, a chain of being. Thus, it will be insisted, the distinction between lord and peasant is a natural distinction between two links in the chain. My reply to this argument is simply that it is the poem itself which undermines the doctrine of the chain of being at the same time that it appears to implement it. For as we have seen, the poem is concerned not only with the representation of a hierarchy on the estate; it is also, perhaps primarily, concerned with an opposition at the same level or "link" in the chain. That is, the poem contests the present state of the chain (the status quo) by equating one kind of nobility (the Sidneys) with Nature and another kind ("other lords") with Culture. Moreover, the status of the chain of being is undermined at two levels in the poem; not only is the position of one kind of aristocracy contested and that of another supported, but the position allotted to poets in the present chain is also called into question. For in developing the concept of the chain of being on the estate, Jonson places himself in a position next to the king (the poet makes his appearance as a guest at Penshurst in lines 64–75; King James and Prince Henry appear in lines 76–77). This is hardly consistent with the order of being prescribed by tradition, and I shall have more to say about this particular break in the proper linking of the chain in a moment.

The ambiguity concerning the "walls" of Penshurst is developed further by the negation of their function as *walls*, or barriers; instead they are described as open so that "all come in" (line 48) who so desire. The reader too is brought by the description into the house, and the remainder of the poem describes what occurs in the interior. Yet the distinction between interior and exterior environment remains blurred. The architectural appearance of the interior is undefined; and, just as the outer features of the house were subordinated to a description of the natural environment beyond its walls, so are its inner features left undelineated in favor of a description of what is conceived to be the natural environment within.

Those who enter are farmers and their families. They are depicted as having nothing to ask of the lord and the lady of the house, but as bearing gifts themselves (these gifts are products of Culture, that is, of Nature cultivated and transformed by human labor, though that aspect is never allowed to emerge clearly):

> Some bring a capon, some a rurall cake,
> Some nuts, some apples; some that thinke they make
> The better cheeses bring 'hem . . .
> (lines 51–53)

What all of this seems to be referring to in actuality is the payment of *rent in kind* by peasants on the Sidney lands; but its quality as rent and as the product of human labor is hidden, and instead the process is represented as the peasants' free bestowal of "gifts" of Nature as expressions of "their love" (line 57) upon the lord and lady who have no "neede of such" (line 59). Yet the most startling indicators of an underlying hidden referent for this elaboration of Nature at the interior of the house occur in the next lines:

> . . . or else send
> By their ripe daughters, whom they would commend
> This way to husbands; and whose baskets beare
> An embleme of themselves, in plum, or peare.
> (lines 53–56)

"*Ripe* daughters," coming at the end of a catalogue of products of rural husbandry, is a significant metonymy in itself. But we remember too that earlier, in line 44, the fruit growing in the orchards of Penshurst was said to hang in such a way "that every child may reach." I suggest that that "child" which, we remarked, was associated with the images of "blushing apricot, and woolly peach" (line 43) is also related to the "ripe daughters" of line 54 who "beare an embleme of themselves, in plum, or peare"; so that by an interesting substitution, the child that picks the fruit becomes the child that *is* the fruit, and when "ripe" the "child" is also ready to be picked by a husband. My assumption that this substitution is by deliberate design is supported, I believe, by the fact that Jonson made a very significant change from his probable source for this part of the poem. The source is Martial's epigram describing the Baian villa and farm of Faustinus (III,lviii). Martial writes:

> et dona matrum vimine offerunt texto
> grandes proborum virgines colonorum.
> (lines 39–40)

which Ker translates: "And the strapping daughters of honest farmers offer in a wicker basket their mother's gifts."[11] In Martial's poem there is, at the most, a slight implication that the "strapping daughters" may be themselves "their mother's gifts." Jonson takes the implied metaphor identifying the daughters with the contents of their wicker baskets and literalizes it so that now the daughters are "ripe" and their baskets literally "beare / An embleme of themselves."

This reference to "ripe daughters" is also metonymically related to the lady of the house, Barbara Gamage, who is identified with fertility throughout the poem. (For example, line 18: "thy Ladies oke" is believed to refer to a tree under which a story had it that Lady Sidney first went into labor; line 19: the lady is identified with the "copp's . . . nam'd of Gamage" which provides an unending supply of deer for Penshurst's table; and line 90: "fruitfull" is central among the three essential qualities for which Lady Barbara is praised—"Thy lady's noble, fruitfull, chaste withall.") Here again, the association points to an ambiguity in the representation of

Penshurst. We have seen that the lord is said to "dwell" within walls of Nature and is thereby partly identified with the peasants who "dwell about them." Similarly, the "fruitfull" lady of the house is partly identified with the farmers' "ripe daughters." While the latter association is made somewhat more indirect by the use of the adjectival form "fruitfull" in the case of the lady as compared with the implied nominal "fruit" for the peasant girls, the connection is nonetheless clear, whether consciously or unconsciously intended by Jonson.

Actually, at the time of her marriage in 1584, Barbara Gamage was an extremely valuable and rare "fruit." She had just succeeded to the fortune of an old and powerful Welsh family. Her father, John Gamage, died on 8 September. Events of the next few weeks indicate the urgency with which high-ranking members of the Elizabethan aristocracy treated the circumstance of an unattached woman of gentle birth with a large inheritance. There is evidence of a scramble at court to control the young heiress's marital prospects. Even the queen took an active interest in the arrangement of an appropriate alliance. But the object of all this attention was at some remove from the court, in the custody of her guardian, Sir Edward Stradling, at his seat St. Donats, Glamorganshire. There, on 23 September, she was married to Robert Sidney whose family was already well established in Wales as a result of Sir Henry Sidney's long tenure as lord president of the Council in the Marches. Word of the marriage had not yet reached the court on 26 September when Sir Walter Ralegh, a kinsman of Barbara Gamage, wrote to her guardian demanding information on behalf of the queen. Ralegh's letter is also of interest because of its reference to this business of matchmaking as a process of buying and selling, with the young woman as the object of exchange:

> Her Majestye hath nowe thrise caused letters to be written unto you, that you suffer not my kinsewoman to be boughte and solde in Wales, without her Majesties pryvetye, and the consent or advise of my L. Chamberlayne and my selfe, her father's cousin germayns: consideringe she hath not anie nearer kyn nor better . . . I doubte not but, all other perswasion sett aparte, you will satisfie her Highnes; and withall do us that curtesie as to acquaint us with her matchinge.[12]

The lord chamberlain to whom Ralegh refers was at this time Charles Howard, second Lord Howard of Effingham, soon to be appointed lord admiral (he would command the English fleet that defeated the Armada in 1588). Howard wrote to Stradling twice concerning his cousin Barbara Gamage: on 21 September 1584 he urges "that you doe not suffer anie to have recourse unto heer touchinge mariadge till yow know farder of heer Majesties pleasur"; and on 26 September, angry at Stradling's silence on the matter, he complains that "the strangnes of your dellinge towardes me in this cause hath moved some other good frend of mynde to aquaynt me with your manner of dellinge with my cosyn, which I dowe nothinge at all allowe of, and so shall you well knowe when I shall have opportunitie."[13] Howard was probably acting in the interest of Sir James Croft, a personal servant of long standing to the queen and the comptroller of her household. Croft had sought to match Barbara Gamage with his grandson, Herbert Croft, and mentions that he has Lord Howard's approval in a letter to Stradling dated 15 December 1583. Subsequently, on 17 September 1584, Croft writes from the court, accusing Stradling of forcibly detaining the young woman "as a prisoner" at his house in Glamorganshire.[14] Meanwhile, Walsingham, in his role as secretary, writes on 20 September informing Stradling of the queen's explicit instructions that Barbara Gamage be brought to the court and "that this younge gentlewoman . . . be not suffred to have anye suche accesse to hir as wherby shee maye contract or entangle hir self for mariage with anye man." Yet in another letter to Stradling, dated the very next day, Walsingham, whose daughter had married Philip Sidney a year earlier, discloses his personal interest in the matter: ". . . beinge nowe secreatly geven to understande that for the good will yow beare unto the Earle of Pembrocke, you meane to further what yow may younge Mr. Robert Sydney, I can not but incorage yow to proceed therin, for that I knowe her Majestie will noe waye miselike therof: besyds the L: Chamberlaine, Mr. Rawley, and the rest of the younge gentlewoman's kynsfolkes, doe greatly desyre yt." The latter claim is not supported by the letters of Lord Howard and Ralegh written a few days later and quoted above. Eventually, on 27 September, Walsingham writes to Stradling assuring him that powerful men at court will defend him against "what so ever blusteringe woords are geven owt against you by younge Mr. Croftes and his frends there," and providing him with an alibi for his failure to obey the queen's directive that he bring the young heiress to court before negotiating her marriage: "The messenger affirmeth that he came to your howse two howres after the mariadge sollempnised."[15] Such fortuitous timing evokes a wedding scene out of a romantic stage comedy. But Stradling probably did know of the queen's wishes prior to the union of Barbara Gamage and Robert Sidney; and even if he did not deliberately ignore her order, he certainly shunned the counsel of his ward's relatives at court and avoided seeking royal approval of his own plans for a marriage. Instead, he appears to have conducted swift and secret negotiations with Henry Sidney and his son-in-law, the earl of Pembroke (who provided part of a bond of £6,000 as Barbara Gamage's jointure, which Stradling held in trust and passed on to his heir, Sir John Stradling, in 1609).[16] In risking the queen's displeasure, Stradling seems to have acted with the confidence that he would be protected by powerful men like Pembroke and Walsingham who had a personal stake in the fortunes of Henry Sidney's sons.

Jonson may not have been aware of the intrigue connected with the wedding of Barbara Gamage to Robert Sidney, but he must have known how valuable a commodity she was at the time of her marriage. Moreover, there is another historical fact to which the poem refers and of which Jonson and his readers could not have been unaware: that is, that Barbara Gamage was indeed extraordinarily "fruitfull." She gave birth to twelve children, eight girls and four boys. And, since two of the boys died in infancy, in essence the marriage of Robert Sidney and Barbara Gamage issued mainly in "ripe daughters," suitable wives for courtiers of no mean stature and fortune.[17]

However, Jonson's praise of Lady Barbara is not confined merely to her childbearing ability. He also celebrates her qualities as a wife and mother. There is evidence, moreover, that in the latter regard Jonson did not need to exaggerate. By the standard of the times, Lady Barbara appears to have been an extraordinarily attentive mother. In April 1597, during a long stay in Flushing where he had succeeded his brother Philip as governor, Robert

Sidney wrote to his wife at Penshurst relating his plans for her to come over on a visit. He insists that she not bring the three older children: "They are not so yong now, but that they may wel bee from their mother. Mary is almost ten, and Kate almost eight; and though I cannot find fault hether unto, with their bringing up, yet I know now every day more and more, it wil bee fit for them to bee owt of their fathers hows. . . . For the boy [William], I would faine have him with Sir Charles Morison. . . . For I know there shall bee care had of him there, as much as I would wish. And in the meane time I pray yow disuse him from lying with his mayd. For it is not good for him, and I will have him taken from it. I know that these things are nothing pleasing to yow; but yow must remember, I have part in them, as wel as yow, and therfore must have care of them. I know also, that a better, and more carefull mother there is not, then you are; and indeed, I doe not feare any thing so much as your too much fondnes. But having so many as now God hath sent yow, yow may wel spare the bigger, and mind them which be yonger . . ."[18] The tone of the letter is mildly chiding. In Robert's view, and by Elizabethan convention, the children were ready to be weaned socially—the girls from "their fathers hows" and the boy from the care of women—and Barbara's attachment to them was a bit excessive. But there is also a tender recognition here "that a better, and more carefull mother there is not." Two years later, Robert Sidney's servant and regular correspondent Rowland Whyte expresses admiration for Lady Barbara's care and education of the children: "My Lady sees them well taught, and brought up in learning, and qualities, fitt for theire birth and condicion."[19]

It appears, then, that Jonson's praise of Barbara Gamage is not unfounded. He represents her as the paragon of the role of wife and mother by the standards of a concept of the family that is relatively recent historically. As the lady of the house she bears a large measure of the responsibility for the upbringing of her children; and she is especially responsible for training her daughters, largely by the example of her own piety and "her high huswifery," to perform, eventually, the duties of wife and mother in households and families belonging to husbands of their own.

In this respect, Jonson's poem is congruent with the iconography of the period. As one facet of his study of the emergence of the modern concept of the family, Philippe Ariès writes of the shift from a manner of family portraiture that is essentially "a sort of *ex-voto*," to one that is more concerned with conveying a new notion of the nature of the family itself: "These pictures are no longer intended for churches: they are meant to adorn private homes, and this secularization of the portrait is undoubtedly a most important phenomenon—the family contemplates itself in the home of one of its members." Ariès proceeds to distinguish stages in the development of family portraiture in Europe during the sixteenth and seventeenth centuries. At first, members of the family are arranged stiffly; they "are juxtaposed, and sometimes linked together by gestures expressing their reciprocal feelings, but they do not join in any common action." Eventually, artists begin to portray the family around a table laden with fruit, or joined in a common activity such as the making of music. In the Netherlands, in particular, where painters relied primarily on middle-class patrons, the family portrait became a kind of genre painting that depicted a representative moment in everyday domestic life: "The men gathered round the fire, the women taking a cauldron off the fire, a girl feeding her little brother."[20]

But in England portraiture remained an aristocratic art oriented toward the effect of solemnity and timelessness rather than verisimilitude. At Penshurst there is a painting of Barbara Gamage and her children, six in number at the time (ca. 1596), which is attributed to Marcus Gheeraerts the Younger (Fig. 8). This family portrait is of the first kind described by Ariès. The arrangement is stiff, the effect rather austere, though there is a certain warmth of facial expression and of gesture. Such formality is typical of Elizabethan portraiture even where, as in this painting, we may detect a changing image of family and of maternity.

Despite the requisite formality of presentation, however, the artist has achieved here a sense of bonding among the represented figures. What is even more striking is the idea, conveyed by this painting, of the social value of mothering, a value which, together with "huswifery," is similarly celebrated by Jonson in his praise of Barbara Gamage. These are very early representations of the institutional function of mothering and housekeeping as a way of maintaining the existing social order and the sexual division of labor.[21]

Figure 8. Barbara Gamage (Lady Sidney) and Her Children, *attributed to Marcus Gheeraerts the Younger (ca. 1596). Reproduced by permission of Viscount De L'Isle, V.C., K.G., from his collection at Penshurst Place.*

In Gheeraerts's painting we can already observe the beginnings of an articulated ideology in which nurturing is designated as the social role of women, and in which children are socialized according to gender. Mothering, and its reproduction in the next generation through the identification of daughters with their mother's role, can be said to be thematized here, especially in view of the father's conspicuous absence from this family portrait. All of this is suggested by means of a simple kind of gesture: the mother's hands rest on each of her sons; and the four daughters are arranged in two pairs, with the older daughter in each pair duplicating the mother's gesture (and imitating her role) by holding the hand or the shoulder of her younger sister. Compositionally, the figures have been joined by making them overlap. Yet, at the same time, the composition serves to maintain hierarchy and differentiation of gender roles: the mother is positioned in a way that suggests her primary concern to be for the nurturing of her sons; the eldest son, William Sidney, is in the foreground and at the center of the group; and while all the figures do overlap, William's body is set off from the rest by an object at each side—to his right a hat, to his left a sword which is superimposed upon the figure of his older sister, Mary (who is also distanced from him by a larger space than that separating any of the other figures)—as if to reaffirm William's rightful place as eventual successor to his father and as the future patriarch of the family.

In effect, "To Penshurst" combines the stately formality that persists in Gheeraerts's painting with a suggestion of the domestic activity that characterizes the middle-class Dutch family portraits. Jonson's poem aims at a conception that is similar to that of the painters, a notion of the family as father, mother, and children joined in a common activity which is seen as the moral and spiritual foundation of the larger body politic; and of the house as the dwelling where such activity takes place, that is, as a *home*.

Thus far it has been evident that the "chain of being" at Penshurst is also a chain of giving: the land gives of itself, animals give of themselves, peasants give of themselves, ripe daughters give of themselves, ladies give of themselves to lords, lords give of themselves to kings. Moreover, the giving is voluntary and constitutes an equivalent exchange in kind; hence, nothing and no one is exploited. Of course, all this "giving" is an idealization of real relations of exchange at Penshurst. But like the force of labor mentioned earlier, these relations of exchange are kept hidden by the notion of wealth as the gift of Nature and by the principle of spontaneous and disinterested "giving" in imitation of Nature. In fact, Jonson's poem provides a remarkable seventeenth-century illustration of what the anthropologist Marcel Mauss has described in his classic study of the disparity between the theory and practice of gift giving in many cultures: "The form usually taken is that of the gift generously offered; but the accompanying behaviour is formal pretence and social deception, while the transaction itself is based on obligation and economic self-interest."[22] However, in continuing to treat Jonson's poem as a celebration of the tradition of disinterested generosity and gracious "hospitality," literary critics have often ignored what "hospitality" might actually mean. Once again, this suggests that such criticism shares the discourse and the ideological closure of the poem. The ideology involves a romantic idealization of a feudal, hierarchical social order, where there is no class conflict and where all exchange is represented in the form of prestations that are voluntary, disinterested, and spontaneous. What is obscured by this representation is, nevertheless, still evident from elements of the poem that allude to an emergent system of commodity exchange in which human relationships have also begun to take on a commodity form, especially where women are concerned.

It is significant, too, that although nearly everyone who enters the house at Penshurst bears a gift ("all come in . . . / And no one empty-handed, to salute / Thy lord, and lady, though they have no sute"), there are two exceptions to this rule. These exceptions occur at the conclusion of the delineation of the chain of being on the estate, at the point where the poet presents himself next only to the king. Jonson appears as a "guest" beginning at line 61. Neither he nor the king is represented as bearing tangible gifts; instead, they receive gifts. Twice it is suggested that at Penshurst, all is "as if" it belonged to the poet (lines 63–64: "Where the same beere, and bread, and selfe-same wine, / That is his Lordships, shall be also mine"; and line 74: "As if thou, then, wert mine, or I raign'd here"). Jonson's statement here must be understood in contrast to poems by both Martial and Juvenal in which patrons are attacked for having humiliated and insulted their guests (and their poets) by serving them a dinner that is inferior to that eaten by the patrons themselves.[23] As Cubeta has argued, Jonson's point is that "the Sidneys disregard rank before their untitled guests, such as the speaker, who is treated as an equal, sharing the same meat and wine as his host."[24] At the same time, however, Jonson implies an important difference among those who are untitled. Not all commoners deserve to share the same meat and wine as the host; and certainly not all commoners deserve to share the same table as a king. Jonson is careful to distinguish between himself and all those who are not quite the same kind of commoner that he is:

> . . . nor, standing by,
> A waiter, doth my gluttony envy:

But gives me what I call, and lets me eate,
He knowes, below, he shall finde plentie of meate.
(lines 67–70)

Furthermore, although he is clearly praising the Sidneys for their hospitality and, by implication, for their patronage, there is also in these lines a profound sense of the poet's desire for all that is celebrated in the poem as the property of Sir Robert and his lady (and perhaps, too, the sense that he deserves it). This "wish" is barely hidden in the lines which conclude the passage referring to the poet himself, immediately followed by the reference to King James:

As if thou, then, wert mine, or I raign'd here:
There's nothing I can wish, for which I stay.
That found King JAMES, when hunting late, this way. . .[25]

Moreover, the fact that Jonson does not conclude the passage referring to himself with a couplet, but rather makes the last line devoted to him (line 75) rhyme with the first line devoted to the king (line 76), enforces a sense of the poet's special status, even suggesting that perhaps he does deserve to "raign here." Finally, as a last support for my reading of the self-referential part of the poem, I would note the resumption here of negative constructions the predominance of which points to desire or longing for something that is felt to be lacking: (beginning in line 61) "Where comes *no* guest"; "*Without* his feare"; "And I *not faine* to sit"; "Here *no* man tells my cups; *nor*, standing by"; "Thy tables hoord *not* up for the next day, / *Nor*, when I take my lodging, need I pray / For fire"; "There's *nothing* I can wish, for which I stay." By contrast, the passage which follows and is devoted to the king contains not a single negative construction. The king literally does "raign here," when he is here, as anywhere else in the realm. The poet can only "wish," and his wish points to a lack. Thus, once more in the poem, negative constructions reveal something hidden behind the mask of an ideal, tranquil social order. An imaginary identification of poet and king through the device of juxtaposition and the rhyming of lines 75 and 76 is rendered unstable by the contrast of negative constructions in connection with the former and positive constructions in connection with the latter. This contrast points to the real and insurmountable difference between commoner (poet notwithstanding) and king.

The Presence of the Poet: From Description to Narration

From the point at which we have entered the Great Hall (line 48), the mode of representation has changed. The earlier parts of the poem are descriptive; and although description continues in the interior of the house, there is a gradual change from a descriptive to a narrative mode. From the beginning of line 48 ("But all come in . . .") a shift occurs from the topographical overview of the preceding lines to the image of a kind of processional: farmers, their wives and daughters, bearing gifts. The interior is presented in a panoramic view with figures moving across a horizontal plane, meeting the lord and lady and presenting their gifts. The quality is still mythic here; the figures move before the reader as in a diorama, performing a dumb show, like the play-within-the-play in *Hamlet*, or like the dancing in one of the masques that Jonson wrote for the court, a stylized, ceremonial and emblematic representation of real social relations. But when Jonson himself appears in the first person (line 65: "And I not faine to sit . . ."), the dumb show has ceased, and a true narrator has begun to speak. The panorama now broadens to include history as well as myth, a poet and a king who are individualized in relation to specific historical events in contrast to the farmers who have been presented as eternal but undifferentiated types (*the people*). We have seen that Jonson attempts to identify himself with James I here; but this part of the poem is also designed to assert the Sidneys' loyal service to the king and to the realm, and to locate the house as having an essential historical and political function in the state as a whole.

In the concluding fourteen-line section, a synthesis is made between the descriptive and the narrative forms of the earlier parts, and between Nature and history. The description is again of Nature, this time of Nature in an interior, human, and social form which finds its embodiment in the Sidney family. But the essence of that Nature is less easily described than was the natural environment of the estate. Virtue, nobility, fidelity, chastity, innocence are all attributed to the family; but these abstractions cannot adequately delineate the essence to which they refer. That delineation is made through a narrative *telling* of the activities that are the outward expression of that essence:

> His children thy great lord may call his owne:
> . . . .
> Each morne, and even, they are taught to pray,
> With the whole houshold, and may, every day,
> Reade, in their vertuous parents noble parts,
> The mysteries of manners, armes, and arts.

The union of description and narration is the yoking also of other principles that are otherwise in opposition: realism (details of daily events) and allegory (the book of "their . . . parents noble parts"); history (progression in time from day to day and generation to generation) and myth (the timeless cycle of "morne, and even"); private (the family) and public (the state); Nature (the Sidneys' "vertuous" essence) and Culture ("manners, armes, and arts"). Ultimately of course it is the "I" of the narrator, Ben Jonson, that has brought about this synthesis of the descriptive and the narrative portions of the poem, and of the mythic and the historical elements they contain respectively. Thus, in a sense, Jonson achieves his aim—it is the poet who speaks, and his power is perhaps greater even than that of a king. Every time the king utters the royal "We" he speaks for all that is present in the realm. But the poet speaks for "posteritie" as well as for the present;[26] he is a witness to all that is present in the king's realm and his "I" is the sign of a power to represent that "present" for all time to come. The poet is as much creator of that "present" as he is its chronicler. What the narrator says the children "reade" is, at the same time, constituted by the poet here and in other poems devoted to the Sidneys. A poem of this sort legitimizes nobility, and a new nobility has a special need for poems of this sort.

Thus, what appears to be a commentary by Jonson on an already existing text and its readers—the "book of Sidney" as it were—is at the same time a very significant part of what produces that text. As in other respects, the poem here simultaneously makes assertions and denials about its own ontological status: it is description and it is narration; it is the presentation of an already present, nontemporal *presence*, and it is the "becoming-present" of something new and different;[27] it states that the poet is merely a chronicler, and that the poet is a creator, that Ben Jonson is effaced by what the poem contains and that Ben Jonson is all that the poem finally contains. This multiplying of contrary and contradictory assertions concerning the status of the poem with respect to its subject matter contributes to a complex logic that obscures certain historical (diachronic) and social (synchronic) distinctions. The "present" that is finally handed down to "posteritie" in "To Penshurst" is history as myth and a myth as history. And yet, this "present" as the poem's essential content is only provisionally final. For at the level of expression or enunciation, the reflexive self-consciousness of the subject-narrator-poet who speaks in "To Penshurst," once recognized by the reader, betrays the ideological function of the poem by reaffirming those historical and social distinctions.

CHAPTER 4

The House

Yet alwaies must such peeces of Lande whatsoever it bee, bee reduced into one certaine breadth and one certain length, or else it can never bee collected or summed into a perfecte contente or number of Acres, and other odde quantities.

—Valentine Leigh, *The Most Profitable and Commendable Science of Surveying of Landes, Tenemens, and Hereditamentes* (London, 1577)

. . . When we mean to build,
We first survey the plot, then draw the model;
And when we see the figure of the house,
Then must we rate the cost of the erection;
Which if we find outweighs ability,
What do we then but draw anew the model
In fewer offices, or at least desist
To build at all? Much more in this great work,
Which is almost to pluck a kingdom down
And set another up, should we survey
The plot of situation and the model,
Consent upon a sure foundation,
Question surveyors, know our own estate,
How able such a work to undergo,
To weigh against his opposite; or else
We fortify in paper and in figures,
Using the names of men instead of men:
Like one that draws the model of a house
Beyond his power to build it . . .

—Shakespeare, *Henry IV, Part 2*

Before beginning to rebuild the house in which one lives, one must not merely pull it down, and make provision for materials, and for architects (unless one does one's own architecture), and

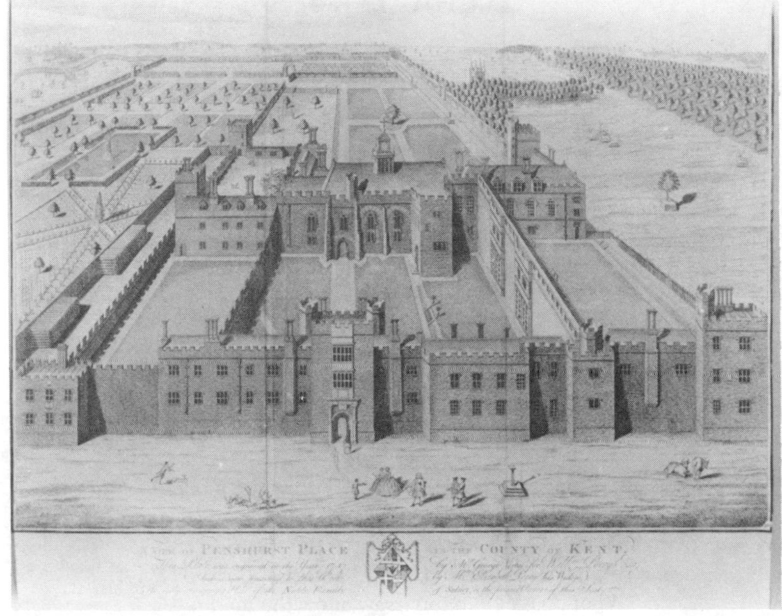

Figure 9. *Penshurst Place, engraved in the year 1747 by George Vertue. From Edward Hasted,* The History and Topographical Survey of the County of Kent *(Canterbury, 1790).*

besides have ready a carefully drawn plan; one must also have provided oneself with another house where one may conveniently stay while the work goes on.

—Descartes, *Discourse on the Method of Rightly Directing One's Reason and of Seeking Truth in the Sciences* (1637)

Topographical Coordinates

BEFORE DISCUSSING the final fourteen-line section of the poem, which seems to stand by itself like the opening eight-line section and which is the epitome as it were of the previous summation of natural and social order at Penshurst, I should like to turn now to the estate itself. A glance at the map (Fig. 10) will make it apparent that the descriptive portion of the first half of the poem is

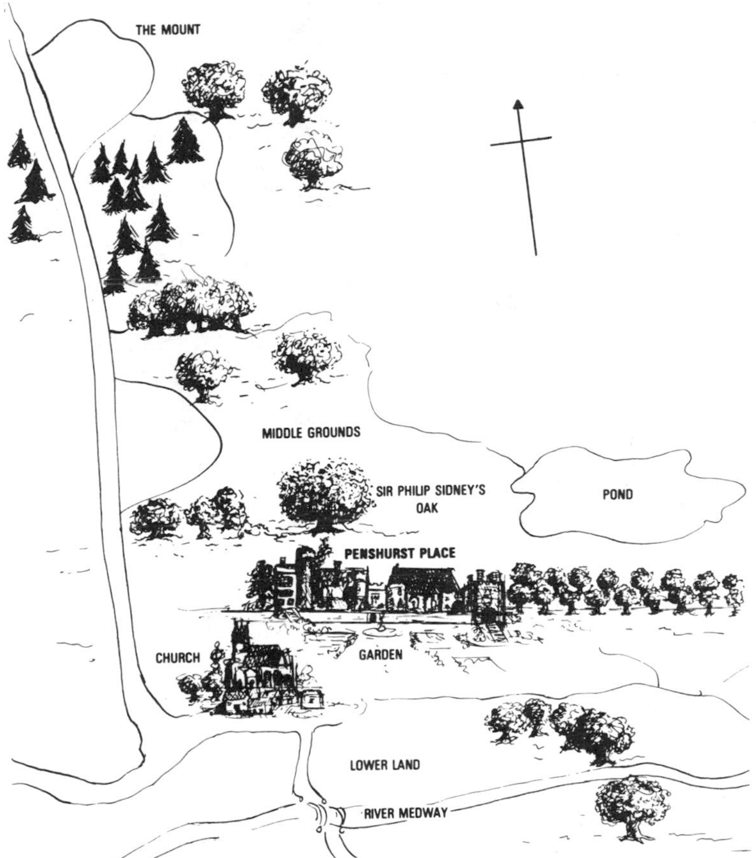

Figure 10. *Map of Penshurst Place and environs with some of the locations referred to in Jonson's poem. Adapted from a pamphlet entitled* Penshurst Church and Village *(London: Ashmead Press, 1970), by permission of the Rector of Penshurst.*

Figure 11. *Penshurst Place. Aerial photograph from the north, taken June 1950. British Crown Copyright Reserved.*

itself a kind of map. That is, beginning with the reference to "thy Mount" in line 10, and moving to the passage into the house itself (lines 45 ff.), the poem maps the estate from the outer limits of the surrounding land to the walls of the house. The major points identified in "To Penshurst" can be traced from north to south on the map. The poem first scans the estate from its northern limit, the "Mount," to its southern boundary, "the river," presenting a preliminary bird's-eye view of the topography, and then gradually closes in to focus on its central feature, the house. The sequence is: the mount, Sidney's oak, Lady Leicester's oak (presumably also in the vicinity of the tree planted to celebrate Philip Sidney's birth), the "lower land," the river, the "middle grounds," the "topps," the park, the ponds, the orchards, the gardens, the walls, and the house. Roughly, the movement of this description can be traced on the map in the form of a whorl that starts in the north and ends in the center, at the house.

Thus, while it describes a magical and mythical Nature, this part of the poem also entails the mapping of a real topography. If Jonson wanted to represent merely a magical Nature at Penshurst (like that of Cockaigne), it would not have been necessary to identify specific locations on the estate; and even if it is argued that such identification is a conventional device to enforce the reader's association of this magical Nature with Penshurst and with the Sidney family (which is indeed part of its function), it would still not have been necessary to describe these actual locations in this particular order. Why, then, does Jonson choose to "map" the estate by reference to certain features, described in a sequence that moves from north to south? Because this particular order corresponds to a movement by degrees from the untamed nature at the outer limits of the estate to the tamed nature at the interior of the house itself.

We may get a clearer picture of that movement and of the topographical order it describes by comparing the poem with a view of the house and its immediate grounds in an eighteenth-century engraving and in modern aerial photographs (Figs. 11, 12, 13). Lines 10–44 of the poem take us from the trees and lake at the extreme north to the north front of the house and its adjacent walls surrounding the orchard. Lines 45–47 describe the walls themselves. At line 48 we read, "But all come in": obviously, Jonson had in mind here the main entrance to the house, that is, the north gate in the "King's Tower" which was part of the additions built by Sir Henry Sidney, though probably supervised by his son Philip, in around 1585 (Fig. 14). Passing through the gate of the King's Tower and through the main court we enter the north door of the "Great Hall." This is the center of the house. It is the literal center of activity in the house and on the estate, the place where nature's abundance is consumed by the lord and lady and their guests; and topographically, it is roughly at the center of the walled perimeter. But it is also the mythical center of the *home*; for the hall is not merely a place where food is consumed, but one where a tradition of hospitality and feasting is maintained. The function of this tradition is primarily symbolic; it is a sign of responsibility and order, justifying authority and power. As the oldest portion of the house, the Great Hall at Penshurst could be felt by its seventeenth-century owners and their tenants as the direct link with a mythified past. Built in the fourteenth century, it is the only truly Gothic portion of the house, though later additions were generally designed to maintain the Gothic style. Today, the Great Hall at Penshurst is usually given as the most typical extant example of a medi-

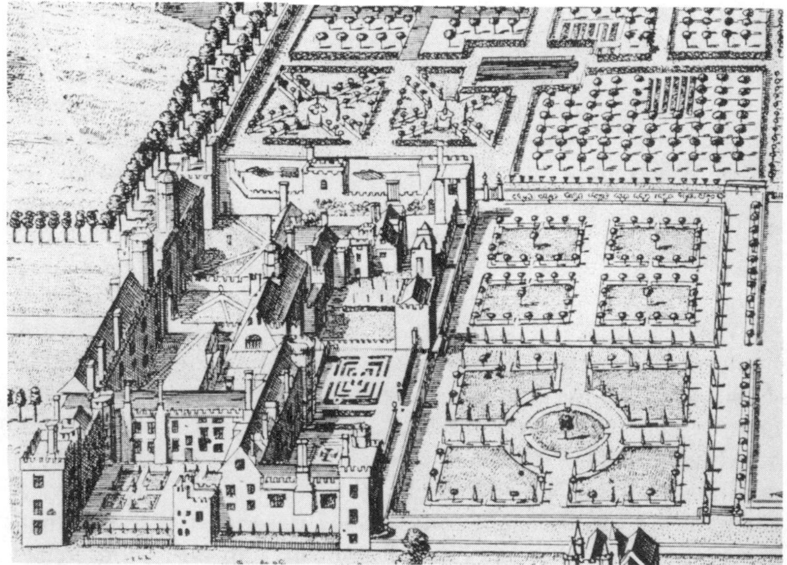

Figure 12. *Penshurst Place. Bird's-eye view from the west, in a detail from an engraving by Johannes Kip, published in 1728.* Country Life.

eval manor house. It is the only remaining hall with a central hearth, and its tables and benches are the oldest of the kind that have survived (Fig. 18).

The Hall: Perpendicular Gothic

Even in Jonson's time, the Great Hall at Penshurst would have been thought an outstanding example of an ancient architectural form. Men who could afford to build new homes in the Elizabethan and Jacobean periods designed them according to a fashion which reflected priorities that were different from those that governed the building of the fourteenth-century manor house at Penshurst.[1] But why did the Sidneys not build their additions according to new styles? Well, one very important reason was that they could not afford to. While certainly a prominent family by the 1580s, the Sidneys were not wealthy. Nevertheless, there was at least one way in which Henry Sidney could turn his limited financial resources to

Figure 13. *Penshurst Place. Modern aerial view from the west.* Country Life.

a certain advantage. By maintaining the Gothic style of the original building, Sir Henry was able to keep within a growing fashion for the revival of Gothicism. He may even, perhaps, have considered his plan for additions at Penshurst an assertion that his house observed a purer adherence to Gothic forms and what they represented than did any of the newer houses.

For through most of the Tudor period, and particularly during the last quarter of the sixteenth century, there was a medievalist trend in English art, literature, and in the life at court. In literature, as is well known, two of the most important works of the period, Sir Philip Sidney's *Arcadia* and Edmund Spenser's *Faerie Queene*, returned to the chivalric motifs of medieval romance. Philip Sidney participated actively in the frequent tournaments that were an integral part of Elizabethan pageantry, and he assumed mythical proportions in contemporary references which depict him as, in Spenser's words, "the president of noblesse and of chivalry." As Sidney's biographer Roger Howell points out, a definite ideological function was served by this imagery: "There can be little doubt that the emergence of Sidney as the Shepherd Knight was more than mere show or literary convention. Sidney was . . . aware . . . that serious meanings could be conveyed through the

Figure 14. *Penshurst Place. North Front (with the sixteenth-century King's Tower at center) and park. Reproduced by permission of Viscount De L'Isle, V.C., K.G.*

imagery of chivalry and that it was indeed possible to translate the Catholic chivalry of the Middle Ages into a Protestant device in the sixteenth century."[2] Such image making was itself part of a larger and ongoing program undertaken by the Tudors to secure and to legitimate their power, a goal which required the obscuring of certain fundamental social changes that were taking place in England. Art and architecture as well as literature were powerful tools in the service of that goal.[3]

It is true that for a brief period, in the middle of the century, English builders had experimented with Renaissance designs borrowed from Palladio, Serlio, and du Cerceau. Perhaps the best example of this influence is the house at Longleat (Fig. 20), built by Sir John Thynne, one of the wealthiest of the "new men." But by the 1580s the tendency in country-house architecture was toward a revival of the Perpendicular Gothic forms which had already seen one revival in the court architecture of the reigns of Henry VII and

Figure 15. *Penshurst Place. South Front (with the fourteenth-century hall and the Garden Tower) and garden. Reproduced by permission of Viscount De L'Isle, V.C., K.G.*

Henry VIII. An interesting pattern can be observed here: at the beginning of a new dynasty the architecture of the court entailed the renormalizing of an old form to legitimize a new content; a hundred years later the buildings of a new nobility, brought to power largely through the policies of the new royal line, reflect a similar attempt to legitimize power and authority by identification with the ruling class of an earlier epoch through an association of architectural forms (Figs. 21, 22).[4]

Compared with the designs of Serlio and du Cerceau adopted by the builder of Longleat, the native Gothic was an undecorated style. According to Eric Mercer, the High Renaissance features of Longleat were not widely admired during the sixteenth century; Thynne's preoccupation with decoration, his "continual alteration of details—of the order of a column, of the carving of a frieze" were ridiculed.[5] Mercer suggests that Sidney's description in the *Ar-*

Figure 16. *Penshurst Place, North Front, main entrance to the King's Tower. Above the doors can be seen the arms of Edward VI surmounted by an inscription placed there by Sir Henry Sidney, which tells of the king's gift of Penshurst Place to Sir William Sidney. The inscription is dated 1585, presumably the approximate date of the completion of the King's Tower. Reproduced by permission of A. F. Kersting.*

Figure 17. *Penshurst Place. Perspective of arches (King's Tower—Great Hall—Garden Tower) viewed through the open doors of the main entrance at the North Front.* Country Life.

Figure 18. *Penshurst Place. Interior, the Great Hall.* Country Life.

cadia of Kalander's house can be read as a negative evaluation of ornamental facades like that at Longleat:

> The house it selfe was built of faire and strong stone, not affecting so much any extraordinarie kinde of finenes, as an honorable representing of a firme statelines. The lightes, doores and staires, rather directed to the use of the guest, then to the eye of the Artificer: and yet as the one cheefly heeded, so the other not neglected; each place handsome without curiositie, and homely

Figure 19. *Penshurst Place. Portion of the screen in the Great Hall with Dudley and Sidney badges, the bear and ragged staff and the broad pheon's head, above arch. Engraving from F. T. Dollman and J. R. Jobbins,* An Analysis of Ancient Domestic Architecture, *Vol. 2 (London: Atchley and Co., ca. 1863–64).*

> without lothsomenes: . . . all more lasting then beautifull, but that the consideration of the exceeding lastingnesse made the eye beleeve it was exceeding beautifull.[6]

It is especially interesting from my viewpoint that Mercer should see Sidney's description as an attack upon the style represented by Longleat, since this same passage has been frequently cited elsewhere as an encomium to the house in which Sidney spent his childhood, that is, Penshurst. This suggests that Longleat and Penshurst would have been seen by Sidney and his contemporaries as polar opposites stylistically. And I suspect this was indeed the case. It is significant that the original buildings at Penshurst antedate both of the Gothic revivals that took place under the Tudors. They are older Gothic constructions of the kind which probably

Figure 20. *Longleat, Wiltshire. The beginnings of the classical style in England (1572–80). Reproduced by permission of A. F. Kersting.*

served as models for those revivals, models for the ideal of plainness, utility—in Sidney's words, "a firme statelines," "handsome without curiositie." The ideal is stated again by Bacon, succinctly and not without irony, in the opening sentences of his essay "Of Building":

> Houses are built to live in, and not to look on; therefore let use be preferred before uniformity, except where both may be had. Leave the goodly fabrics of houses, for beauty only, to the enchanted palaces of the poets; who build them with small cost.[7]

The virtue of utility as opposed to ornament and uniformity (or symmetry) of appearance was consistent with an emerging Protestant (and a bourgeois) ethic. It was a virtue advocated in opposition to a wealthier class of aristocrats who were seen as parasites on the still-precarious social, economic, and political order of Elizabethan and Jacobean England. Those who managed their own wealth by the principle of utility were represented, by Bacon and others, as the more responsible segment of the aristocracy and the segment most capable of joining with the monarch in governing the country.

Figure 21. *Richmond Palace, Surrey (ca. 1501). From Mark Girouard,* Robert Smythson and the Architecture of the Elizabethan Era *(London: Country Life, 1966).*

Figure 22. *Burghley House, Northants, as remodeled in the 1570s and 1580s. From Mark Girouard,* Robert Smythson and the Architecture of the Elizabethan Era *(London: Country Life, 1966).*

But along with the principle of utility, another significant aspect of Sidney's description of Kalander's house is the emphasis on "lastingnesse"—"more *lasting* then beautifull, but that the consideration of the *exceeding lastingnesse* made the eye beleeve it was exceeding beautifull." Here, as in Jonson's "but stand'st an ancient pile," the joint connotation of solidity and antiquity is employed to serve a double function. On the surface, "lastingnesse" appears to express a traditional esthetic norm in opposition to newfangled designs, the first and perhaps the most extreme of which was Longleat.[8] But we can detect another purpose behind the assertion of that ideal: it is after all Sir Philip Sidney who is speaking, a paragon of the new aristocracy that has risen through the favor of a new ruling dynasty and at the expense of an older baronage. A taste for "lastingnesse" can be seen as a device of these men for denying to the world, and perhaps to themselves, the fundamantal fact of *nonlastingness* upon which their fortunes, their titles, and their power are based. The fact that Longleat was also built by one of the "new men" does not alter this view. Its owner and builder, Thynne, was not active in the great political events of his day, though he had powerful friends in the highest places. He was an exception to the general rule, and his house was looked upon by his contemporaries as an extravagant and tasteless testament to his vast wealth. On the other hand, the man who built the main additions to Penshurst, Sir Henry Sidney, was an active servant of the Tudors throughout his life, though receiving little in the way of financial remuneration for his devoted service.[9] It is no wonder that Sir Henry chose to maintain the style of the earlier buildings at Penshurst. In so doing he was able to turn the limited finances at his disposal into a virtue by calling attention to the past from which his family and the class to which it belonged were supposedly descended rather than to the break with that past which had actually brought them to power.

Neither Longleat nor Penshurst was important as an explicit model for direct imitation by other houses of the period. Rather, they are representative extremes: the former constituted the first significant attempt to introduce High Renaissance patterns into the design of an English country house; the latter strictly maintained the traditional Gothic style with its irregular plan, its country stone, its crenellations, and its towers. The other great houses built toward the end of the century combine lavishness, the tendency toward uniformity, and the ornamental facade, with motifs that continue to be recognizably Gothic. It was not until the following century, beginning in the buildings of Inigo Jones, that pure Renaissance classicism began to replace the variegated style combining Gothic and classical motifs in English building. Jones was the first professional architect in England, and enjoyed the patronage of the Stuarts. As Eric Mercer has suggested, in the early seventeenth century the classical style though radical esthetically was tied to conservative political and ideological interests. On the Continent it was the artistic expression of the Counter-Reformation; in England it was the style of the court. By contrast, conservatism in architectural taste tended to be the norm for those who were radical or revolutionary in politics.[10]

This situation was not necessarily paradoxical. Though Gothicism in sixteenth-century architecture was closely associated with medieval castle and church architecture, it was by no means the expression of a sympathy or a desire to return to feudalism and to the Roman Church. On the contrary, the staunchest supporters of the Gothic and medievalist fashion were often men of Calvinist sympathies.[11] The appreciation of the Gothic, the archaism of the revivals, were closely linked to the nationalist character of Protestantism in England. Perpendicular Gothic was admired not because it was the style of the old church, but because it was the only style that was a native one. It is partly for this reason that the ultrarational style of Palladio, which Jones introduced to Londoners in his Whitehall Banqueting House of 1622 (Fig. 23), did not become the norm in English architecture until about fifty years later.[12]

It would appear, then, that rationalism, normally associated with Protestantism and with the rise of the middle class, in this instance gave way to a principle of higher priority in late-sixteenth-century England, i.e., nationalism. But in drawing such a conclusion we may be misled in the same way that Englishmen in the sixteenth and seventeenth centuries often misconstrued the nature of their own past. For the middle class was not a sudden new phenomenon in the sixteenth century. In England as on the Continent, a burgeoning middle class had been playing an increasingly important role socially and culturally for several centuries. It is not surprising, therefore, to read Nikolaus Pevsner's argument that

Figure 23. *Whitehall Banqueting House (1622), by Inigo Jones. Reproduced by permission of A. F. Kersting.*

rationalism comes into English architecture not with Palladianism in the seventeenth century but with the Perpendicular style itself during the late Middle Ages, and that "the Perpendicular was the first great break in the development of English art."[13] Thus, what may appear as a rejection of Palladian rationalism in favor of nationalism as the motive principle of late-sixteenth-century English architecture is really a revival, or rather, perhaps, a survival, of an earlier form of rationalism inaugurated by the Perpendicular style. And it is not without interest for us that Pevsner cites the Great Hall at Penshurst as an example of that style in fourteenth-century domestic architecture and notes the fact that the house was built by a London merchant.[14]

The Sidney Additions

Three general aspects of the architecture at Penshurst have emerged so far in this discussion: first, that even in comparison with the preclassical Gothicism of other Elizabethan houses, Penshurst seems still more conservative, more authentically medieval; second, that the source and center of this authentic Gothic appearance is the original fourteenth-century manor house; and third, that the latter, while truly medieval, is not simply emblematic of a feudal society and values, but is a prime example of the Perpendicular style which articulates a conception of the rational that is at least protobourgeois. As we shall see, the fact that the first owner and builder of Penshurst was a London merchant lends a certain irony to the motives of its sixteenth-century owners, the Sidneys, in building additions that kept to the original style.

These additions were built of the same stone from local quarries as the medieval house, "the countrey stone" to which Jonson refers, occasionally interspersed with Elizabethan brick. The style is deliberately plain; in fact portions added by the Sidneys are even less ornamented than the Great Hall, an outstanding feature of which is the scrollwork characteristic of Gothic windows. (The windows of the Great Hall at Penshurst are particularly impressive for a domestic building.) The estate was given to Sir William Sidney by Edward VI in 1552. It passed to Henry Sidney on his father's death in 1554. Nigel Nicolson has suggested that the accounts record indicates "unusual activity by masons, carpenters, and tilemakers, 'working on my lord's work,' " as early as 1560–62. It is likely that this was when construction began on the wing extending north from the Buckingham Building (which dates from ca. 1430–35 but is confusingly known by the name of the dukes of Buckingham who owned Penshurst from 1447 to 1521). In addition to this wing, Sir Henry Sidney probably built most of the North Front. His son, Robert, completed the Long Gallery (which extends south from the Buckingham Building) in 1607.[15]

The North Front (Figs. 11, 14, 16) is of particular interest for a number of reasons. In the first place, its length and relatively flat facade, facing out on the park and the woods to the north, present the house openly and directly to the world. And although the style of the North Front elevation is consistent with the fourteenth-century hall, its openness to the outer world makes it consistent as well with an important innovation in the design of most of the newer Elizabethan houses. As Mercer observes, the builders of medieval houses were constrained in their designs by military and economic exigencies. Their buildings were fortresslike centers of feudal estates, facing inward upon interior courtyards and protected by strong outer walls. By contrast, in the houses of the sixteenth century "one can trace a process at the end of which they turn their backs on the courtyards and face the world, while symmetry and decoration, that had at first been reserved for the courtyard, appear on the exterior."[16] The elevation of the North Front at Penshurst lacks symmetry and decoration. But it still constitutes a turning inside out of the original, exterior-walled manor house design. While Sir Henry Sidney preserved a small closed court, the broad facade of the North Front displayed the house to the world, an advertisement as it were of its contents—the family that dwelled there. In addition, the design of the North Front was a solution to the Sidneys' problem of trying to build in a way that would be economic and still serve the symbolic function performed by other, more opulent houses. For its length, combined with the massive and imposing effect created by the simple, rectilinear, and perpendicular arrangement of country stone and glass, gave to the visitor arriving from the north the impression of a much bigger house, the space between the narrow wings being kept hidden from view.

I have said that the North Front is asymmetrical. This is the result of a deliberate and significant decision on Henry Sidney's part to displace the main gate and the King's Tower slightly to the east of the center of the elevation. The reason is recorded by Sir Henry's steward who wrote that his master had the tower and gate erected slightly off center "so that he might see clear through the porch and service corridor of the hall to the garden."[17] The eye of the visitor arriving at the main gate would thus be met by a perspective of arches leading through the King's Tower, through the court, through the service passage behind the screen of the Great Hall, through an inner "office court" (which has since become the upper terrace of the garden),[18] to the south Garden Tower and the formal garden. (See Fig. 17.) This perspective depends, of course, on all doors being open from the main gate to the garden, a nonfunctional arrangement (except perhaps in the heat of summer) but one that may have obtained on occasions when guests arrived. The design is therefore primarily symbolic or representational. Its purpose is, in part, to further suggest the opening up of a closed architectural structure which had previously kept its back to the world.

But there is a more important purpose behind the perspective arrangement at the entryway of the house. Passing through the main gate the visitor is led immediately to the ancient north door of the Great Hall and into that portion of the house. Thus, the prospect which meets the eye at the main entrance, and the direct passage which the gate affords to the Great Hall, urge an association of the new building with the old and the new aristocracy with the old. This association is enforced by the continuity of style and of the materials used in the additions, and especially by the continued use of crenellations. Like the battlements, towers, and drawbridges of the "sham castles" of the period, the crenellations at Penshurst are decorative and deliberately anachronistic. They were not built of the thickness required for real fortifications. And since they served no useful purpose, they could only have been meant to constitute a *sign*; that is, they function as an essential part of the total system of representation at Penshurst, a system designed to convey a message to the occupants within and to the world without. The crenellations lead the eye along the upper length of the new buildings to certain key places in the asymmetrical, rambling "pile" of the system as a whole. They operate as visual connectives between the various parts of the house and between the various periods of its construction. As such, they have a metonymic relation to the central metaphor which is enunciated in the perspective of the main entrance. The crenellations at the roof line which lead the eye from building to building, period to period, suggest continuity between contiguous elements; they are metonymies which are comprehensible only by reference to the metaphor that relates the main gate of the King's Tower to the north portal of the Great Hall. This metaphor is designed to achieve a relation of continuity that associates the Sidneys with the fourteenth-century owners of Penshurst. Thus, in a manner similar to the technique of itemization that is used in the different sections of the poem, the repetition of stylistic elements in the architectural scheme constructs a sequence of metonymies that supports an ideological metaphor: King's Tower (Sidney) = Great Hall (old nobility).

Another example of the use of architectural anachronism for an ideological purpose is evident in the interior of the Great Hall (Figs. 18, 19). I am thinking of the screen which extends across the east end of the hall and which may have been used as a platform for musicians, as well as for protection against drafts. It is Gothic in style and seems, at first glance, to belong to the fourteenth-century interior. However, closer observation reveals that the screen includes Renaissance design motifs[19] and contains the Dudley emblem of the bear and ragged staff, adopted by Henry Sidney after his marriage to Mary Dudley in 1551, as well as the Sidneys' own badge of the broad arrow.

It can be seen, therefore, that while continuity with the older design of the house was stressed, no attempt was made to deny the anachronism of the newer parts. Indeed, it was a necessary sign of the Sidneys' stature and of their legitimate title to the estate that they build additions to the house. The Dudley and Sidney badges on the screen of the Great Hall, and similar marks including initials and dates of construction which appear on moldings and tablets of the newer buildings, are clearly in evidence for a reason. In order that the central metaphor be understood, it was essential that continuity and difference be united in the representation. The function of the metaphor was not to establish a relation of identity between the old and the new; it was not meant to create the illusion that the Sidneys had owned the estate from the beginning—this they could not possibly have perpetrated—but only to enforce the illusion that they were a family of rank at least as old as the estate, and therefore legitimately entitled to it. (And it is worth recalling here that Sir Henry Sidney went so far in foisting that illusion as to have a false genealogy drawn up in support of the same claim.)[20]

So we see that in Sir Henry's design at Penshurst the Great Hall was preserved as the center of the house, the center of a "feudal" estate and the marker of an authentic feudal past; the main gate of the North Front was the center of a different structure, and the marker of a mythical past constituted by a metaphorical relation to the Great Hall. It is now possible to explain what might otherwise appear to be an anomaly in the representation. I am referring to the coat of arms and the inscription which Henry Sidney placed above the arch of the main entrance, in 1585, presumably the year in which the King's Tower was completed (Fig. 16). The arms are those of Edward Tudor (Edward VI, son of Henry VIII), and the inscription reads as follows:

> The most Religious and Renowned Prince Edward the sixth, Kinge of England, France and Ireland, gave the House of Pencester with the Mannors, Landes and Appurtenances, there-unto belonginge unto his trustye, and wellbeloved servant Syr William Sidney, Knight Banneret, serving him from the tyme of his Birth unto his Coronation in the Offices of Chamberlayn and Stewart of his Household; in commemoration of which most worthie and famous Kinge Sir Henrye Sidney, Knight of the most Noble Order of the Garter, Lord President of Councill, established in the Marches of Wales, Sonne and Heyre to the aforenamed Sir William caused this Tower to be buylded and that most excellent Princes Armes to be erected. Anno Domini 1585.

As I have said, this seems an anomaly, even a contradiction in the representation as interpreted so far. For if Sir Henry was attempting to use an anachronistic architectural scheme as the vehicle for a metaphor relating his family to the one that built Penshurst, why would he betray that vehicle right at its point of origin in the archway of the King's Tower? I suggest that rather than betray the metaphor, the inscription above the main gate assures its success. By this contrivance Sir Henry avoided calling attention primarily to himself, his ancestry, and his heirs. Rather, it is to the Tudors and to their genealogy that attention is first directed. Now this is an interesting displacement. We have seen that the entire system of representation is designed to convey a message to the occupants of Penshurst and to the world outside, a message which confirms the Sidneys' mythicized or imaginary relationship to their historical context. In other words, the representation is an ideology. By the placement of a reference to the king who granted the estate to Sir William Sidney at the point from which that ideology is generated, any criticism of the metaphor upon which it is founded is immediately suspended. For if anyone were willing to doubt the veracity of what the message conveyed about the family, that their title to Penshurst was legitimate, no one would be likely to doubt the legitimate title of the Tudors to the throne of England. As every student of the period knows, the question of legitimacy was one that haunted Englishmen in the sixteenth century. It was the touchiest of issues for Tudor chroniclers who were bound to assert, in the same breath, a justification of usurpation in the past and an insistence upon primogeniture in the present and for all time to come. No one could have read the arms and inscription at the entrance to Penshurst and *not* have repressed, consciously or unconsciously, his awareness of the real function of the metaphor that was enunciated there.

Thus, the King's Tower, with its coat of arms and inscription referring to an earlier Tudor king, served to neutralize criticism, to suspend disbelief, the first condition for the actualization of the metaphor. And now, if we look again at Figure 17, we can see beyond this first point in the perspective a second arch also bearing a coat of arms. This is the crest of the Sidneys, placed by Sir Henry or by one of his descendants above the north portal of the ancient Great Hall, that is, at a point further into the perspective and a point in the representation that is further back in time. Here the metaphor is completed. History, which would mark a difference between the time of the Great Hall and the time of the King's Tower, is replaced by a mythical time which represents the two buildings as continuous and synchronic. This substitution works because if a king (and the origins of a royal line) cannot be called into question, then neither can a reading of history which presents the Sidneys as members of the same feudal nobility that previously held title to the house.

Yet it is not just the Sidneys' pedigree and their property rights that are established with the completion of the metaphor. The Great Hall has a symbolic function which is temporal; it is the link with the past which valorizes the Sidney genealogy. But it also has a potential for symbolic representation that is determined by its relation spatially to the rest of the house. The hall is located at the center, and it is the space within which the central social activities of the house are performed. It has already been observed that these activities took on a different form in the sixteenth century as compared with the period and the social order for which the hall was originally constructed. The fourteenth-century hall housed a lord who "was not merely a proprietor, but a prince" with dominion over the lives of those who dwelled on his manor.[21] But the owner of a landed estate in the sixteenth century was more proprietor than prince, though he still held considerable power over the lives of his tenants. As Christopher Hill among others has pointed out, the Reformation in England led to a "secularization of the parish" and, conversely, a "spiritualization of the household."[22] In this period, the father of the family replaced the priest as the chief representative of ethical and spiritual authority. The household rather than the parish became the fundamental unit of society. The significance of this change and the extent to which it penetrated all of Elizabethan society can be judged from the fact that it was true not only for Protestant households but for those which remained Catholic as well.[23] A household included servants by definition, but its nucleus was the family of the "householder." At this time, a landed aristocrat came to be viewed as the head of the chief household and the father of the chief family on the estate. The lady of the house would be celebrated above all for her "high huswifery," as Jonson put it. Thus, while the Great Hall at Penshurst symbolized the Sidneys' connection with a feudal past, it was also a place where domestic activities were performed that were represented as exemplifying the civilizing force of family life.

The Garden

We have yet to mention what lies at the south end of the house, that is, the garden. But first, let me summarize the brief passage we have made across the topography and the architecture of the estate, following the route which is mapped in the poem. We have approached the house from the north, moving from the open, untamed nature of the woods at the northern boundary, past a park, fields, and ponds, a grove of oak trees, an orchard, past the walls of the newer buildings by way of the arched gate of the King's Tower, through the court, into the Great Hall, out through the gate of the Garden Tower (which is the final arch in the perspective first seen at the main entrance), and finally, into the garden where Nature reappears but in a different guise. Here we are in the midst of a tamed, civil Nature; a Nature controlled by symmetry of design and by the trimming and pruning of a good husbandman, and a Nature contained within distinct boundaries marked by hedges and fences and outer walls.

In his essay "Of Gardens," Bacon writes: "And a man shall ever see that when ages grow to civility and elegancy, men come to build stately sooner than to garden finely; as if gardening were the greater perfection."[24] It is quite likely that Henry Sidney and his sons designed their house and its garden with a similar idea in mind.[25] But gardening, in contrast to architecture, is a highly ephemeral art form; and it is therefore difficult to say anything very precise concerning the Sidneys' garden plan. Still, we can be guided by some basic principles derived from Roy Strong's pioneering study of Elizabethan and Jacobean gardens. Strong discusses the influence of humanism and of the Italian Renaissance gardens on the development of gardening in England. He writes that in Italy, by the middle of the sixteenth century, the garden "drew to itself visions of the idyllic whether expressed in terms of poetic yearning for the Golden Age or of the ideals of the pastoral life of Vergil's *Eclogues*. . . . [It] evolved into a series of separate yet interconnected intellectual and physical experiences which required the mental and physical co-operation of the visitor as he moved through them. Strange though it may seem to us, plants become almost incidental, apart from their contribution towards achieving a symbolic effect." This attitude toward Nature is evident, too, in the designs of gardens for some of the great houses and palaces of the later Tudor period. Moreover, as Strong points out, such garden symbolism could function "as a means of intertwining the natural world with a dynastic apotheosis."[26]

In Sir Philip Sidney's *Arcadia*, the description of Kalander's garden exemplifies these principles—though this fictive garden is of a relatively modest design when compared with the actual ones studied by Strong. Sidney's depiction proceeds from a terrace down a flight of stairs, through an Edenic bower—"a place cunninglie set with trees of the moste tast-pleasing fruites"—and "into a delicate greene." The latter is bordered by shrubs behind which are "newe beddes of flowers, which being under the trees, the trees were to them a Pavilion, and they to the trees a mosaical floore: so that it seemed that arte therein would needes be delightfull by counterfaiting his enemie error, and making order in confusion." This self-conscious control of nature by art is further symbolized by a reflecting pool "whose shaking christall was a perfect mirrour to all the other beauties." Direct classical allusions follow in the form of a fountain with a sculpture of Venus and her babe Aeneas, and in the paintings of classical divinities on the walls of a nearby garden house. Finally, the function of dynastic legitimation appears unambiguously in another painting, a portrait of

Basilius, the reigning prince of Arcadia, and his family.[27] If Sidney based his description of Kalander's garden on an actual model, it would most likely have been the garden at Penshurst or, perhaps, that at Wilton, the country house of his sister Mary, countess of Pembroke, where Sidney stayed in 1580 and where he wrote part of the *Arcadia*.

We can get an approximate idea of the design of the garden at Penshurst from Kip's eighteenth-century engraving (Fig. 12). Though many of its details may have been altered from the time of Henry, Philip, and Robert Sidney, the general layout appears to be consistent with Renaissance practice. It follows the pattern of the fourfold plot—Philip Sidney's "mosaical floore"—which was common in Elizabethan gardens and which had ancient origins of practical and mythical significance in the gardens of the Middle East. Elizabeth Burton has attributed this design to an originally functional consideration in Eastern gardens which, "due to the constant need for irrigation, were invariably laid out on this plan; a plan which may still be seen in the design of certain Persian carpets. Briefly, it was a cross of water dividing the garden into four squares or rectangular plots. . . . The 'chessboard' gardens of Western Europe from the Crusades to Stuart times follow this pattern, although, certainly, there can have been very little need for this kind of close irrigation in England. . . . The Elizabethan garden was, therefore, a square divided into four plots, not by water but by walks and paths."[28] Burton also identifies the mythical locus of the fourfold plot which is especially striking since it comes from Genesis: "And a river went out of Eden to water the garden and from thence it was parted and became into four heads" (2:10). This is a reference which would not have been lost to any Elizabethan Protestant contemplating a country-house garden.

It can be seen that the actual layout of Penshurst contains an implicit, underlying "map" which charts the transformation of Nature from the wild state of the surrounding forest, through the Arcadian fields and park, into the paradise of the garden. The meaning of the transformation is "read" in the passage through the house and particularly through the Great Hall. But it is what the hall contains that is understood as the agent of the transformation, i.e., the Sidney family. In fact, two transformations are required (see diagram). The first (T_1) is accomplished by the metaphor which we have analyzed as relating the King's Tower to the Great Hall. A second stage (T_2) is reached in the passage from the hall to the Garden Tower and the garden beyond. Here another metaphor is completed, relating the Great Hall to a place and a time before the Fall. Once we have reached this point, the house and the hall through which we have passed achieve new significance as the medium through which paradise, or a portion of it, has been regained. (The double arrows in the second part of the diagram indicate this interrelationship in which the garden functions as both the end of the progress and the origin of its essential meaning.) The progression ends at the garden; but the most important element in the sequence, a view of which Henry Sidney took care to provide the visitor immediately on his arrival at the main gate, is the Great Hall at the center. Paradise is represented at the end of the progress as a sign of the relationship between the Great Hall and the family that is installed there. The transformation which we have witnessed has involved an exchange between the fourteenth-century hall, crusty with tradition, and a sixteenth-century family representative of a new ruling class and acknowledged by contemporaries as a model of domestic virtue. In other words, the Great Hall has lent the Sidneys its history, bestowing upon them their pedigree and their destiny; and the Sidneys have lent to the hall their virtue which is natural, innate, and timeless, and which bestows upon the house the power to transform Nature into paradise.

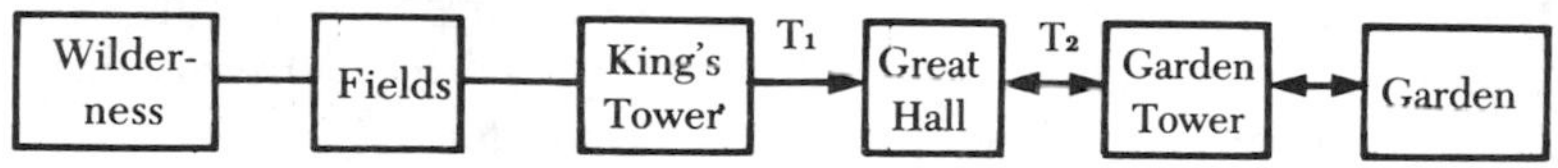

A[n Ex]Change of Value: New Doctrines of Nature and History

This relationship is not merely an exchange of attributes represented by the house for those represented by the family; it is an exchange of *value*. And, moreover, it is an exchange of value between two different systems of value. The change appertaining to the Sidney family is obvious; it becomes identified with the nobility of a previous era. The Sidneys are now valorized in accordance with an older system within which they previously had no value—they receive a pedigree. The Great Hall, in turn, is valorized in terms of a new system, one based not on a tradition of descent ordained and sanctioned at the moment of its inception by God, but on the notion of a universal and innate Nature. Thus, while the Great Hall retains its function as the sign of a historic past, "historic" has begun to assume a new and different meaning. Just as the Gothic style of the hall no longer serves its original function within the preternatural, allegorical tradition of the Roman Church, but instead comes to be seen as a natural and domestic architecture in opposition to the artificial and foreign Renaissance style, so too the "history" of which the hall is a sign is now understood as a *natural history*.

This new conception of history, which is embodied in the design of Penshurst, is very important and warrants some consideration here. By means of this conception the "nobility" of the families that previously held title to the house is now understood as a nobility of essence, a nobility based on the essential and innate virtues of the families concerned, rather than on mere lineage. It may appear rash to suggest that there is in Sir Henry Sidney's design of Penshurst a deliberate implementation or reflection of a developing contemporary shift in historiographical perspective. Yet the Sidneys were closely involved with some of those writers who were responsible for this shift from a theocentric historiography to one based, in Sir Walter Ralegh's words, on "naturall reason . . . [the criterion of whether a doctrine or principle] in every question of Nature, and finite power, may be approved for a fundamentall law of humane knowledge."[29] The theocentric view, consistent with a feudal monarchic system under the guidance of the Church at Rome, concerned itself primarily with interpreting the past as an unfolding of the judgments of God. But with the Reformation, and the need to justify royal supremacy in matters both temporal and spiritual, came a corresponding need for new historiographical principles.[30] To this end, the Calvinist theocratic ideal, with its emphasis on obedience to the "magistrate," was useful.[31] Though the aim here was by no means to divert attention from God as the "First Cause" of all events in this world, the mediation of law and lawyers became the basis for a notion of history concerned with secondary causes or "natural laws."[32]

One of the most influential historical writers of the late sixteenth century was Jean Bodin, the son of a lawyer and himself trained in the law. In his *Methodus* (1566), Bodin divided history into three categories: human, natural, and divine. Bodin then argued that although the "history of divine things" should be the central aim of historical inquiries, yet,

> since in man mother nature engenders first the desire for self-preservation, then little by little due to awe of Nature's workings drives him to investigate their causes, and since from these interests she draws him to an understanding of the very Arbiter of all things—for this reason it seems that we must begin with the subject of human affairs. . . . So it shall come about that from thinking first about ourselves, then about our family, then about our society we are led to examine nature and finally to the true history of Immortal God, that is, to contemplation.[33]

Later, having discussed methodology and the work of past historians, Bodin argues that disagreement among the latter requires that "we must make some generalizations as to the nature of all peoples or at least of the better known, so that we can test the truth of histories by just standards and make correct decisions about individual instances. . . . [L]et us seek characteristics drawn, not from the institutions of men, but from nature, which are stable and are never changed unless by great force or long training, and even if they have been altered, nevertheless eventually they return to their pristine character."[34] The naturalistic emphasis in Bodin's theory of history here takes the form of a description of the "natures" of different peoples on the basis of geography and climatology.

Bodin's naturalism is evident, too, in his *Six livres de la république* (1576), where he sets forth one of the earliest modern theories of unlimited sovereignty. Book V contains a historical and comparative analysis of legal institutions that relies, once more, on the notion that climate and geography determine the characters or "*naturels*" of peoples of different nations.[35] But, from our perspective, what is most significant about Bodin's theory is that he locates the origin of all forms of civil society in the family, conceived of as a "natural" community. This influential work went through ten French and three Latin editions during Bodin's lifetime. In 1606 an English translation by Richard Knolles appeared, from which I quote here.

Bodin defines the family as "the right government of many subjects or persons under the obedience of one and the same head . . . and of such things as are unto them proper [i.e., property attached to the household]."[36] Later, he asserts that there is a necessary natural and historical basis for his conception of the family as the essential unit of the state, since "the beginnings of all civill societies are derived from a familie, which is (as we say) it selfe a naturall societie, and by the father of nature it selfe first founded in the beginning together with mankind."[37] This is not the place to enter into a lengthy critique of Bodin's normative, patriarchal notions of "nature."[38] I wish only to point out that in his view the family and the property required for its subsistence came into existence with man and were part of that Nature "founded in the beginning" by God the Father. Consequently, the foundation of the well-ordered state is a "natural societie": the family unit composed of wife, children, servants, and private property, under the authority and government of the father who is, in himself, "the true Image of the great and Almightie God the Father of all things."[39] In this "natural" form—that is, rightly governed by the father—the family is the primary source of moral, intellectual, and religious virtue and is, therefore, the essential component of political order, for "the first and principall end of everie Commonweale ought to consist in vertue."[40]

Though Bodin was, nominally, a Catholic, his work was compatible with the interests of a new ruling English family with Puritan sympathies like the Sidneys. They would have been particularly sensitive to a conception of history based on natural law and stressing the investment of property, virtue, and, ultimately, sovereignty, in the family. Moreover, there is much evidence that they were active in promoting the new historiography in England. Henry Sidney's brother-in-law, Robert Dudley, earl of Leicester, was one of the most important patrons of historical writings in the sixteenth century. Sir Henry himself patronized works on the history of Ireland where he served as lord deputy.[41] Philip Sidney and the intellectual circle which surrounded him showed great interest in the writings of radical Protestant historians and political theorists, most notably George Buchanan.[42] That Sidney read and, to a degree, appreciated Bodin's *Methodus* is evident from a letter written in October 1580 to his younger brother Robert: "For the method of writing Historie, Boden hath written at large, yow may reade him and gather out of many wordes some matter."[43] Although Sidney is critical of historiography in his *Apology for Poetry*, his aim there is not to condemn the study of history outright but to contest the view that the historian's chief function is as a teacher of morality, a role which Sidney claims for the poet.

Sidney's attitude reflects a shift in humanist thought away from the idea of history as primarily moral instruction toward an emphasis on its political usefulness.[44] In this conception, the proper function of historiography is to analyze the causes and effects of past events and, thereby, to derive practical examples of military and administrative strategy. Sidney commends the *reading* of history to his brother as being in itself a form of historiography, founded on the doctrine of imitation:

> So generally doe the Roman stories follow the Greeke, and the perticuler stories of present Monarchies follow the Roman. In that kinde yow have principally to note the examples of vertue or vice, with their good or evell successes, the establishments or ruines of greate Estates, with the cawses, the tyme amd circumstances of the lawes they write of, the entrings, and endings of warrs, and therin the strategems against the enimy, and the discipline upon the soldiour, and thus much as a very Historiographer.[45]

He urges Robert to set down a "Table of Remembrance" of his reading, organized in Ramist fashion into "logicall subdivisions": "So likewise in politick matters, and such a little table yow may easelie make, wherwith I would have yow ever joyne the historicall part, which is only the example of some stratageme, or good cownsaile, or such like."[46] Underlying this pragmatic conception of historiography is the notion of a universal and natural law governing human affairs.

It is worth bearing in mind, too, that Ralegh, whose *History of the World* (1614) treats secondary causes as the sufficient basis of historical explanation, was closely connected to the Sidney circle. Francis Bacon does not appear to have been active in the group of intellectuals that gathered around Sir Philip Sidney; but he had friends among members of the circle, including Ralegh and Fulke Greville, and definite connections with the group through mutual involvement in the support of scientific and technological experiments as well as through commercial ventures.[47] And, of course, it is in Bacon's work that the principle of the sufficiency of secondary (i.e., *natural*) causation would be harnessed to the concepts of utility and progress in a new historiography and in a general program for the "advancement of learning."

I have digressed on this development of a species of naturalism in Elizabethan and Jacobean historiography, and particularly on the Sidneys' connection with this movement, in order to support my reading of what the house at Penshurst in its final state was designed to represent. Behind all the medieval trappings of the age, the armor, emblems, banners, and blazonry of the Accession Day tilts, the revival of Arthurian romance, the preservation of Gothic forms, lie the beginnings of a modern, naturalist conception of history. If this view is granted, then I think it not at all unlikely that Sir Henry Sidney and his sons consciously maintained the Gothic style at Penshurst in order to represent their accession to the estate as part of a natural historical continuity.

The identification of the Gothic as a "natural" style is generally thought to have first occurred in the eighteenth century as part of a revolt against a dogmatic classicism.[48] Yet as we have seen, already in the late sixteenth century something of a "revival" of the Gothic took place. We have located the reason for this persistence of the Gothic during the Elizabethan period in the principle of nationalism. Perhaps now it can be said, in addition, that even at this early date, another principle lay behind the Gothic revival, that of naturalism. This naturalism was not of the kind associated with the neoclassical doctrine of imitation, but rather arose out of a self-conscious awareness of the English countryside, the English yeoman farmer, and the shepherd whom the concurrent fashion of pastoral verse would celebrate, the English home, and the English family within—a Protestant family in which a husband and father was the minister of God and of Government in his own household. It is not surprising that the title of a book by Andrew Boorde, the earliest published work in English on the subject of building, should read: "The boke for to lerne a man to be wyse in buyldyng of his howse for the helth of body, and to holde quyetnes for the helth of his soule, and body. The boke for a good *husbande* to lerne" (ca. 1540).[49] The word *husband* derives from the Old Norse *hūsbondi* (for householder) formed from *hūs* (house) + *-bondi* (freeholder, yeoman); *-bondi* derived from the earlier *būandi*, the past participle of *būa* (to dwell). The "soule and body" of Boorde's "husbande" would include a wife and children, perhaps servants, and property; and so the house would be understood as the enclosure for a family, a natural community upon which the community at large was founded.

The concept of the family in such sixteenth-century writings may not yet be the "conjugal" family which Ian Watt claims to have emerged only in the eighteenth century.[50] But neither is it the traditional patriarchal community of the Middle Ages. I have already discussed the heightened degree of domesticity and the increasing value attributed to marital and filial devotion which became evident by the end of the sixteenth century.[51] In this period we have the beginnings of the notion of house as *home* in the special sense that the latter term has come to enjoy in England. And through a metaphorical relation between the "stately homes" of the aristocracy and the more "humble homes" of the free farmer or the craftsman, this naturalism based on a changing concept of the family became the foundation of a form of nationalism that is peculiarly English. Jonson's poem, with its comparison of the farmers who "dwell about" the house at Penshurst to the lord who "dwells" within, is an early example of the metaphor. Some of the epigraphs to this book provide evidence of its persistence and of the ideological use to which it continues to be put. The principles of nationalism and naturalism may thus be related motives for the survival of the Gothic style in Protestant England. And the ideal of the country house built not for show, or for the lavish entertainment of a queen, but "built to live in" as Bacon put it, and for "lastingnesse" in Sir Philip Sidney's words, is an ideal and an image upon which the British tradition of paternal, benevolent government would be based.

CHAPTER 5

The Home

Built in 1611, Hatfield House now confronts at close quarters the modern world. . . . Yet—as the visitor discovers, when he has taken his eight minutes' walk and is face to face with it—Hatfield House has not been subdued by its twentieth-century situation. It may represent the past, but not the dead past. Like the plays of Shakespeare, this massive architectural monument of Shakespeare's age somehow still manages to speak to us with a living voice.

Who should recognize this voice better than I? I spent my childhood there and, because I was the youngest of my family by seven years, my relation to the house was close and private. . . . In company or in solitude, gradually I was penetrated by the spirit of the place; thus I grew intimate with its changing moods and the varied aspects of its complex personality.

Complex partly because it is both public and private. It was designed to be the house of a great nobleman, when great nobles ruled the country. This means it has something of the palace about it, with its grand staircase and huge ornate rooms intended for state occasions and semi-public gatherings. All the same, the impression it leaves is not that of a palace; it is also a family home with the characteristics of a family home. There are plenty of private-seeming rooms, moderate-sized and intimate, full of pleasant untidiness and the spirit of relaxation; and this spirit can overflow into the big rooms, making them intimate and untidy too. I remember Hatfield as a house where books and newspapers were strewn about the floors, and on the tables of the pillared front hall lay tennis rackets and mackintoshes and old hats.

—Lord David Cecil, *The Cecils of Hatfield House: An English Ruling Family* (Boston, 1973)

The Garden Metaphor Displaced

I HAVE said that the ensemble of relationships composing the topography and the architecture of Penshurst is an implied "map" of a transformation of nature from a wild state into the paradise of the garden. Jonson's poem is a reading of that "map." In most respects, the reading is consistent with the estate. Thus, for example, like Sir Henry Sidney's perspective of arches from the King's Tower through the Great Hall to the garden, the poem is organized around the family as the center of the house and as the ordering principle of Nature at Penshurst. Yet there are significant differences between the poem and the prior order of representation to which it refers. I have already pointed out that hardly any allusion is made to the architectural features of the house. At the same time, bare mention is given to the garden which we saw was central to the system of representation at Penshurst. This may be attributed to several factors. The poem's concern with the right *use* of wealth may have led Jonson to shift emphasis from the garden to the greater utilitarian value of the orchards. Another reason may be that Jonson did not wish to call attention to the symmetrical garden at Penshurst; contemporary evidence suggests that while symmetry was becoming the norm in building it was already considered unnatural in gardening. This inversion of the standards for houses and gardens is advocated by Sir Henry Wotton in his *Elements of Architecture*: "As fabriques should bee regular, so gardens should be irregular, or at least cast into a very wilde regularitie."[1]

That Jonson would concur with this view is suggested by the notion of Nature which is implicit in the form of "To Penshurst." We have seen that the poem is characterized by an asymmetrical structure with the exception of the first eight lines, and these are devoted mainly to a description of those houses which are considered unnatural. From line 8 on, the poem has a quality of openness and irregularity, limited only by the rhymed couplets; this is not unlike the irregular garden advocated by Wotton, more park than garden really, which would become the norm of the "English garden" in the eighteenth century.[2] Furthermore, the titles of two of Jonson's collections of poems reflect this concept of Nature as an ordered disorder: *The Forrest* and *Under-wood*. Both titles refer to the classical *Sylva*, as Jonson explains in a note "to the reader" at the beginning of *Under-wood*:

> With the same leave, the Ancients call'd that kind of body Sylva, or ῞Υλη, in which there were workes of divers nature, and matter congested; as the multitude call Timber-trees, promiscuously growing, a *Wood*, or *Forrest*: so am I bold to entitle these lesser Poems, of later growth, by this of *Under-wood*, out of the Analogie they hold to the *Forrest*, in my former booke, and no otherwise.

It is possible, therefore, that the function of the garden at Penshurst as a metaphor for paradise would not have appealed to Jonson. Indeed, he seems to have shifted the metaphor from the garden to the estate as a whole. In the poem the house is surrounded by a park, fields, ponds, orchards; the image of paradise is that of a magically ordered disorder, an image corresponding to Wotton's phrase "wilde regularitie," surrounded by the wilderness at the outer limits of the estate, the disordered disorder of unnatural chaos.

The Family

As we have seen, the garden at Penshurst functioned as a sign of the "nature" of the Sidney family—a family whose innate virtue gave to the ancient Great Hall the power of transforming untamed Nature into paradise. The garden was primarily the operator of a transformation and of a transvaluation of the notion of nobility from a concept based on hereditary descent and wealth, to one based on natural virtue. In order to achieve this transvaluation, the representation had to entail a passage across the estate from north to south, and it had to conclude with the passage from the house into the garden. Only then, in retrospect, could the house take on its new meaning; only then could the Sidneys' status be valorized. But the poem is of a different order of representation. It too surveys the estate from north to south; thus, for the reader, reading the poem is like reading a map. But only up to a certain point; once the poem has brought us to the interior of the house it does not have to take us beyond the Great Hall and into the garden in order to accomplish its message. Because its medium is language, the poem can *tell* us what the house contains and what is the nature and the power of its contents. It can tell us that what translates *house* to *home* is the family that "dwells" within. This is in fact what we are told in the last section of the poem; and this is why the conclusion is not consistent with the "topographical" method of the earlier section. The *cultured Nature* of lines 9–44, and the *natural Culture* of lines 45–89, have been mapped; it remains for the poem to reveal to us the agency through which both Nature and Culture are transformed at Penshurst and by which the contradiction between them (pointed to in lines 1–8) is resolved. For this, topography is no longer necessary; the answer lies within the house, and we have no need to progress further.

And so this "topographical poem" never reaches what would have been the most important part of the topography in the first order of representation; in the final fourteen-line section of the poem, the garden as emblematic of the agency of paradise regained is replaced by the agency itself, the family that dwells in the house:

> These, PENSHURST, are thy praise, and yet not all.
>   Thy lady's noble, fruitfull, chaste withall.
> His children thy great lord may call his owne:
>   A fortune, in this age, but rarely knowne.
> They are, and have beene taught religion: Thence
>   Their gentler spirits have suck'd innocence.
> Each morne, and even, they are taught to pray,
>   With the whole houshold, and may, every day,
> Reade, in their vertuous parents noble parts,
>   The mysteries of manners, armes, and arts.
> (lines 89–98)

This is a virtuous family maintaining a civilized "houshold." Its knowledge and observance of "the mysteries of manners, armes, and arts" are signs of its civility and of its legitimate title to rule.[3]

The turning inside out of the old manor house is complete; its new essence has been bared to the reader, and by extension, to the world. And as the word beginning the next line suggests, "now" a conclusion is possible:

Now, PENSHURST, they that will proportion thee
  With other edifices, when they see
Those proud, ambitious heaps, and nothing else,
  May say, their lords have built, but thy lord dwells.
(lines 99–102)

The final word, "dwells," brings all the preceding details together into a general significance. The opposition of "dwells" to "built" would not make very much sense without the long chain of metonymies which has come before and which has established a *context* within which "dwells" connotes a home, a family, the bearing and rearing of children, a natural community governed by natural law and natural rulers, and the fundamental unit of a natural social order in the state at large.

The Sanctioning of Property

The differences between the two orders of representation, the estate and the poem, can be explained in part by reference to the different historical periods in which they were respectively conceived. The estate, with the completed North Front, dates from around 1586; the poem was first published in 1616 and was probably written not long before the death of Prince Henry in 1612. As I have said, the primary ideological function of the house with its surrounding grounds and its garden, as Sir Henry Sidney left them, was to legitimate the name of Sidney. But by the time Jonson was writing, this was no longer a primary concern. The status of the Sidney family was already firmly established, and their financial condition was somewhat improved as well, though, as J. C. A. Rathmell has demonstrated through extensive quotations from Sir Robert Sidney's letters, financial problems continued to make it difficult to maintain the tradition of hospitality at Penshurst.[4] Nevertheless, whereas Sir Henry Sidney had refused a barony in 1572 because the offer did not include the remuneration necessary to sustain the title, his son Robert was able to accept such a title from James I. He became Baron Sidney of Penshurst in 1603; in 1605 he was made Viscount Lisle; and in 1618 he received the title of earl of Leicester which had lapsed with the death of his uncle,

Robert Dudley.[5] Moreover, the name Sidney already had mythical status by the second decade of the seventeenth century, largely as a result of the astonishing effect that Sir Philip, "the shepherd knight," had had upon the imaginations of his contemporaries. So a poet like Jonson, seeking the continued patronage of the Sidneys by writing an encomium to their "ancestral" home, would not be likely to concern himself with a rationalization of their titles. Instead, as I suggested earlier, the poem is an attempt to rationalize the accumulation of wealth and the maintenance of certain relations of exchange. Thus, where the estate as Sir Henry left it was a representation designed to legitimate the family's name, the poem attempts to sanction its wealth in relation to those who are poorer, and its position in relation to those who may be wealthier but are not necessarily of higher rank.

But it is not just Sidney wealth and position that Jonson attempted to legitimate in "To Penshurst." Rather, he sought to rationalize a general norm for the accumulation and use of wealth. Here I realize that I am deviating somewhat from the accepted view put forth by L. C. Knights in his *Drama and Society in the Age of Jonson* (1937), not only an important book to any student of Jonson, but also one of the exemplary instances of a sociological criticism in English.[6] Knights treats Jonson as a social critic working in a long tradition of classical and Christian "anti-acquisitive" thought. I do not take issue with this view; but I do claim that it is incomplete, that in order to do justice to the complexity of Jonson's work we need to account for elements that differentiate it from the "anti-acquisitive" tradition. "Acquisitive" is primarily a moral term; it is a judgment referring to a voluntary subject as the agent of a process. On the other hand, "accumulation" refers primarily to the process itself, a process which was intensified, particularly in agricultural production and in the consolidation of estates, during the early stages of capitalist development in England. Now it seems to me that Jonson could be, and indeed was, both possessed of what Knights calls an "anti-acquisitive attitude" and, at the same time, engaged in an attempt to provide a rationale for a normative conception of accumulation. Knights fails to appreciate the extent to which the satire of acquisitiveness in Jonson is carried out in the name of values and norms that are part of the same system the satire claims to reject. These values are embodied in the *forms* which Jonson takes to be natural and normal, and these forms are characterized by a version of the principle of accumulation.

We have seen that the poem evokes the Sidney estate through a catalogue of its attributes. These are primarily natural in the first half of the poem; the grounds are well stocked, well kept, abundantly productive. Paul Cubeta has suggested that "in all these physical details connotations of moral values, the solidity and integrity that give genuine worth to character, reinforce the ethical suggestions of 'reverenc'd' in line six, the key to Jonson's attitude here."[7] Perhaps so, but it is important to notice that the natural wealth that connotes "solidity and integrity" here is signified by a process of itemization and quantification at both the syntactic and the semantic levels of the poem, the same process that serves to designate the fantastic wealth imagined by Volpone and Sir Epicure Mammon and which Jonson represents in his plays as unnatural and excessive.

Thus, after having rejected the ornament associated with Culture in the first eight lines, the remainder of the poem comprises a series of metonymies the ultimate effect of which is the substitution of a new overall metaphor, a new *kosmos* (the term originally meant "ornament" as well as "order" in ancient Greek) for the old. This accounts for the abrupt break between the first eight lines and what follows. Culture is first defined negatively as ornament, and it is so defined within a tightly symmetrical poetic unit suggesting the artificiality of the *kosmos* described there. Then, at the end of this section, Penshurst's "better markes" are described as natural, unfragmented, continuous, unified, and universal; yet in the section that immediately follows (lines 9–44), Nature on the Penshurst estate is enumerated in a style characterized by fragmentary details which constitute a different kind of ornament from what is common in Renaissance poetry. Eventually, *kosmos* and Culture are renormalized in the final two sections of the poem. The new *kosmos* appears in the form of the plain style in which the rhetorical figure of metaphor is restrained and ornament is achieved primarily through heightened description (*ekphrasis*) and the accumulation of detail.

In this, Jonson anticipates the literary naturalism of a later age.

In the view of Angus Fletcher, naturalism involves the displacement of one allegorical tradition, one form of *kosmos*, by another. For a postscientific world, *kosmos* takes the form of an obsession with "natural" details.[8] Moreover, Fletcher's study suggests that in all instances the operation signified by the verb *kosmein* is ideological: "Notice that there is nothing neutral about the process: to adorn, in the rhetorical sense of *kosmein*, means to elevate a lower rank to a higher one."[9] In Jonson's poem ornament, identified with the houses of wealthier lords, is degraded, while Penshurst is elevated by giving it the better name of Nature and by enumerating the attributes of that name. And, of course, the latter process achieves its emotive effect on the reader in part by hiding the fact that it is a new form of *kosmos*. Thus, writes Fletcher, "the naturalistic type of allegorical fiction . . . builds a whole world out of documentary detail, which at first appears intended solely to inform the reader, but which on second view appears intended to control the reader."[10]

"To Penshurst" controls the reader by such an accumulation of "documentary detail" and by the implementation of that detail in a set of logical operations that require the reader's participation in the enforcement of an ideology. But this process is more complex than the ordinary use of *kosmos* to provoke adulation or envy (the process which Jonson attacks in attacking the other houses, and the process which is satirized in characters like Sir Epicure Mammon). It is more complex and more subtle because the naturalistic details of "To Penshurst" preserve the function of *kosmos* and of allegory as control, while denying their allegorical nature.

The Double Articulation of Nature

Of course the wealth of the Sidney estate is not seen as an *acquisition* of the Sidneys, but rather as something that is given to them by Nature. As I mentioned earlier, unlike the Cockaigne poem, "To Penshurst" represents a magical, abundant Nature through affirmative rather than negative constructions. In *The Land of Cockaigne*, only the underlying *lack* is real. In "To Penshurst," although the magical element is fantasy, the abundance referred to is real. There is no sign of longing for the goods of

Nature; indeed, if there is longing expressed for any goods at all, it may be the ambivalent longing for those goods which are identified in negative constructions as useless, unnatural, Culture in the opening lines of the poem.[11] Just as the Sidneys built additions to the estate to represent nobility (their own) as natural and innate, so too Jonson's poem represents a certain form of wealth and a certain form of exchange as natural phenomena. In "To Penshurst," Nature's abundance is a sign of the Sidney's *natural* right to their domain; it is the just reward of landlords who oversee their lands according to *rational* principles, principles which are themselves the direct reflection of what is natural; and of these, the most preeminent is the principle of the right *use* of Nature.

In architecture, this principle of *use* as opposed to the *abuse* identified with ostentation has already been noted in Sidney's description of Kalander's house, and in Bacon's essay "Of Building." But in Jonson's poem the house is not spoken of as designed for use; instead, the house is addressed by apostrophe as the *user* of Nature. As such the house is a metonym for the family. It is personified, transformed into a subject capable of willfully and rationally possessing and using its environment. One reason for the personification is that it attaches directly to this house the active principle of *use* in contrast to the passive and static attribute of "envious show." This vital principle distinguishes Penshurst from other houses and contributes to making it not merely a house but a *home*. The personification of the house is thus a device for enforcing the ideological statement or proposition in the poem. But the device also performs a function at the level of articulation or expression, that is, where the ideological proposition is produced, which has to do with the relation of the poet to his patron and to the reader. Just as all economic exchange within the representation is suppressed (all exchange at Penshurst is represented as voluntary and symbolic, rather than necessary and economic), so too, in the very mode of enunciation, the economic content of the exchange between Jonson and the Sidneys, the commodity nature of the poem, is suppressed. By addressing a house instead of a patron the exchange is made purely symbolic.

The active use of wealth at Penshurst is opposed to the static hoarding of it elsewhere, an opposition which is in reaction to the recrudescence of feudal forms of accumulation and exchange which a middle-class ideology would identify with sumptuous and ornamental architecture. The Sidneys' wealth is represented as being within a certain limit to accumulation, a limit that marks a qualitative difference between the natural and the unnatural (and "acquisitive"). Theirs is wealth used and administered according to the doctrine of moderation, the "Golden Mean" which Jonson adopted from Horace and from the Stoic philosophers. Yet this qualitative difference can only be understood as a difference in quantity, since Nature is also treated here as a rationally ordered plenum in which quality is a matter of measurable quantities. It would seem then that the limit to quantification marks an arbitrary boundary. The territory beyond this boundary is that of *excess, un-Nature, acquisitiveness*, while included within it is the *norm, Nature, quantification* [or accumulation].

The term *accumulation* appears in brackets here because it is kept hidden in the poem. In fact, part of the function of "To Penshurst" is to negate or to hide the element of accumulation which is a necessary component of the concept of wealth and exchange that Jonson represents as both natural and normal. It may be argued that even if one were to concede the existence of a principle of quantification in Jonson's description and evaluation of the estate, there is still no element of accumulation involved precisely because Nature's "free provision" is said to be used and circulated rather than displayed and hoarded. But this argument confounds the poem's two levels of meaning, and particularly, the two general meanings of the implied term *Nature* which the poem endeavors to define. The poem as a whole is an extended metaphor; and the tenor of this metaphor is the actual condition or "nature" of Penshurst. As I have already mentioned, while the magical way in which Nature gives itself to the Sidneys is fantasy, those things that it gives, the things that signify Nature in the poem—soil, air, wood, water, sheep, cows, fish, foul, fruit, flowers, capons, cakes, nuts, cheeses, daughters—i.e., the goods themselves and their abundance, are real. And while the absence of accumulation may be "true" at the level of fantasy, that is, at the level of the imaginary *vehicle* of a magical Nature, the *tenor* of the overall metaphor is a real condition of abundance that would depend upon the existence of a surplus. In other words, while the poem opposes use and "free" exchange to ostentation and hoarding, the possibility of "freely" using and exchanging the bounty of Nature depends on the existence of a real surplus which could be derived only through accumulation.

This analysis points in turn to another hidden problem concerning the condition of Nature at Penshurst. Since the magical Nature is only imaginary, the real surplus to which it refers must have a source that is also real. Abundance depends on more than just Nature; it depends on cultivation, the working of Nature, on *labor*. And the accumulation of a surplus depends on a level of production beyond the amount required for the sustenance of the producer. Since rent was no longer being paid primarily in labor by the end of the sixteenth century, but was rather paid "in kind," or even in some instances in money, it was at least possible for the tenant farmer to appropriate a portion of the surplus production of his labor to his own economic development.[12] But more often than not, the major portion of the surplus produced by tenants and freeholders was consumed or even sold at a profit by their lord.

So we finally uncover the reason for the double sense in which the poem refers to Nature. In a real sense the elements of Nature are present on the estate. But they are only *potentially* available to the nonproducers whose title to Penshurst is an assertion of private ownership of Nature. According to the poem, what makes the elements of Nature available to its owners is magic. But this magic is not real; it is only a substitute for the real process that produces abundance, and for the relation which allows the Sidneys to be the beneficiaries of that abundance. The "magical Nature" at Penshurst is a surrogate for surplus labor and for the Sidneys' power over the labor of others. As Raymond Williams has observed in an eloquent discussion of the country-house poem, the "magical extraction of the curse of labour is in fact achieved by a simple extraction of the existence of labourers."[13]

With perhaps the single exception of Williams, critics who have attempted to interpret "To Penshurst" have failed to distinguish between the two Natures implied there. This lapse is a consequence of the fact that most of the criticism has been limited by some of the same assumptions that govern the discourse of the poem. The double semantic reference to the implied term "Nature" is contradictory; but it does not appear so in the poem. Instead, the contradiction is suspended in the oscillation that Jonson managed to set going between our apprehension of the connotations of the magical and of those of the real. In this way we are made witness simultaneously to a magical Nature which bestows itself freely upon an Edenic "lord" and "lady," and a real Nature that the poem legitimates as the property of an actual ruling family. But the contradiction becomes evident only when we add what the poem omits: that is, that the real Nature is available for its owners' consumption solely through the transforming power of human labor.

This absent signifier of the text—the curse of labor, but also the potentiality inherent in labor—continues to be repressed in those interpretations which easily transfer the attributes of a magical Nature to the real Nature of the estate. Such interpretations evince a desire for order and coherence which is sustained by the text's apparent resolution of social contradictions.[14] The capacity of "To Penshurst" to activate this desire in the reader is an example of that poetic power recognized by Sir Philip Sidney when he argues that poetry, rather than philosophy, is the highest vehicle of moral doctrine: "For who will be taught if he be not moved with desire to be taught; and what so much good doth that teaching bring forth . . . as that it moveth one to do that which it doth teach?" It is precisely because, as Sidney claimed, "the poet, he nothing affirms," that poetry has the power to lead the reader into affirming a great deal.[15]

But this nonaffirmative rhetoric of the fictive text is also the vehicle of poetic irony and ambiguity; it is what finally can carry us beyond the initial pleasure—that state of being moved, which is the necessary condition for entering into a poem's universe of discourse—to a more self-conscious, critical activity. Most criticism has been accurate and even eloquent in paraphrasing the sense of "To Penshurst." But it has also been incomplete in failing to detect the ambiguities of the code through which that sense is communicated. When G. R. Hibbard writes that the poem "presents in concrete terms a whole and consistent view of life in which not only man's relation to man, but also to God on the one side and to nature on the other, are given due place";[16] when Paul Cubeta writes that the "physical details" of Nature provide "connotations of moral values, the solidity and integrity that give genuine worth to character";[17] when Hugh Maclean writes that the poem depicts "the social attitudes and actions befitting a 'ruling class' which thoroughly understands the nature of its responsibilities and desires to make them effective";[18] they are all speaking about the poem in abstract versions of the poet's own discourse. Within that discourse, "connotations of solidity and integrity" can go unquestioned. But what critics have continued to speak is at best a diluted variant of the discourse of the poem and of an ideology which was already anachronistic in Jonson's time.[19] The poem's artistry, the imaginative power that is concealed by the casual "amble" of the plain style in which it is written, is perhaps responsible along with its content for the imitations it called forth later in the seventeenth and eighteenth centuries, and for its continued appeal. But "To Penshurst" is interesting also for the way in which it seems to undermine its own discourse. The poem's ambiguous relation to its occasion, and the poet's ability to expose and to place in question his ideological function on that occasion, are essential aspects of the knowledge and the pleasure we may derive from reading it. The same cannot be said, however, for most of what has been written about "To Penshurst." And our acceptance of such criticism as complete, on the assumption that it is inclusive of the poem's relevant contexts, may be an expression, more than anything else, of our own desire and willingness to accept and to share the discourse and the ideology it speaks.

CHAPTER 6

Beyond the Ideology of the Text: The Rhetorical Strategy of Jonson's Classicism

The arts [*technê*], or productive forms of knowledge [*poiêtikê epistêmê*] . . . are potencies inasmuch as they are the initiating principles of change in another thing (or in the artist or craftsman himself under the aspect of otherness).

—Aristotle, *Metaphysics*

For books . . . doe contain a potencie of life in them to be as active as that soule was whose progeny they are.

—John Milton, *Areopagitica* (1644)

When [man] has comprehended himself and has grounded his life in real democracy without renunciation and estrangement, then there arises in the world something which appears to us all in childhood, and in which none of us yet was—home.

—Ernst Bloch, *Das Prinzip Hoffnung* (1959)

Limits of Ideology and Potentialities of the Esthetic

AND YET, there is more to Jonson's poem than the pressures of an ideological function and the constraints of a discourse conceived to perform that function would indicate. Rhetorically, the poem is addressed to the place; pragmatically, the addressee is the reader for whom the place, personified and idealized, becomes the emblem of the *integer vitae*. Jonson serves his patron well in making his family the tenor and his country seat the vehicle of a metaphor enunciating the moral virtues and the social value of a *home*. Yet we still need to account for the capacity of readers, even today, to recognize the quality carried by the metaphor and to respond to it in terms of their own personal and historical situations. This capacity cannot be reduced to a mere reflex of discourse and ideology.

There must be a further significance carried by the text, a surplus of possible meaning and a pleasure, beyond what was historically comprehensible to readers of the society and culture within which the poem was produced, and, no doubt, beyond what the author himself could have understood. What I mean is not adequately accounted for by theories of the relationship between art and ideology that employ Louis Althusser's notion of "internal distantiation." It is an important concept and I shall touch on it briefly in this chapter, but it is limited by the restrictive conception of the subject on which it is founded. What I have in mind involves a more affirmative esthetic, something closer to Georg Lukács's concept of *potentiality*, or to Ernst Bloch's notion of *utopian fulfillment*, or, in a different but not necessarily uncomplementary way, to the active pleasure of the text which Roland Barthes calls *jouissance*.[1] I would add, however, the important qualification that this potentiality of the esthetic needs to be analyzed not just as a progressive sociohistorical "content" thematized in the text, or as a principle of "Hope" allegorized in it, or as a form of the "will to power" embodied in the acts of writing and reading, but as a mode of social *praxis* activated primarily through the text's formal operations in relation not only to its content but to a prior system of conventions, styles, genres, and so on. To be more precise, it is a question of rhetorical and narrative strategies which, while often aimed at the resolution or containment of social contradictions, have the effect of revealing them in a new light. To say that social contradictions are revealed by the work of art does not mean that ideology is thereby exposed nor that it is miraculously transcended, but rather that it is focused in a way that enables alternative forms of praxis in the wider social sphere to be perceived as possible. This conception is not unrelated to the more traditional notion of esthetic distance, though it must insist that logically such distance, like ideology itself, can be only partial. This amounts to saying what is, perhaps, obvious though it is not always acknowledged in the practice of criticism: that art (or, at least, Western art since the later

Middle Ages) is generally *polyphonic*.[2] I take it as axiomatic here that works of art do provide such indices of alternative possibilities for human praxis, and that this potentiality constitutes the primary basis of pleasure and cognition in the esthetic activity.

The problem of localizing such a principle in specific works is in significant ways more difficult with respect to a poem like "To Penshurst" than it is in connection with the architecture of Penshurst Place.[3] Therefore, I intend to concentrate on the poem, or rather, on its literary context, in this concluding chapter. The difficulty in question is in part a matter of a special case: that is, "To Penshurst" is one poem in a corpus of works by an author who rarely appears to speak through a persona, but rather employs the first person pronoun most often as a sign of his own presence. The text is therefore deceptively "plain." On a first reading it is likely to seem univocal, to lack qualities that would distantiate it from the ethic or the ideology it expounds.

In addition, there is a more general aspect to the problem, having to do with the very nature of this poem as a literary text, a piece of writing, that is, an artifact in which the temporality of the verbal "utterance" appears to be arrested and contained in a static "text." From its earliest use as a technology for making lists and keeping records, writing has been an especially powerful cultural device because of its unique capacity to integrate the intelligibility and perceptibility of an authoritative "voice" within a semipermanent form. The twofold effect of this technological transformation of the dynamic "utterance" into the static "text" is described by the anthropologist Jack Goody: "By making it possible to scan the communications of mankind over a much wider time span, literacy encouraged, at the very same time, criticism and commentary on the one hand and the orthodoxy of the book on the other."[4] This striking observation suggests that there is in the very medium of the written word, at its most fundamental level, a tension between ideology and historicity.[5]

I don't mean to suggest that poetry is necessarily more complex than the other arts, nor that the written is more complex than the oral; but I do think that beginning in the early modern period, the referent of the written word in European cultures becomes more difficult to identify because the development of these cultures was such that writing became the primary vehicle of a subject in search of itself. This dislocation and division of the subject (the necessary condition of subjectivity in the modern sense) constitutes a response to historical disjunctions in the social organization of reality. The most obvious symptom of such division is the fragmentation in religion. Its psychological manifestations are evident in the visual arts, beginning with Mannerism in the sixteenth century and culminating in the Baroque. There we see a self-conscious preoccupation with the medium of representation that places in question the power of communication and the authority of that which is communicated in the very act of realizing it. But it is in the written word, where the subject that says "I" has begun to interrogate its own status in the discourse into which it inserts itself, that this self-consciousness takes its most involuted form; that is, in religious writings of all sorts, in the early autobiographical texts, and in poetry.[6] And it is, above all, through writing that the conflict is played out between the orthodoxy of the book, on the one hand, and the capacity to criticize (and to rejoice in the power to criticize), on the other. In analyzing a specific instance of such conflict, we are likely to find that what first appears as a writer's adherence to an orthodox view may be complicated by other elements in the text. I have already suggested as much concerning Jonson. It now remains to explain how the rhetorical strategy he adopts in "To Penshurst" involves the sort of potentiality described above.

Jonson's strategy, to the extent that it was ideological, was also constrained by what he was describing. Therefore we might be tempted to ask whether there is indeed a historical truth to what he tells us of the Sidneys, and we might seek further empirical evidence to help us determine whether his description was valid or invalid. However, it is difficult to make such a judgment where human relations, in the house and between members of the household and the people of the surrounding community, are concerned. As we saw earlier, attempts by commentators to do just that have led to anachronistic expressions of faith more than anything else. Here, we find ourselves in the same dilemma as the modern historian, caught between his desire to reconstruct the past and his knowledge that he is always to some degree constructing *a* past.[7] His predicament is all the more difficult when he tries to understand the social and psychological aspects of interpersonal relations in a time when the large majority of people were still denied the power of writing, and when those who had it gave only the most stylized indication of their innermost thoughts and feelings. Among the aristocracy in the sixteenth and early seventeenth centuries, even the most personal occasions for writing—letters exchanged between husbands and wives or parents and children, or between close friends—are highly conventionalized. Perhaps there are moments when the conventions of the age are breached, when the modern reader may glimpse a gesture of more spontaneous feeling than is permitted by the prevailing code—one finds, for example, in the correspondence between Robert Sidney and his wife, Barbara, striking instances in which expressions of conjugal intimacy manage to come through the otherwise formal prose, and this perhaps helps to confirm the accuracy of Jonson's depiction of the family.[8] But such moments do not provide sufficient evidence in themselves for generalizing about conjugal relations in the family, and they certainly don't tell us much about relations between the classes on a country estate like Penshurst. Moreover, even if there were more of this kind of "documentary" textual evidence to support claims as to Jonson's "grounding of this poem in actuality,"[9] I don't believe the poem's meaning for a modern reader, which would entail a certain capacity to transcend its original occasion and its immediate ideological function, can be explained in terms of the purported authenticity of the attitudes, values, and behavior it describes. Such a view, whether of the historicist, humanist, or Marxist variety, remains naively reflectionist.

Another possibility worth consideration is the evidence afforded by the estate itself, which provides a somewhat more concrete record of the constraints upon the poet's capacity to mystify social relations at Penshurst. This is, of course, one of my reasons for studying the place as well as the poem. A visit to Penshurst will confirm, even today, the legitimacy of certain utopian elements in Jonson's text: the atmosphere is still bucolic; the buildings are relatively integrated into the landscape and into the community (i.e., the estate is indeed on the same plane as the village, not above it, and there is evidence in the earliest extant surveyor's map that the lord's dwelling was in close proximity to the village and to the homes of his tenants);[10] compared with the more extravagant "prodigy" houses built in Jonson's time, the Sidney estate is certainly a modest country home.

Finally, there are the constraints of the literary tradition. That is, one might argue that this poem of formal praise is written in a tradition of epideictic rhetoric involving certain rules and conventions with respect to both content and form. Such a reading of "To Penshurst" would attempt to show that the pleasure and meaning of the poem for a modern reader derives from an intertextual knowledge of the tradition in which it is written. Presumably, too, such a reading would hold—at least implicity—that the poem espouses timeless values that transcend ideology, values that appear in different cultures and in different historical epochs, and are somehow transmitted, perhaps even created, by the particular genre or rhetorical tradition to which the poem belongs. Certainly, Jonson was writing under such generic and rhetorical constraints (see Chapter 2 above). But with some exceptions, notably two recent studies by Richard S. Peterson and Thomas M. Greene, which are far more subtle than earlier discussions of imitation in Jonson,[11] the tendency of the intertextual approach has been to promote a naive conception of the relationship between form (literary genre or style) and content (ethical, metaphysical, or psychological verities of the human condition). Indeed, Greene's analysis of tensions and conflicts inherent in the "heuristic" and "dialectical" modes of imitation through which some Renaissance writers read and appropriated the texts of antiquity would suggest that we need to be more cautious about our own easy assumptions concerning the transmission of enduring values through literary forms.[12] Yet even at its best—where it is employed to interpret and explain the sense of distance and conflict as well as the continuity that exists in the relationship between a text and its literary sources—the intertextual approach depends on a type of knowledge that is rarely found today outside the relatively small community of literary scholars. An intertextual interpretation will give access to the ways in which a text relates to its antecedents, and may even reveal ways in which the text projects a sense of its own future readership. But in order for this kind of information to prove helpful in understanding the possible significance of a poem like "To Penshurst" for a modern reader, it will have to be incorporated into a critical method that moves beyond the confines of a strictly *literary* history.

Such factors as these—the available historical evidence concerning the Sidneys, the symbolic and practical significance of the topographical and architectural organization of space at Penshurst, the conventions of the literary tradition—may help us to identify the constraints within which Jonson had to work in writing his poem. But they are not sufficient in themselves to establish some authentic actuality to which we can point as the essential truth of an otherwise idealized or ideological representation. What we can do, however, is to use this kind of information in conjunction with the analysis and interpretation of the tensions and ambiguities in the rhetorical strategy of the text itself. It is important to bear in mind that what is involved in the poem is not just representation but the performance of a strategy for representation. Although Jonson's conception of poetry, of all communication, is committedly if not obsessively representational, much of the strength of his verse lies in the tension between representational and performative levels of utterance.[13]

In the same way that textual ambiguities provide the entry for an ideological analysis, they may also lead us to an understanding of how ideology is, in a sense, superseded, if not transcended, by other elements in the text's formation. And this may help to explain the pleasure and the illumination that a seventeenth-century poem, which appears to be transparently ideological in its immediate purpose, can bring to a modern reader. Of course, for some readers, the pleasure will involve the security and comfort provided by the poem's mythic validation of institutions and practices that are still, however transformed, central to our lives—the proprietary conception of self, family, and home, justified in the image of responsible, benevolent, yet authoritative management. But there is also another source of pleasure involved here. It derives, I believe, from our ability to recognize in the ambiguities and contradictions of the rhetorical strategy a certain disfunction, an opening as it were in the apparent esthetic closure that establishes the boundaries of an ideology (the topographical metaphor is, once again, especially apropos, since both house and poem are self-consciously topographical in their respective depictions of an order of things).

Implied here is a notion of the esthetic that is somewhat at variance with tradition, a notion that does not emphasize unity, resolution, and closure, nor even the tension of *concordia discors*; rather, a notion of the esthetic in terms of conflict, discontinuity, rupture, and, ultimately, the opening up of more problems than are ever resolved by the work. This is not the place to embark on a lengthy discussion of the possible forms such an esthetic might take.[14] Nevertheless, the Althusserian conception requires mention because of its direct concern with the relation between art and ideology and, too, because its influence is being felt at the present time in Anglo-American literary studies. Althusser has sketched the bare outlines of an esthetic in some remarks intended as a qualification of his global theory of ideology. He claims that works of art "allude" to reality in such a way that "they make us 'perceive' (but not know) in some sense *from the inside*, by an *internal distance*, the very ideology in which they are held."[15] The concept is a provocative one though it remains undeveloped in Althusser's work. While I have been influenced by it in the writing of this book, I am not convinced that notions like internal distantiation, or internal dissonance, or the idea that art deforms an already deformed (i.e., ideological) representation of the real necessarily exclude the concept of *potentiality*. By the latter I do not mean some sort of "transcendence" of ideology; I mean a process whereby not only are contradictions within a given ideological context rendered perceptible (if not knowable), but alternatives to the existing ideology are figured in the production of the work of art. This implies a notion of the subject that is more active than what Althusser allows, a notion of the subject as locus of an ongoing, changing system of relationships (both the subject inscribed in and through the work of art, and the subject that intervenes in that inscription, inevitably modifying and modulating it in the act of interpretation). To the degree that the latter conception is problematic, it is not because the subject is conceived of as active rather than as passively constituted or "interpellated by ideology," as Althusser puts it. It is only because we still tend to think and to behave according to an image of the subject as occupying a place *within* the individual.

This positioning of the subject in the individual is itself a cultural phenomenon of the Renaissance.[16] In the plastic arts the invention of focused perspective is both a symptom of this development and a means by which such an image of the subject is fixed in Western thought. Erwin Panofsky writes:

> The decisive innovation of *focused perspective* epitomizes a situation which focused perspective itself had helped to bring about and to perpetuate: a situation in which the work of art had become a segment of the universe as it is observed—or, at least, as it could be observed—by a particular person from a particular point of view at a particular moment.[17]

Stephen Orgel and Roy Strong have shown that in Renaissance theaters perspective staging was the instrument of more than one ideology centered in the individual. Devices for representing uniqueness of viewpoint could serve both absolutist and protodemocratic social models.[18]

In literature, the differentiation and secularization of the "voice" of the text helps to constitute the reader as a more individualized subject as well. Certainly the power of the written word continues to play an important role in the service of a dominant ideology, that is, as the vehicle of a sovereign and universal subject, a point of view, an order that is represented as continuous, fixed, and unchanging. But the antithetical function of writing also gathers momentum at this time as part of the individual's attempt to establish a personal identity free of ideological constraint. If, as I believe, such a conflict does exist in the individualized subject of the literary text from that time onward, it is not a resolvable conflict since neither absolute constraint nor absolute autonomy is finally possible. What is significant, however, and what writing—poetry preeminently, in the broadest sense of the term—embodies, is a dialectic between these communicative functions involving repetition (i.e., the reproduction of ideology), on the one hand, and innovation (i.e., the modeling through formal means of new modes of perception and practice), on the other. I realize that this is a highly abstract proposition. It is best to elaborate further at this point by returning to the example of Jonson, whose divergence from an earlier stylistic tradition illustrates the kind of dialectic described here.

From Sidney to Jonson: Classicism as Contestation

In "To Penshurst" two spatiotemporal modes converge: the one mythic, analogical, signaling the presence of a divine Being that is both transcendent and immanent; the other historical, analytic, perspectivist, governed by the central viewpoint of a unique, individual human observer. The mythic mode is the vehicle of a magical Nature of inexhaustible abundance and of an immutable temporal dimension in which classical and Christian allegorical motifs are blended with references to contemporary personages and events into a single, continuous surface. The essential quality attributed to Penshurst approximates to the state of grace; it is a quality that is decentered, shared by the land and its inhabitants regardless of rank, permeating the entire estate but also bounded by its perimeter. By contrast, the historical mode is the vehicle of a specific social and cultural referent. It conveys the sense of a definite, irreversible time, of actual persons, and of an actual place described in topographical detail. Moreover, it establishes a perspective on an entire nation and its history. While the represented center of this social and historical perspective is Penshurst (and the family that dwells there), its center at the level of representation itself is the eye and the "I" of the poet who is identified with the same precision as the topographical details of the estate.

We noted earlier that the poem recapitulates an opposition between myth and history that is already evident in the house itself. The building carried out by Henry Sidney in the 1570s and 1580s was deliberately anachronistic, alluding to a feudal nobility identified with the Gothic style of the older baronial hall. Sir Henry's buildings were constructed as the mythic representation of unbroken continuity with the past and of the eternal presence at Penshurst of the essential quality of *nobilitas*. At the same time, the self-consciousness with which Henry Sidney employed this anachronism—indicated in the heraldry of the screen in the Great Hall and by the careful identification of the newer buildings on entablatures containing his and his wife's initials or their respective family crests, together with dates of construction—marks a historical perspectivism centered in an individual point of view that is structurally equivalent to the position of the "I" in Jonson's poem.

But we have also seen that there is a fundamental difference between Jonson's neoclassical esthetic and the Gothic style to which the Sidneys adhered. Up to now I have explained this difference as the result of a historical shift in ideology, Jonson's esthetic being acceptable to the Sidneys in 1610 or thereabouts because they no longer had need of the legitimation provided by a metaphor connecting them to an earlier feudal nobility. There is, however, another aspect to this shift which may help us to understand *how* Jonson's text manages to distance itself from its immediate ideological function.

Again, the form of "To Penshurst" is antithetical to the form of the house. More significantly in the present context, the style of Jonson's poem is antithetical to the kind of poetry produced by the previous generation of Elizabethan poets, including Sir Philip Sidney himself. The difference is marked by Jonson's self-conscious assumption of the mantle of *classicist*.

To the extent that there is a classical component of English Renaissance literature prior to Ben Jonson,[19] it is evident at the level of the *signified*, but rarely is it a facet of the *signifier*. During the sixteenth century, English humanists may have been diligent in their employment of classical subject matter; but, save perhaps for experiments in quantitative prosody, they tended to be less interested in classical forms.[20] In nondramatic literature as in the visual arts, allegory—even when it entailed allusion to classical mythology—tended to override any sustained interest in the formal principles of classicism. English resistance to classicism was, in part, a consequence of Protestant and nationalist rejection of forms identified with Italian popery, and, in part, an aspect of the retrospective feudalism through which Tudor ideology rationalized the dynasty's claim to legitimacy. I have already mentioned some of the more overt, spectatorial forms of such legitimation: the persistence of the Gothic style in architecture; the building of "sham" castles, in which crenellation served a symbolic rather than a military function; the emphasis in painting on heroic portraits of the ruling elite and of their real or imagined ancestors; the vogue for heraldry; and, of course, the elaborate ritual of the Accession Day tilts.[21] We find the literary analogues of this tendency in pastoral romance like Sidney's *Arcadia* and in the deliberate archaism of Spenser.

The self-conscious medievalism of Tudor culture sought expression in forms and images that represented history as an unbroken tradition and a providential succession—with all the important connotations of rightful inheritance the latter term implied for sixteenth-century Englishmen. By contrast, for the classicist, who looked back beyond the actual or mythic feudal past to the "Golden Age" of antiquity, *succession* was a far less important component of the representational code than were the principles of *identity* and *uniformity*, principles shared by classicism with its claim to the timeless validity of ancient forms (and the ethical norms that these were held to embody) and by the new science in its search for universal laws of nature. Jonson's poetry is founded on these principles and, as such, constitutes a significant break with the sixteenth-century tradition of English humanism.

For an analysis of Jonson's relation to the previous generation of English poets, the poetry of Sir Philip Sidney provides an especially interesting basis of comparison since Sidney is a mediatory figure for Jonson in more than one respect: as a poet and literary theorist, and as the heroic and legendary member of an aristocratic family that Jonson counted among his patrons. Sidney's *Astrophil and Stella* already exhibits a significant modification of the lyric tradition in which it is written. As David Kalstone has pointed out, a number of the poems in this sonnet cycle reveal a disturbed awareness of the limitations of the Petrarchan mode as an embodiment of a mythos and an ethos upon which to model behavior in the Elizabethan court: "What had begun as an ideal of conduct had ended as an imperative of courtly affectation."[22] Yet, these reservations notwithstanding, the consciousness assumed by Sidney in the persona of Astrophil is a heroic and a mythopoeic consciousness. Any changes that are traceable in Astrophil's attitude, as the drama of his relationship to Stella unfolds, occur within this heroic frame. Early in the sequence, Astrophil identifies himself with the suffering of Prometheus[23] and associates his "sinfull" love with the noble theft of the celestial fire by this benefactor of mankind:

Alas have I not paine enough my friend,
Upon whose breast a fiercer Gripe doth tire
Then did on him who first stale downe the fire,
While *Love* on me doth all his quiver spend.
. . . .
If that be sinne which in fixt hearts doth breed
A loathing of all loose unchastitie,
Then Love is sinne, and let me sinfull be.
(Sonnet 14, lines 1–4, 12–14)

Even in the final poem, where hope has given way to "most rude dispaire," Astrophil is still identified with the element of fire:

When sorrow (using mine owne fier's might)
Melts downe his lead into my boyling brest,
Through that darke fornace to my hart opprest,
There shines a joy from thee my only light.
(Sonnet 108, lines 1–4)

The poems are also filled with images of knightly service and combat and, whatever their ambiguities in other respects, thus remain consistent with that aspect of the courtly lyric tradition that has been described as "a feudalisation of love."[24]

The most important mythological figure in any of the Renaissance sonnet sequences is, of course, that of Eros, Cupid, or Love. For Plato, writes Ernst Cassirer, "Eros belongs to a middle realm of being. He stands between the divine and the human, between the intelligible and sensible worlds, and he must relate and join them to each other."[25] The association of love and intellect, as developed in the writings of Ficino and other Neoplatonists of the Italian Renaissance, is a frequent theme of Elizabethan poetry. In Spenser's *Amoretti* and in the *Fowre Hymnes*, Love is a beautifully elaborated yet still conventional Neoplatonic figure for the union of reason and desire in the human soul. But in *Astrophil and Stella*, such a union is rendered problematic, especially in those poems where Astrophil struggles with the irony of Love's double connotation as "Desire" and "Vertue" (see, e.g., Sonnets 71, 72).

This ironic treatment of Love is a facet of what Richard C. McCoy describes as the "sexual politics" of Sidney's literary works, involving an unresolved dialectic between the desire for autonomy and the duty of submission.[26] It is also, I believe, a symptom of the anxiety that was widespread among the Elizabethan aristocracy concerning their ancestry.[27] For among the functions of the dynamic and liminal force of Eros in the Neoplatonic cosmos is that of relating the present to an exemplary past. Jerome Mazzaro is right in calling attention to this aspect of the doctrine of love within the English Petrarchan tradition; but he overlooks the irony in Sidney's handling of the theme. Mazzaro claims that the English sonneteers were possessed of a "mythic consciousness" which "like Ficinian 'consciousness' . . . required the mind to divide itself into two—past and present—and to confront itself with the vehicle of a patterned past as the metaphoric tenor for its present mood and then by more knowledge to overcome the separation."[28] His description is illuminating up to a point, but the last phrase is puzzling. For what or where is the "more knowledge" that will finally "overcome the separation?" Mazzaro understands the way in which the Petrarchan lyric embodies a dialectic betwen past and present, but he tends to overestimate the resolutive power of what he calls "mythic consciousness" in the Elizabethan age. It is unlikely that Sidney and his aristocratic audience could have hoped to overcome the separation between themselves and an idealized past. What they attempted to secure through the power of representation was a relation to the past based on notions of resemblance and continuity rather than on identity in any absolute sense. We have already noted one example of this strategy in the deliberate anachronisms of Henry Sidney's additions to the house at Penshurst. Similarly, in Philip Sidney's sonnet sequence the mythic identification with the past is attenuated by a deliberate perspective on literary and cultural history. Astrophil's conflict extends to the conventions and the language of courtship themselves. Nevertheless, the continuity of the principle of Eros in the ambiguous parallel between Petrarch/Laura and Astrophil/Stella remained a way of constituting and retaining a cultural and social connection with the past, and with at least a portion of the European nobility (the latter was a motive of special importance to Sidney and to the faction at court led by Robert Dudley who saw themselves as part of an international movement of Protestant chivalry).

The relation between past and present in Sidney's verse is a self-consciously metaphorical or symbolic one, and this self-consciousness is evidence that the poet feels the separation from the past as intensely as he does the connection with it. Kalstone writes: "The voice of Astrophel is almost the opposite of Petrarch's: recognizing conflicts where Petrarch enforces harmonies; tentative and critical where Petrarch is sure about the relation of beauty and philosophic meditation."[29] But although Sidney can criticize by pointing to the inadequacies of the Petrarchan mode, he can suggest no alternative because the ideological constraints of his social position preclude the assumption of a more personal or "original" voice than that afforded by the Petrarchan persona, however modified it may be. Petrarch's love for Laura thus continues to function typologically as a moment against which Astrophil compares his own feelings for Stella; and the figure of Eros continues to serve Sidney as a poetic and cognitive device for mediating relationships of conflict and contradiction not only in love but in all aspects of an Elizabethan courtier's life.

Recent commentators have analyzed with great acuity the relationship between the allegory of love in *Astrophil and Stella* and Sidney's frustrated personal ambitions at court.[30] No doubt the psychological conflict produced by these circumstances contributed to Sidney's straining against the Petrarchan conventions and, perhaps, against the authority and power represented by the person of the queen. Certainly the poetic medium through which Sidney articulated this conflict brought renewed vigor to the genre of the sonnet. But the particular decorum which he was so careful to observe in transforming social and political ambition into romantic desire is an indication of the extent to which his muse continued to obey an aristocratic and quasi-feudal ethos.

We tend to think of Sidney and of Spenser as representatives of a Renaissance tendency toward the refinement of poetic artifice, and of Jonson as reacting against this tradition by insisting on the placing of "matter" above eloquence. But it is important to realize that the priority Jonson appears to have given to content was part of a broader concern throughout his work with the nature of literary and linguistic forms. The changes he wrought in the literary conventions of the previous generation were no less radical than the more startling experiments of Donne. This may not be immediately evident from our perspective today because the message-transferring function of language which Jonson emphasized has long since become the dominant one in our culture. Therefore, the principles he advocated are likely to seem to us unpoetic, if not downright antipoetic. But in its own time Jonson's poetic theory and his practice as a poet were innovative. Moreover, the innovations involved had as much to do with poetic forms as with thematic content.[31]

Jonson's avowed aim of reorienting poetry in such a way that words would serve as the agencies of "matter" was carried out through a constant effort to define and to codify formal devices. Through his plays, poems, and masques the fixation on the theme of authority and on authority figures has its direct formal counterpart in his insistence on rules or codes in grammar, in orthography and punctuation, in art, and in public morality. Jonson's language and the literary genres in which he chooses to write imply the possibility, indeed the *inevitability*, if one uses language correctly, of an immediate access to knowledge of all kinds. His poem "Why I Write Not of Love," which opens *The Forrest*, can be read not only as a middle-aged man's pathetic farewell to Eros, but as a final rejection of the Petrarchan tradition and of the Neoplatonic doctrines linking all knowledge to an idealized and romantic conception of sexual desire. In Jonson's classical style metaphor is eschewed, matter takes precedence over eloquence, instruction over delight, and the poet lays claim to a more precise identification with antiquity on the grounds that it can be known and can become a pattern for the present directly, through study and imitation. In this view the role of metaphor is rationalized, placed in the service of instruction which is the function of the poet in the present as it was, according to Jonson, in the past. Metaphor is no longer the means of overcoming a separation between the "patterned past" and the present; it is now only one technical device among others whereby the poet-scholar can transmit his knowledge of a pattern that is taken to be natural and universal and, therefore, to be true for the present as well as the past.

Jonson's classicism was motivated in part by a calculated strategy of self-assertion. Quite early in his career we find him proclaiming himself the first true classicist among English poets, and this not only in his attacks on other playwrights during the so-called "war of the theaters," but in the poems as well. In an epistle addressed in 1600 to Elizabeth, countess of Rutland, he writes:

> Then all, that have but done my Muse least grace,
> Shall thronging come, and boast the happy place
> They hold in my strange poems, which, as yet,
> Had not their forme touch'd by an English wit.
> (*The Forrest*, XII, lines 79–82)

The self-conscious distinction Jonson grants his "strange poems" is made more striking by the fact that Elizabeth was the daughter of Sir Philip Sidney whose own poetic skill in the older mode is alluded to in the poem. Here, as elsewhere, Jonson pays homage to Sidney, homage that is perhaps sincere but also obligatory given the status of Sir Philip and the nature of Jonson's relation to the family. An epigram to the same countess of Rutland begins:

> That Poets are far rarer births than kings,
> Your noblest father prov'd: like whom, before,
> Or then, or since, about our Muses' springs,
> Came not that soule exhausted so their store.

Yet the poem ends on a curious turn. Elizabeth wrote poetry herself, and Jonson's praise of her father is complicated by the assertion that if he were alive and could look upon his daughter's poems

> He should those rare, and absolute numbers view
> As he would burne, or better farre his booke.
> (*Epigrammes*, LXXIX)

Later, in 1619, Jonson told Drummond that "the Countess of Rutland was nothing inferior to her father S. P. Sidney in Poesie"

(*Conversations*, lines 213–14). We don't know what those "rare, and absolute numbers" composed by the countess of Rutland were like. But the descriptive phrase is suggestive, and, assuming Jonson wasn't merely engaging in flattery, we may surmise that he was praising her verse for qualities that were closer than her father's to Jonson's own classical standards.

This is speculation. But it is sustained by what we know of Jonson's attitude toward the previous generation of English poets. He could, of course, be more open in his criticism of Spenser than of Sidney.[32] But the comparison of Sidney's poetry with that of his daughter was perhaps a delicate way in which Jonson could pass judgment on Sir Phillip and thereby uphold his own convictions regarding poetic form.

We may detect an anxiety of influence here. But insofar as Jonson's reading of Sidney was concerned, I suspect that the anxiety was brought on as much by the social aspects of the relationship as by the filiation of poet to poet. After all, Jonson was a poet-commoner serving aristocratic patrons like the Sidneys who had helped to establish the norms of Elizabethan court culture in the previous generation. Jonson's deviation from those norms was a way for him, in turn, to establish an independent poetic, psychological, and social identity. In comparing the countess of Rutland's "absolute numbers" to her father's poetry, Jonson expressed his own demand for a more rigorous adherence to classical models and asserted his own authority in matters of esthetic judgment.

Returning now to Penshurst we can see that both the house and the poem involve the convergence of mythic and historical modes, but in different ways. The house is mythic in that it asserts the possibility of a continuous style, the Gothic, which transcends dynastic changes over a three-hundred-year period and which symbolizes a comparable continuity of meaning in social experience. It is historical in that the representation of this continuity is carried out from a perspective that views the present as different from the past but also as linked to it by a logical development. Both the mythic and the historical are evident in the complex symbolic function of the sequence of arches from the King's Tower, through the Great Hall, to the garden (see Chapter 4 above).

The poem is historical in the precision with which it documents what it describes. Not only does it provide a map of the essential characteristics (material and spiritual) of the estate, but it also locates that description as the report of a particular observer (the poet) and suggests a particular occasion for the observation. Further validation is provided by a reference to a visit of the most important single observer in the realm, the king. This empirical and inductive procedure of enumerating instances in which observable data have been recorded is a poetic equivalent of the Baconian conception of "natural history." Jonson shares with Bacon, too, the principle that truth can be arrived at only through the study of both "negative" and "affirmative" instances: as in most of Jonson's writing, "truth" in "To Penshurst" is built on a system of binary oppositions where, as we saw earlier, the absence of certain qualities is used to validate the presence of others. It is upon this base of observed "data," coupled with the authority of classical allusion, that the abstract values of the estate and of the Sidney family are asserted.

At the same time, however, these values and the place where they are located are taken in the poem to be particular realizations of universal "laws" of human nature. Here Jonson's historical method reverses itself and constitutes a new myth, that of an essential and immutable "order of things." Again, we can relate Jonson's way of thinking to seventeenth-century science which involved, according to one study, "a view of Nature even more static and fixed than that of medieval Europe."[33] Jonson takes the particulars he has observed and enumerated and then dissolves them into a transcendent, uniform, and static unity. Historicist critics have often noted this reductive—and potentially repressive—tendency within classicism. Erich Auerbach associates it with the rise of absolute monarchy; he contends that neoclassical doctrines of nature threatened to undermine the humanist sense of historical perspective that had been developing in European culture since the time of Dante. Arthur O. Lovejoy, in a comparative study of classicism and deism, constructs an outline of Enlightenment ideology the first and last categories of which are "Uniformitarianism" and "a negative philosophy of history."[34]

But before we dismiss classicism as dogmatic or unhistorical we ought also to recognize that for the poet, as for the philosopher and the scientist of the early seventeenth century, the appeal to a universal and objective "order of things" was an assertion of the right to think and to speak with relative freedom. This was especially true of those who were not aristocratic "amateurs" but who wrote as professionals. For Jonson and his contemporaries, such an assertion could not yet have resulted from a fully formed, conscious egalitarianism. Nevertheless, within the ideological limits of the time it constituted a legitimation of the ontological status of the writer as an independent subject in spite of his subjection to others within the prevailing social order.[35] In this respect too, a correlation can be drawn among literary, philosophical, and scientific texts of the period. The poetry, satire, and criticism of Jonson, with its emphasis on individual judgment based on an understanding of "Nature" and acquired through careful study of the classics; the principles of discovery and invention through observation and experiment in the writings of Galileo; the method of Descartes, grounded metaphysically in the concept of the *ego cogito*—all share an implicit notion of quality which, carried to its logical conclusion, transcends immediate class, cultural, and national distinctions. In a still rigidly hierarchical social system, it was the appeal to rigor in method and to an authority in knowledge based on the norms of Nature and Reason that gave the writer a certain freedom and transcendence. While he remained dependent on the king and the nobility, and while he may have consciously adhered to the ideology of those he served (as did Jonson), the writer nonetheless, and often in spite of himself, became the means of calling that ideology into question.

In England as elsewhere in seventeenth-century Europe, the condition of this new kind of writer, the professional, was inherently one of tension and conflict. Sartre's description of the situation is instructive: "Free from material cares, the members of the governing elite are sufficiently detached to want to have a reflective knowledge of themselves. They want to retrieve themselves, and they charge the artist with presenting them with their image without realizing that he will then make them assume it. . . . Thus, the writer is a parasite of the governing 'elite.' But, functionally, he moves in opposition to the interests of those who keep him alive."[36] Neither the writer nor his patrons need have been conscious of this dialectic for it to have been at the center of their relationship. Yet it is difficult to imagine a professional writer, even at this early stage, being as blind as his patrons to the conflict that defined his condition. There is certainly evidence in Jonson's writing that he was aware of the nature of this conflict, that he recognized, perhaps with some anguish, the dilemma of having his function as a poet and, consequently, his freedom depend on the subjection of that function to the power of others.

My point here is that seen from within, that is, in terms of its avowed premises, classicism appears as Lovejoy described it, antihistoricist and uniformitarian. But viewed in the context of a more inclusive historical frame, these very characteristics of classicism at its inception become their own opposites. They are recognized as strategies for confronting and contesting an older, outmoded structure of behavior and belief, and for enunciating a new conception of the subject. It is ironic, though hardly paradoxical, that classicism's reliance on a uniform, static notion of Nature was an inherently historical gesture; it marked the introduction of a potential difference (if not of diversity in the more modern, liberal conception) into the prevailing sense of quality that depended on inherited titles and property and on revealed rather than rationally derived doctrines.

For Ben Jonson, the appeal of classicism was mediated by a complex network of social and psychological relationships. In the first place, the role of classicist enabled Jonson to distinguish himself from other common poets and playwrights, and to assume a superior attitude in the theater toward those of his own social class. Second, it is probably the case, as Auerbach suggests, that classicism served as an ideological support for absolutist political doctrines and practices. This would help to explain the favor Jonson enjoyed under James I. By identifying himself with the king (as we saw him doing in lines 74–76 of "To Penshurst"), Jonson may have sought to establish a position of relative autonomy with respect to those, other than the monarch himself, who were above him in rank. But "relative" is an essential qualification here, for as a playwright writing mainly for the private theaters and the court, and as a poet seeking patronage where he could find it, Jonson could not remain independent of the aristocratic elite.

There is, then, yet another facet to the appeal of the classical mode for Jonson, having to do with his relation to aristocratic patrons. And here, his response to the poetry of the previous generation, especially the courtly amateurs among whom Sidney was preeminent, takes on special significance. Classicism was a representational code grounded in an epistemology that was different from, if not antithetical to, the system of knowledge and belief on which the architecture at Penshurst and the poetry of Philip Sidney were based. The "strange poems" Jonson claimed to have first brought to English carried with them in their very formal constraints (that is, in the stress on "matter" over eloquence, on imitation, on judgment and decorum) the fundamental principle that truth was unchanging. The capacity to represent this truth was situated in the mind of the individual who trained himself to decipher the classical forms. Not only did this mean the ability to employ classical subject matter allegorically, which had already been essential in the poetry and art of the sixteenth century, but it required as well a precise understanding of the decorous use of poetic device and genre. For a poet in Jonson's situation to proclaim himself a classicist was to adopt a literary persona that allowed him to go beyond the existing hierarchical system for grounding social and psychological identity, to derive his truth and his being from a prior order, a natural order first codified in the texts of antiquity.

Jonson Agonistes

Moreover, although it may have been personally motivated, Jonson's strategy of claiming a measure of freedom from an existing system of authority and power by appealing to a prior one had potentially far-reaching effects. The defining characteristics of classicism as both style and epistemology were such that any implicit assertion of personal transcendence on Jonson's part became immediately extendable to those readers or members of the theater audience who shared his understanding and his judgment. Jonson acknowledged such an elite among his interlocutors, addressing them as "hearers," "readers," or "understanders," and distinguishing them from the mere "spectators" whom he described as coming to the theater "to see, and to be seen."[37] This was a different elitism from the *noblesse* or *gentillesse* of the later Middle Ages, concepts that grounded hereditary privilege and status on a Christian foundation of ethical duty and on chivalric rituals sanctioned by the Church.[38] Jonson's conception was not necessarily less Christian in its underlying assumptions, but it was more directly founded on reason than revelation. In this respect, his neoclassicism was, like the new philosophy, potentially if not intentionally egalitarian.[39]

The rules or laws governing classical form were understood as immutable and universal, as was the human capacity to discern them, that is, the capacity for reason. No one was deprived of such capacity by nature, but many were impeded in its exercise by the corruptive effects of one or more of the passions. Jonson's diagnosis of the moral ills of his age is in this respect closely allied to Bacon's notion of the "distempers of learning" that infect men's minds. "The human understanding," writes Bacon, "is no dry light, but receives an infusion from the will and affections; whence proceed sciences which may be called 'sciences as one would.' For what a man had rather were true he more readily believes. . . . Numberless, in short, are the ways, and sometimes imperceptible, in which the affections color and infect the understanding" (*Novum Organum*, I, xlix). A similar conception provides the basis of the psychology of "humors" according to which Jonson drew the characters in his satires. It is also given as the root of sinfulness in an epode focused on the roles of reason and passion in human nature:

> For either our affections doe rebell,
> Or else the sentinell
> (That should ring larum to the heart) doth sleepe,
> Or some great thought doth keepe
> Backe the intelligence, and falsely swears,
> They're base, and idle feares
> Wherof the loyall conscience so complaines.
> Thus, by these subtle traines,
> Doe severall passions still invade the minde,
> And strike our reason blinde.[40]

While this view is certainly Christian in essence, it is important to distinguish it from the traditional notion that humanity was depraved and all of earthly Nature in decay since the fall from paradise. Bitter and disdainful as Jonson could be in his satires, his understanding of human nature was on the whole more optimistic than the doctrine of the decay of Nature.[41] Implicit in Jonson's adoption of classical forms was the notion that the governance of reason is potentially available to *all* human beings. Thus while neoclassical principles of uniformity and universal law could be placed in the service of absolutist political doctrines, it is also the case that neoclassicism complemented the new science in anticipating the democratic aspects of Enlightenment ideology. We are not duty bound to celebrate this rationalist, progressivist ideology uncritically; but we do need to remind ourselves that the liberal, humanist ideals on the basis of which classicism is denounced as a conservative, uniformitarian world view are themselves ushered in by the classicist strain within Renaissance humanism.

Jonson is generally regarded as a traditionalist and a conservative. On the surface this is an adequate appraisal. In poems like "To Penshurst," and in his masques, he provided the aristocracy with idealized images of the organic society on which their privileged status was supposedly founded. Critics have often cautioned against thinking of such literature in terms of flattery; they point out that poets who wrote in praise of kings and lords did so out of a sense of moral conviction and social responsibility, and in the belief that they were providing their patrons with learned counsel. The principle is stated by Jonson in the form of a dignified ratio: "Learning needs rest: Soveraignty gives it. Soveraignty needs counsell: Learning affords it" (*Discoveries*, lines 65–66). But while we need to be alerted to the dangers of anachronism, we cannot pass so easily over the issue of flattery. It is no anachronism to say that even as the seventeenth-century poet claimed the poetic license to instruct, he was obliged to hold up a flattering mirror to his patron. Jonson goes to great lengths to disclaim the role of flatterer; but at times he protests too much, and one senses that he was oppressed by a keen awareness that what status he did possess depended on such a function. Where this anxiety comes through in his writing it reveals Jonson to be more realistic about the actual situation of the Jacobean poet than some modern commentators have tended to be. I am not suggesting that Jonson was a democrat in disguise, but I do believe that his conservative and legitimist pronouncements mask a deep sense of injustice concerning his own position in society.

Given the social context in which Jonson proclaimed himself a classicist, the forms he employed were not as conservative as they might otherwise seem. Nor were the ideas that the classical forms brought with them. In the epistle to *Volpone*, where Jonson addresses yet another audience, the intellectual elite of the universities, he makes explicit his concern not just with classical form but with doctrine:

> I have labour'd, for their instruction and amendment, to reduce *not onely the ancient formes*, but manners of the scene: the easinesse, the propriety, the innocence, and last, *the doctrine, which is the principall end of poesie, to informe men in the best reason of living* [my emphasis].

The ethical doctrine implied here is hardly subversive, but the norms of Reason and Nature on which it is founded are potentially so. At times, this critical potential surfaces from within the apparent conservatism of the "ancient forms." So, for example, in an epigram, "To Sir William Jephson," Jonson writes:

> Thou wert the first, mad'st merit know her strength,
> And those that lack'd it, to suspect at length,
> 'Twas not entayl'd on title. That some word
> Might be found out as good, and not *my Lord*.
> That *Nature* no such difference had imprest
> In men, but every bravest was the best:
> That blood, not mindes, but mindes did blood adorne:
> And to live great, was better, then great borne.
> (*Epigrammes*, CXVI, lines 5–12)

The idea of nobility based on "merit" rather than on "title" has classical origins in the Stoic philosophy. It also appears earlier in English literature, but rarely, if ever, with the force of personal conviction and the precision that Jonson gives it in his handling of the epigrammatic *point* in the poem to Jephson.[42] Moreover, while an aristocrat might conjoin intellectual merit with blood as necessary conditions of *nobilitas*, he would not conceive of them in the oppositional relationship that Jonson sets forth here.[43] Such criticism of the prevailing ideology is only obliquely evident in Jonson's poems addresed to the Sidneys. But, as we saw earlier, it is there as an undercurrent in "To Penshurst," surfacing briefly in the poet's self-representation as a guest at the estate, and providing a tension and complexity that make the poem far more than just a graceful encomium.

The breaking through of this critical attitude in both the form and content of Jonson's classicism, and the figuring in verse of alternative notions of nobility and virtue, are aspects of the "potentiality" I referred to at the beginning of this chapter. In considering the extraordinary outpouring of literature during the Tudor and Stuart periods, we need to be wary of generalizations concerning the differences between "aristocratic" and "bourgeois" modes of thought. Cultural change is a complex phenomenon, involving an interplay of endogenous and exogenous processes. Still, given what has been shown thus far, I think certain general propositions can be made. While Jonson remains politically conservative, his insistence on a rationalist basis to all discourse, poetry included, and to all social intercourse, points the way to new doctrines of sovereignty and of social organization in England. The humanist ideal of intellectual merit, which had been assimilated into an aristocratic, courtly culture under the Tudors,[44] is eventually pushed to its limits in Jonson. To paraphrase Sartre again, Jonson makes his patrons *assume* the image which he is obliged to reflect for them. Although he did not, or could not, abandon Renaissance notions of hierarchy, his texts do give forceful articulation to the idea of intellectual merit as the standard of an individual's worth.

We have seen, too, that within a mythicized and heroic setting of aristocratic domesticity at Penshurst, Jonson managed to give verbal form to other emergent middle-class values: the home, the conjugal family, the administrative responsibilities of persons of rank to the state as representative of the whole of society. In dramatizing such values Jonson's poems and plays contributed to the formation of new institutions that would, in turn, legitimate the new forms of social interaction. Viewed in this light, a poem like "To Penshurst," despite its traditional, aristocratic theme, can be said to liberate a potential for future social praxis along bourgeois egalitarian lines.

However, the potentiality that lifts Jonson's poetry above its immediate ideological function does not end here. Consciously or unconsciously, to have projected bourgeois values into an aristocratic setting would have been simply to oppose a dominant ideology with an emerging one. As we saw earlier, "To Penshurst" involves a representation of such conflict and an attempt to contain it, and illustrates the extent to which portions of the aristocracy were susceptible to an infusion of bourgeois ideas and practices. But what complicates Jonson's poetry even further is that while it contributes to this process of infusion, it is, at the same time, already engaged in revealing the limits of the new ideology before it has come to fruition.

We may take the connotations of the opposition between "merit" and "title" in the poem to Jephson, and resonances of the same distinction elsewhere in Jonson's works, as an example of what I mean. Advancement on the basis of "merit" is a doctrine that reflects the self-conscious individualism which we conventionally associate with the Renaissance. Individualism is, in turn, related to competition as a motive force in human affairs. In England, as the centers of culture shifted from the monastery and the university to the court and the city, competition for favor and patronage became an essential aspect of intellectual activity. Like flattery, competition was now a more or less inescapable fact of life for the poet. This is already evident in the culture of the court, where the doctrine of *sprezzatura*, the ingenious allegorical devices, the games, the tournaments, and the romantic conflict of Sidney's Petrarchan hero, all mask a fiercely competitive struggle among courtiers for the preferment of a powerful prince.[45]

But where the cultural form of this conflict at court is sublimated and refined in allegorical lyric and romance, competition among the new professional writers in the city is more openly individualistic. The infamous "war of the theaters" involving Jonson, Dekker, and Marston at the turn of the century is evidence to that effect. Circumstances may have been extreme that led Jonson to send out a prologue in armor at the beginning of *Poetaster* (1601), to proclaim

> . . . 'tis a dangerous age:
> Wherein who writes, had need present his scenes

> Fortie-fold proofe against the conjuring meanes
> Of base detractors, and illiterate apes. . .

But such defensiveness is only an exaggerated form of a more general attitude. Even where he bestows praise on fellow poets and playwrights, one senses that for Jonson the recognition of merit and the honor it brings is a result of comparison and competition; therefore, to praise another is an act filled with anxiety and ambivalence. As with the role of flattery in the poet's relation to his patron, we need to understand such competition among poets in its proper historical context. But I don't believe we can dismiss the anxiety that is apparent in the poetry as a distortion produced by our own historical perspective. Nor can Jonson's defensive posture be explained away as an intrapsychic disorder, an aspect of the "anal eroticism" that Edmund Wilson has described in a well-known essay.[46] Jonson's aggressively competitive relation to other poets may be a matter of personal temperament, but it is a temperamental response forged by historical and social conditions.

Here, again, comparison with Sidney is fruitful. As a poet, the competition in which Jonson found himself was fundamentally different from the courtly struggle for place and power that is sublimated in the romantic sexuality of *Astrophil and Stella*. Sidney could refer with characteristic nonchalance to the *Arcadia* as "my toyfull booke," and to the *Apology* as "this ink-wasting toy of mine"; and his Astrophil can say, in mock remorse, "My youth doth waste, my knowledge brings forth toyes."[47] There is, of course, a good deal of tongue-in-cheek irony to these remarks, Sidney being ultimately as serious in his conception of the office of the poet as Jonson. Still, his amused rhetorical self-irony is revealing of the extent to which poetry was a necessary, but hardly a sufficient, condition of Sidney's identity and of his station in life. To excel in the art of poetry was for him one of the many outward signs of an inner quality that ostensibly originated in birth and breeding. By contrast, for Jonson poetry was a singular means of achieving identity and status. In this regard Spenser, whose social origins are much closer to Jonson's than to Sidney's, provides something of a precedent. But it is not likely that Spenser, who began writing poetry at about the time Jonson was born, could have set out to make a career primarily as a poet. It took what Spenser had actually achieved by the 1590s, coupled with the legitimacy officially conferred on poetry by its most eminent champion, Philip Sidney, for Jonson not only to claim for the poet the status of an "arbiter of nature" (George Puttenham had claimed as much) but to attempt to live in accordance with that claim.[48]

Poetry's ascendancy as an honorable profession cannot be separated from the ideological value it had come to serve both in the theaters and in the occasional verses and masques written for the monarch and the court. The historical conditions that made it possible for Jonson to claim greater autonomy for poetry and to seek to define his own social identity as a poet entailed, too, a change in the status of the object of what he liked to refer to as his "studies." In addition to its other attributes, culture was now becoming a commodity. The poet's skill and his learning had begun to assume the form of intellectual property in a client system of exchange that was rapidly turning into a marketplace.[49] Patronage steadily increased throughout the reigns of Elizabeth and the first two Stuart kings. But the combined effects of economic inflation, wasteful expenditures of the court, and the sheer growth in number of those who sought the protection of a patron contributed to an intensification of competition among scholars, artists, and poets. In reading Jonson we can sense the strain generated by these circumstances. The intensity of competition for a share of the new but, as yet, limited literary market is suggested by the proprietary tone of Jonson's frequent and worried references to plagiarists and poet-apes. And, in a more deeply disturbing way, it is evident in the anxiety already mentioned as to how his own work measures up against the poetry of contemporaries whom he praises such as Donne, Francis and John Beaumont, Drayton, and, of course, Shakespeare. Jonson's persistent disavowal of his flattery of patrons and his envy of fellow poets suggests that the opposite was in fact the case, or, at least, that he suspected it might be the case and wished to persuade himself as well as his reader that it was not.[50]

Remarkably, Jonson shows a certain awareness of the extent to which in his time intellect and craft were coming to be thought of as private property, and the product of the intellect as a commodity. Despite his satires on acquisitiveness, he is not averse to employing the metaphor of accumulated wealth for the process that leads to accomplishment and honor. So much is evident in the following passage from "An Epistle to Sir Edward Sackville, Now Earl of Dorset" (ca. 1624), where coincidentally, and yet, as might be expected, the figure of Philip Sidney stands as the model:

> . . . he must feele and know, that will advance.
> Men have beene great, but never good by chance,
> Or on the sudden. It were strange that he
> Who was this morning such a one, should be
> *Sydney* e're night! . . .
>
> 'Tis by degrees that men arrive at glad
> Profit in aught; each day some little adde,
> In time 'twill be a heape; this is not true
> Alone in money, but in manners too.
> Yet we must more than move still, or goe on,
> We must accomplish: 'tis the last key-stone
> That makes the arch. . .
>
> (*Under-wood*, XIII, lines 123–37)

Since this passage is nearly a direct translation of classical sources, the money imagery borrowed from Plutarch and the keystone that makes the arch from Seneca, we must be careful not to confuse the type of "profit" it evokes with more modern senses of the term. There is little evidence here of a specifically bourgeois conception of capital accumulation and commodity exchange. If anything, the positive value attached to the term "heape" is more likely to be associated with a recrudescent feudalism than with the incipient capitalist ideology with its doctrine of *use*; in this context, the effect of "heape" is precisely the opposite of its negative effect in the phrase "proud, ambitious heaps" in "To Penshurst." The contrast is made all the more interesting by the fact that the name Sidney is associated with both of these antithetical contexts. But aside from this inconsistency, what is most striking about the passage from the epistle to Sackville is that the regular ("by degrees"—with a possible pun intended) storing up of "money" is an image there for the acquisition of "manners," i.e., virtuous qualities which bring, in turn, honor and the recognition of others.[51] The equation may be borrowed from classical sources, but it is especially significant that Jonson should elect to employ it in a poem that reflects as much upon his own self-image as on the benefactor to whom he offers praise and thanks.

Elsewhere, the economic imagery used to describe virtue and talent is indeed more clearly related to early capitalist institutions of finance and trade. The conclusion of a commendatory poem on William Browne's *Britannia's Pastorals* (1616) reads:

> And, where the most reade bookes, on Authors' fames,
> Or, like our Money-Brokers, take up names
> On credit, and are cossen'd; see, that thou
> By offring not more sureties, than enow,
> Hold thyne owne worth unbroke: which is so good
> Upon th' *Exchange of Letters*, as I would
> More of our writers would like thee, not swell
> With the *how much* they set forth, but th' *how well*.
> (*Ungathered Verse*, XXI, lines 9–16)

Despite the distinction between quality and quantity in the last line, and the pejorative reference to "Money-Brokers" followed by the contrastive pun in "Hold thyne owne worth unbroke," it is ultimately the phrase "Exchange of Letters" that sets the tone and establishes the metaphorical, not to mention the real, context of the entire piece.

The market metaphor in the poem to William Browne is derived from a relatively recent sense of the term *exchange*,[52] and is already an index of the commoditization of culture. Another poem, in praise of Chapman's translation of Hesiod's *Works and Days* (1618), carries the logic of such imagery a step further. After a series of metaphors describing Chapman's translations of Homer and Hesiod as the transporting of Greek treasure to English shores, the poem concludes:

> If all the vulgar Tongues, that speake this day
> Were askt of thy Discoveries; they must say,
> To the Greeke coast thine onely knew the way.
>
> Such Passage hast thou found, such Returnes made,

As, now, of all men, it is call'd thy Trade:
And who make thither else, rob, or invade.
(*Ungathered Verse*, XXIII, lines 7–12)

The central image here is not only that of voyage and discovery, but also that of capturing a particular market on the "Exchange of Letters." In his edition of Jonson's poems, George Parfitt glosses "Returnes" as "a mercantile image which refers to the profit on an investment in a voyage."[53] The idea of intellectual property and proprietary interest in the fruits of intellectual labor is clearly stated in the last two lines.

Such imagery exposes a painful contradiction that is generally characteristic of Jonson's work: that is, while merit based on intellectual accomplishment is the means through which the poet-commoner asserts his freedom, and while the accomplishment is held to be an external sign of the interior quality of the man, the recognition of such merit depends finally on the same system of rationalized commodity exchange that Jonson satirizes in its more obvious acquisitive forms. This correlation is obscured by the manner in which worth is delineated in Jonson's poems of praise. As in "To Penshurst," the usual mode of description is through negative and comparative constructions. When value is described affirmatively it is usually in a highly abstracted form; virtues like integrity, honesty, intellectual ability are imputed, but more often than not justification of the quality comes in the form of a comparison. Satirized figures therefore take on special importance in Jonson's works because they constitute images of the Other against which a socially sanctioned ethical and behavioral norm is maintained. This structure is more obvious, perhaps, in the plays than in the poems.

In *Volpone*, for example, Venice is represented as a place where the qualities that predominate among men are appetite, acquisitiveness, and self-interest, a place against which the upright trading commmunity of London can measure itself. William Empson imagines the reaction of contemporary Londoners to Jonson's Venetians: " 'Terrible pigs, that tyrannous Council of Ten; they never think of anything but money.' Jonson could rely upon getting this reaction even from the business men in his audience while most of the audience were enjoying the play as a satire upon business men."[54] In the poems, the figure of the poet-ape occupies a similar place as the Other of legitimate intellectual property and trade. Of course there are real differences between poet-apes and poets, just as there are differences in motive among patrons; yet Jonson has a difficult time making these distinctions concrete. All he can do is attach the verbal sign of the better quality to the name of the person or place being praised.

The qualities that most often distinguish good from bad in his poems are the cardinal humanist virtues of honesty and integrity. Ironically, it may be Jonson's own fidelity to the logic of this ethic that leads him to reveal a certain overlap in the criteria of value that govern the behavior of those who are the objects of both his satire and his praise. However, to treat such a revelation as the direct consequence of Jonson's own honesty and integrity would be to assume a deliberate and conscious choice made prior to the act of composition, an intention that cannot be documented. It is more likely that such ambiguities are revealed by the text as a consequence of the interplay of conflicting ethical and rhetorical decisions in the process of composition; that is, they are the result of a logic internal to the text's development—a development realized for us in the act of reading—and to the relationship that this temporality mediates between the authorial subject, the "I" of the text, and its implied reader.

Since for Jonson the good poet must, by definition, also be the good man, he could demonstrate his rightful title to the office and function of poet only by making his own work the concrete embodiment of the qualities of honesty and integrity. This he accomplished more through the structure and the rhetoric of his texts than at the level of statement, and this despite the fact that we tend to think of Jonson's poetry as a "poetry of statement." To the extent that Jonson's vaunted empiricism is observable in the poems of praise as well as in the satiric works, it is found primarily not in what is stated about those who are praised but in the imagery employed to make the statement and in the rhetorical stance adopted toward the addressee. The effect of the logic inherent in his rhetorical strategy is a dislocation of the tidy order of distinctions between virtue and vice that he otherwise appears to expound. In sum, the integrity of the body of the text on which

Jonson staked his identity as poet depended on the revelation of a loss of integrity in the system of values that the text was supposed to transmit.

Jonson's poems succeed both in exposing the arbitrary, if not irrational, basis of the traditional doctrines according to which a man of quality was identified, and, at the same time, in providing a disturbing glimpse of the consequences attendant upon the loss of such intrinsic and spontaneously recognized criteria of nobility and honor. In the "Epistle to Sir Edward Sackville" the metaphor comparing the acquisition of manners to the acquisition of money is attenuated by the lines

> Yet we must more than move still, or goe on,
> We must accomplish: 'tis the last key-stone
> That makes the arch . . .

Yet the question remains as to what distinguishes the stage of accomplishment from the process that leads up to it; what *is* the keystone that completes the arch? Presumably, it is an activity or use to which the acquired manners are put. Jonson harks back here to the traditional Aristotelian ethic adopted by Sidney: "For, as Aristotle saith, it is not *gnosis* but *praxis* must be the fruit."[55] But, whereas for Sidney's generation praxis was still determined by a code of honor, by the reign of James I the code had lost much of its power to compel belief. The thirty-nine years from the accession of James to the execution of Charles I constitute the exemplary instance of what Lawrence Stone refers to as "Tawney's Law," i.e., "that the greater the wealth and more even its distribution in a given society, the emptier become titles of personal distinction, but the more they multiply and are striven for."[56] Honor was now becoming something to be bought and sold. This had been true among the Tudors as well, but never to the same extent. The important distinction here is not an ethical, but a pragmatic one. It is not a question of the superior moral fiber of the Elizabethan nobility as compared with the men elevated by the Stuarts. Rather, it is a matter of an ideology's being unable to keep pace with changing socioeconomic conditions.

As we saw earlier, in the sixteenth century the claims of many noble families to title and to quality on the basis of primogeniture were highly questionable. Yet despite his anxiety in this regard, Philip Sidney apparently believed that the pedigree his father had purchased from the heralds was authentic. And, what is more important, he and his contemporaries behaved as though the outward signs of honor were indeed proofs of authenticity. Here again an abstract ideal can be seen to be validated through habitual behavior which is itself governed by tacit belief, by the "background expectancies" (see my Introduction) of the group that shares the ideal in question. By Ben Jonson's time, however, the inflation of honors had reached the stage at which belief in the correlation between "honor" and its outward signs was strained to the breaking point. In his satires, Jonson could represent the confusion of material and spiritual value as an aberration. Yet Volpone's assertion that money is "virtue fame / Honor, and all things else," only reflects what was rapidly becoming a new norm governing social praxis in England. In the 1650s Gervase Holles looked back on the recent history of his own family with poignant and self-conscious irony:

> For after the entrance of King James the sale of honours was become a trade at Court. . . . Nor indeed did that way of merchandise cease all the raigne of our last martered King, which was one cause (and not the least) of his misfortunes. I have heard the Earle of Clare [Sir John Holles] . . . often inveigh bitterly against it, and he would usually call it temporall simony. I remember I once tooke the liberty (hearing him so earnest upon that subject) to aske him why he would purchase himselfe seeing he condemned the King for selling. He answered "that he observed merit to be no medium to an honorary reward, that he saw divers persons who he thought deserved it as little as he (either in their persons or estates) by that meanes leap over his head, and therefore seeing the market open and finding his purse not unfurnished for it he was perswaded to ware [spend] his mony as other men had done."[57]

The phrase "temporall simony" is a residuum of the aristocratic belief in the inherent spirituality of the outward signs of gentility. Metaphors of mercantile exchange are employed with deliberate irony. And yet, finally, the earl of Clare's answer is a compromise of the most fundamental sort; fundamental not just because he has decided "to ware his mony as other men had done," but because of the way he justifies his decision, i.e., according to the new doctrines of rational self-interest, competition on an "open market," and contractual exchange.

This attitude eventually receives formal codification in Hobbes's famous assertions that "Desire of Power, of Riches, of Knowledge, and of Honor [may all] be reduced to the first, that is Desire of Power," and that "the *Value*, or Worth of a man, is as of all other things, his Price."[58] For Jonson and his contemporaries, the alternative to such a cynical reduction was to retain some notion of an inherent spiritual value manifesting itself in forms of praxis that would constitute authentic outward signs of merit. The problem remained, however, as to how to validate such outward signs in the face of the steady disintegration of the homogeneous tradition of revealed doctrine which had previously served to provide the necessary criteria of validation. Jonson's solution typifies one of the major strains of thought in the literature of his age, a blending of Christian humanism and Stoicism that is evident as well in Shakespeare's later plays. But, in contrast to Shakespeare, Jonson's insistence on rigorous imitation of his classical sources suggests a deep-felt need to find an authoritative basis for a revision of the Elizabethan courtiers' code of honor. Such a revision would entail a shift away from the feudal ethic which, however attenuated, is still central to Sir Philip Sidney's view of himself,[59] toward a conception of honor in which reason reigns unequivocally over desire, and heroic *virtù* is replaced by the concept of virtue as an inner plenitude and integrity of being.

This shift in emphasis within the secular culture corresponds to the tendency in seventeenth-century religious poetry and autobiography to situate the struggle against evil and the search for grace at the interior of the individual. One interesting linguistic trace of this change is the semantic development of the term *conscience* from a substantive denoting a condition, or a function, or a quality of being shared by the members of a community, to a more individualized, personified, and hypostatized sense of the term.[60] Jonson occasionally employs the older sense, as in his "Epitaph on Cecilia Bulstrode":

. . . She was earthes Eye:
The sole Religious house, and Votary,
With Rites not bound, but conscience . . .
(*Ungathered Verse*, IX, lines 9–11)

But the more recent idea of conscience as a property of the individual is more common, as is exemplified in the following:

Whil'st thou art certaine to thy words, once gone,
As is thy conscience, which is alwayes one . . .
(*Epigrammes*, LXXIV, lines 7–8)

So, justest Lord, may all your Judgements be
Lawes, and no change e're come to one decree:
So, may the King proclaime your Conscience is
Law, to his Law; and thinke your enemies his. . .
(*Under-wood*, XXXI, lines 1–4)

With the increasingly complex psychology of faith in Reformation and Counter-Reformation discourse, and with the objectification and internalization of conscience as a property of the individual, the external signs that were formerly presumed to justify status and privilege now become uncertain indicators of the inner qualities that constitute virtue. This is, indeed, a central dilemma of Jonson's time, quintessentially embodied in the figure of Hamlet, and never satisfactorily resolved in the secular literature. The unrealiability of outward appearance as evidence of an inner authenticity of being is reflected in the dissimulation that is a constant motif of both tragedy and comedy in the Jacobean theater. In play after play characters rely on dissembling, either as a necessary ironic device for arriving at truth or as a way of concealing truth in order to advance their own interests. Outside the theater, too, moralists denounce the practices of simulation and dissimulation in one breath, then, in the next, treat it as axiomatic that a capacity to dissemble is a necessary condition of survival even for the virtuous man.[61]

Alienation and Home

Jonson's response to this spiritual crisis was to draw from a classical ethic and from certain humanist commentators, Vives preeminently, the notion of an authenticity and integrity of being founded on reason and judgment. In seeking external, perceptible correlatives of this inner integrity, Jonson bravely insisted that the personality of the whole man was manifested in an order of rational discourse informed by wisdom and, above all, honesty.[62] This is the ideal against which deformities of language and personality are measured in Jonson's satires. But the standard is more a matter of contention than demonstration. In fact, the difficulty of maintaining such a standard with any consistency amidst the realities of power in the hierarchical society of the Renaissance is reflected in the tension of the following passage from the *Discoveries*:

> Wisedome without Honesty is meere craft, and coosinage. And therefore the reputation of Honesty must first be gotten; which cannot be, but by living well. A good life is a maine Argument.
>
> Next a good life, to beget love in the persons wee counsell, by dissembling our knowledge of ability in our selves, and avoyding all suspition of arrogance, ascribing all to their instruction, as an Ambassadour to his Master, or a Subject to his Soveraigne . . . (lines 89–97)

The passage is a translation of Vives, but it has overtones of Machiavelli.[63] While the second paragraph may express a reasonable, indeed a necessary, attitude, given the prevailing social conditions, it is, nonetheless, a compromise of the dictum pronounced in the immediately preceding paragraph.

There is, however, yet another correlative of the notion of inner personal integrity in Jonson's poetry, one that we have already considered in some detail. I am referring to the idea of "home" to which we must return once again, and which we may now view in a somewhat different light. In "To Penshurst" and in the poem with which it is coupled in *The Forrest*, "To Sir Robert Wroth," the idea emerges as the product of a reciprocity between the exterior, ordered Nature of an estate and the imputed interior qualities of its owner. As we saw earlier, this equation is an effect of the metonymic strategy typical of the country-house genre. The connotations of the verb *dwell* figure prominently in that strategy, at the end of "To Penshurst," and in the companion piece addressed to Wroth, husband of Robert Sidney's daughter Mary, depicting his country estate of Durrants, in Enfield:

> Thy peace is made; and, when man's state is well,
> 'Tis better, if he there can dwell.
> (*The Forrest*, III, lines 93–94)

Also, in the latter poem, the phrase "at home" provides literal reinforcement of the distinctions between *home* and *house* and between Nature and Culture which the reader of *The Forrest* has already seen developed in "To Penshurst":

> But canst, at home, in thy securer rest,
> Live, with un-bought provision blest;
> Freed from proud porches, or their gilded roofes,
> 'Mongst loughing heards, and solide hoofes.
> (lines 13–16)

But Jonson's two estate poems are not the only instances in which the idea of authentic being in the individual is correlated with the image of home. The phrase "at home" recurs as a leitmotif elsewhere, as in:

> Nor for my peace will I goe farre,
> As wandrers doe, that still doe roam,
> But make my strengths, such as they are,
> Here in my bosome, and at home.
> ("To the World," *The Forrest*, IV,
> lines 65–68)

and

> Stand forth my Object, then, you that have beene
> Ever at home: yet, have all Countries seene:
> And like a Compasse keeping one foot still
> Upon your Center, doe your Circle fill
> Of generall knowledge . . .
> ("An Epistle to Master John Selden,"
> *Under-wood*, XIV, lines 29–33)

In one place, the essential quality that designates true nobility is brought out by a particularly subtle antithesis:

> Hee's prudent, valiant, just, and temperate;
> In him all vertue is beheld in State:
> And he is built like some imperiall roome
> For that to dwell in, and be still at home.
> ("An Epigram to My Muse, the Lady Digby, on Her Husband . . . ," *Under-wood*, LXXVIII, lines 5–8)

Here the image of a palace (the term "palace" appears literally in the line that follows those quoted) is first evoked, then qualified by both "dwell" and "at home"; indeed, the adverbial "still" tends to do more than just qualify the image of the preceding line—it undercuts it. Sir Kenelm Digby's social status is acknowledged in the compliment that places him in an imperial palace; and yet that status is finally validated by a phrase that denotes a situation comprising relationships and behavior that are by no means exclusively aristocratic.

I call attention to this recurring image of the whole man as one who dwells "at home" in order to establish that it is a pattern of Jonson's thought. In the majority of the poems cited, the central idea is that of being at home with oneself, and the focus therefore tends to be more directly on the person than on his property. But the most complete objectification of what Jonson means by the term *home* is the overall image evoked by "To Penshurst." As we saw earlier, it is a problematic image. And the very fact that the poem is addressed to the place rather than to the person is indicative of the problem. The overt strategy is to establish the qualities of the person by enumerating the qualities of his property. But this displacement has the effect, too, of diverting consciousness away from the precise nature of the relationship between the poet and the patron he addresses. An important aspect of the poem is thus hidden by its rhetorical strategy, just as the function of manual labor and its expropriation by the lord are denied at the level of statement. Yet despite this poetic suppression of real conditions involving the alienation of labor at Penshurst (including the poet's own labor), there is a sense in which the image of a *home* as it is adumbrated in the poem is a potentially liberating one. By correlating personal integrity with this image—which carries with it all the connotations of domesticity and conjugality discussed in the previous chapters—Jonson identifies new criteria of authenticity and virtue which cut across the lines traditionally dividing aristocrats from the rest of society. In short, the image is the product of emergent forms of social praxis which will eventually replace a decaying social order that is no longer sanctioned by viable structures of belief and expression.

Seen in this light, the image of *home* conveyed by "To Penshurst" is more than just an anticipatory representation of a bourgeois notion of the family and of its domain as a fundamental unit of production and social organization. For the idealization of *home* as the center of life marks the beginning, too, of a self-conscious preoccupation with *alienation* in the modern world. According to the *OED*, in the seventeenth century where the term *alienation* denotes estrangement the sense is restricted to a withdrawal of affection and trust, as in Burton's "Alexander . . . saw now an alienation in his subjects hearts," or to an estrangement from the true God as in Milton's "His eye surveyed the dark Idolatries / Of alienated Judah . . . " But Jonson's satiric works provide us with an early and remarkably vivid dramatization of the phenomenon of alienation in the two major senses to which the term has been put in our time: Marx's concept of the alienation of labor in commodity exchange, and the idea in existential phenomenology of the self divided against itself or in search of itself. Both of these conceptions are prefigured in the images of social interaction and psychological or metaphysical introspection produced by Jonson and a number of his contemporaries.

When we place "To Penshurst" beside *Volpone* or *The Alchemist* we think immediately of the traditional antithesis between country and city. Yet we can also discern in this antithesis a new relation between phenomena we associate today with the terms *home* and *alienation*, a relation that is one of the central antinomies of modern (i.e., bourgeois) experience and thought. *Home* and *alienation* thus constitute a unity in Jonson's work, a dialectical unity in which each term mediates the possible meanings of the other. Certainly traditional values play an important part in

Jonson's concept of home—the often cited tradition of "hospitality" or "housekeeping," for example. But it is the general demise of these traditions toward the end of the sixteenth century that is reflected by the idealization of Penshurst. What is more, given the complex of social and psychological factors that contributed to Jonson's ambiguous acts of praise in "To Penshurst" and other poems, we can read his choice of domestic metaphors—home and dwelling—for social and individual integrity of being as a self-conscious index of the difficulty of being "at home" in the new world of seventeenth-century Europe.

In a sense that is less immediately apparent because of the historical context and the constraints of classical decorum, Jonson anticipates the fundamental questions we associate with poetry and philosophy after Romanticism, the questions with which Wordsworth opens *The Prelude*:

> What dwelling shall receive me? in what vale
> Shall be my harbour? underneath what grove
> Shall I take up my home?

Jonson, classicist and realist that he was, and writing long before the age of industrialization, could hardly anticipate Wordsworth's answer. Yet, at the risk of substituting another myth for historical perspective, I suggest that Jonson's work with all its internal tensions between love and fear, gratitude and grudging resentment, admiration and distrust, authority and insecurity, looks beyond Wordsworth to the anxieties of our own age. These tensions are all grounded in a developing awareness of the contradictory effects of the rationalization and commoditization of human relationships: on the one hand, the new freedom, on the other, the isolation of the individual. If anything, what is foreshadowed in Jonson is that self-conscious sense of ontological insecurity, that "lack" of being which post-Romantic poets, philosophers, and literary critics have often described as a feeling of homelessness. One thinks, for example, of the early Lukács, who begins his *Theory of the Novel* by quoting Novalis: "Philosophy is really homesickness, it is the urge to be at home everywhere"; of Heidegger who invokes Hölderlin's "man dwells poetically" (*dichterisch wohnet der Mensch*), deriving out of this assertion a ground of Being that is set in opposition to the description of logocentric man as the being who is "not-at-home" (*unheimlich*); and, in a more immediate literary context, of John Crowe Ransom who writes in one of his many tributes to Kant's esthetic:

> [N]ature when we look hard refuses to be specific and single; it is everywhere itself, a dense "manifold of sense," a tissue of events whose effects are massive and intricate, beyond the grasp of the understanding. It is Kant's monumental achievement to have discerned how it is that nature nevertheless sometimes appears beautiful. These are the times when, filled with our own freedom and purpose, we find that nature too seems free and purposive. . . . The human kingdom and the natural kingdom appear like free and harmonious powers, collaborating with each other in dignity and peace; and in the sequel the poetic imgination is able to set up memorials of art which bear witness to their concord. Or if we require a bourgeois figure: we do not have to keep on feeling that the natural world is our alien habitation, for now it is our home.[64]

Ransom's version is especially striking because his reading of his own image as a "bourgeois" figure reveals in a word the historical and ideological underpinning of the metaphysical and esthetic doctrine. It is a particular historically and culturally determined conception of the homeliness of nature memorialized in art.

I have tried to show that the conception of home involved here can be traced back at least as far as the seventeenth century in English literature, that in "To Penshurst" the idea of an essential ground of Being is situated in the image of property, family, and home. But unlike the recent variants, Jonson's image constitutes a more vigorous assertion of the possibility of overcoming an alienated condition and of being once more "at home" in the world. "To Penshurst" is not primarily a reflection of an internal sense of loss, though there are nostalgic elements in its composition. Nor is it primarily a reflexive image of the capacity of art to restore the homeliness of nature to homeless man, though it does include self-conscious indicators of the poet's power to produce what he purportedly describes. In Ransom's conception, poetry *reconsti-*

tutes a primordial unity of Being by a lyrical or dramatic suspension of the gap between consciousness and its object, a unity that is otherwise elusive in the reified modern world of industrial capitalism and rationalistic technology. On the other hand, "To Penshurst" is an attempt to *constitute* such a unity through the power of the poetic process, a power which, for Jonson, includes the negative function of criticism (the houses with which Penshurst is compared) and the positive one of providing the reader with a model of social praxis in concord with nature. Jonson displays little embarrassment at the utopian aspects of his project, and in this respect he may seem naive by our standards. But it is no less naive to imagine that poetry can remain aloof from an engagement in the fallen world of everyday existence, withdrawn from it or regarding it with cool, contemplative disinterest.

In contrast to the notion that art is the memorial of an original concord between man and Nature, Jonson's poem embodies a more potent and, to my mind, a more satisfactory esthetic. It illustrates an important aspect of Sir Philip Sidney's poetic doctrine in the *Apology*; that is, the unwavering insistence that art is a purposiveness with a distinctly social purpose. But Jonson also manages to differentiate his own esthetic from that of Sidney and the Elizabethan aristocracy, finding in classical forms a rhetorical means for asserting his own freedom. His poem follows upon Henry Sidney's architectural design at Penshurst as a successive stage in the representation of an endogenous process of adjustment and adaptation to social change. In this respect the poem attempts to accommodate a bourgeois image of home and family within an aristocratic ideology. It tries to resolve the contradiction between traditional doctrines according to which house and family are indicative of a superior status in society, and an emerging notion of home and family as a natural, universal condition of sociality. This accommodation is made problematic, however, largely because of the unconcealed tension between the respective social positions of the speaker and those whose house he addresses. The alienation that is repressed elsewhere in the poem resurfaces here; and this, more than anything else perhaps, is what provides the modern reader of "To Penshurst" with a sense of the poem's accuracy and its integrity.

I argued at the beginning of this book that such tensions have been ignored by critics who take the idealization of the place at face value. But we must be careful not to go to the opposite extreme of reducing poems of this kind and the houses they describe to mere ideological reflexes. It is the *proprietary* aspect of the image Jonson produces of home, family, and self that requires criticism. But the ideal of a place in which dwelling is relationship with others, without denial or deprivation of one's own being, and of such a place as a model for humane relationships on a larger social scale, is not easily abandoned. The hope of realizing such an ideal is part of the tension of Jonson's poem, a tension produced out of the conflict inherent for him in the act of writing.

For Jonson, to write was both an acknowledgment of dependency and servitude, and an assertion of freedom. The critical power and the potentiality actualized in the rhetorical strategy of his verse cannot be contained by the conscious directive of performing a conservative social function. In this respect, Jonson's poems of praise and his satires are of a piece.[65] Contrary to what Keats describes as the quality determining literary achievement, the famous "negative capability," it is precisely Jonson's irritable reaching after fact and reason that makes him interesting and that gives his poetry its strength. Which amounts to saying that for Jonson to dwell poetically was to dwell in contradictions, but also to delineate those contradictions rather than to overcome them by means of a more romantic art. In this combined role of critic and poet Jonson managed, uneasily, to be at home.

APPENDICES

NOTES

INDEX

APPENDIX A

A Note on *Deixis* in Descriptions of Penshurst

A prominent linguistic device in any kind of topographical literature is *deixis*.[1] The term, derived from a Greek word for "showing" or "indicating," is used to cover the various orientational features of language that help to provide spatiotemporal coordinates of the situation of utterance. These verbal "shifters"—as they are also sometimes called—include personal pronouns (*I, thou, you, he, she, we, they*), demonstrative pronouns (*this, that; these, those*), and adverbials of place and time (*here, there; now, then*). The person, place, thing, or event to which such a term points is understood by those involved in the act of communication either because the referent has been established earlier in the same utterance, or because it is presupposed within the community of discourse to which the speaker and hearer belong. Under the latter circumstances, at times, the deictic sign can be meaningful "even if the presupposed event or thing does not exist and never has existed."[2] We may readily observe this linguistic function at work in a descriptive poem like "To Penshurst," where a primary concern of the poet is to orient the reader in space and in time (that is, with respect to the representation of place and of history which I have analyzed in the preceding pages).

A brief comparison of Jonson's poem with the language employed in guidebooks and brochures describing Penshurst to the modern-day visitor reveals a similar prominence of deixis but also a pronounced difference in the effect such devices may have on the reader. In "To Penshurst" the orientation provided by deictic signs is often destabilized by other elements of the semantic context in which these signs appear. For example, from the very outset, the "thou" addressed by the poet is known primarily by what it is *not*; it is an absence denominated by the presence ("these" in line 6) of other, antithetical houses. The shift to the first-person pronoun (line 65) occurs at the beginning of a particularly ambiguous passage involving the poet's desire (see Chap. 3 above); and the sense of a lack throughout this passage tends to undermine the immediacy and actuality evoked by the adverbial "here" at lines 67 and 74. Finally, the "Now" at line 99, which is in apposition to the implied "then" of the previous narrative elements, is less stable than the confident tone of the conclusion would suggest because of all the ambiguities that have preceded it in the sequence. In short, while deictic features operate in the usual way here, they are also dislocated by contextual dissonances. The reader who recognizes these dissonances is likely to be disoriented, and will have to work harder to produce an interpretation of the poem. The effect, I would claim, is a heightening of poetic tension and, perhaps, a disrupting of the poem's primary ideological function.

By contrast, consider the rhetoric of a visitor's guide entitled "Penshurst Place: 600 Years of History."[3] A glance at the text reveals a sequence of sentences employing deixis: "It is *this* quality . . . which first impresses the visitor who passes into the Courtyard. . . . *Here*, a house within a house, is the country home of Sir John de Pulteney. . . . *There* is the dais, where the lord and his family dined and *there* along either wall the trestle tables for his household. . . . *Here* the eye travels down from the vaulted roof to the armour set round the room. . . . *Here* furniture and pictures of later times lend an air of greater ease. . . . *Here* is the proud and impressive face of Queen Elizabeth, the noble thoughtful countenance of Philip Sidney and the bold self-confident expression of his uncle Leicester." These deictic terms have the effect not only of orienting the visitor spatially toward the objects of the house, but of giving immediacy to the narrative that unfolds as we pass from room to room, suggesting that indeed we are made witness here to "six hundred years of history."

The visitor who is led passively by the text through the house acknowledges and confirms the deictic signs thereby enacting what appears to be an objective validation of an implied statement: "*This* is history!" In so doing, such a visitor performs a brief ritual that helps to reinforce his or her sense of belonging to a community with a shared past. Certainly, a legitimate social function is served thereby, but this does not constitute an understanding of history. No doubt we all experience something of this sense of community in visiting a house that has become a historic monument. That is an essential part of the pleasure of such a visit. But there is also a pleasure in understanding, which comes from our abilities to construct itineraries and interpretations of our own by means of a reflective activity that combines imagination with a critical knowledge of the place and its history.

In the case of the guidebook rhetoric, deixis tends to reinforce ideology in a one-dimensional way that depends on the reader's passive acquiescence and programmed enactment of an already-present meaning. On the other hand, in "To Penshurst" it is, paradoxically, the failure of orientational features—in a text that depends on such features for its apparent descriptive power—that helps to make the poem an illuminating experience for the reader.

APPENDIX B

A Note on the Advertisements Reproduced in Figures 1 and 2

In the course of working on this study I have found myself becoming interested in advertisements and in books and magazines that seem to recapitulate some of the same domestic themes and images that I had set out to examine in the Penshurst house and poem. I have been struck particularly by the extent to which contemporary advertising relies on a notion of tradition encapsulated in the image of a castle, or palace, or manor house that is still understood as a home. This is certainly true of the sale of housing in the United States, as a glance at the real estate section of a Sunday newspaper will confirm. In Southern California, where I live and work, developers promote tract houses and condominium apartments with names that include the terms "manor" and "estates" or that bear such suffixes as "-hurst," "-moor," and "-worth." And always, the advertised property is referred to as a "home," never a mere house.

Another kind of advertising that employs such imagery is addressed primarily to women and appears in the pages of magazines devoted to homemaking, interior decoration, and gardening. These periodicals also print articles on domestic architecture. In England, a related phenomenon is the tradition of publishing essays in "women's" magazines on the stately homes of the nobility and landed gentry. The reader may have already noticed, in the epigraph to Chapter 2 above, that much of the material in Randolph Churchill's *Fifteen Famous English Homes* first appeared in a magazine entitled *Woman's Illustrated*, which was at that time edited by a man. Implicit in the acknowledgment of Churchill's preface is a social and sexual division of labor between the roles of making a living and making a home.

Generally speaking, advertisements in the American magazines addressed to homemakers employ imagery—verbal and visual—that associates elegance, good taste, graciousness, and even grace itself, with aristocratic status. And, as in other respects analyzed in the preceding pages, here too readers are presented with a paradoxically static view of history. Many of the advertisements contain terms like "classic" or "timeless"; "history" is easily "recreated" for contemporary living; economy, efficiency, practicality, even disposability, are wondrously integrated with grace and permanence.

At the same time, such advertising consistently makes use of images that are associated with doctrines concerning the nature and proper ordering of a home. Often, a central visual element is the image of a hearth, in which case the advertisement will carry resonances, whether or not intended, of the same ancient domestic religion alluded to by Jonson in his reference to the "Penates" of Penshurst (line 79). The Penates were Roman household divinities, guardians of the storeroom, and associated, therefore, with abundance. Their altar was the hearth of the house. The most important of the hearths referred to in "To Penshurst" is the one at the center of the Great Hall (Fig. 18). This is probably also "the harth . . . crown'd with smiling fire" which provides the symbolic setting for Jonson's "Ode to Sir William Sidney, on His Birth-Day" (*The Forrest*, XIV, line 1), composed in 1611 for the festive, ceremonial occasion of the twenty-first birthday of Robert Sidney's eldest son.

The domestic and religious symbolism of the hearth is evident in each of the advertisements reproduced in Figures 1 and 2 above. In saying this I am not drawing an equivalence between these advertisements and the artifacts that are the main subjects of this book. I mean only that the complex structure of belief and expectation that enables such advertising to work is a repetition and development of the sixteenth- and seventeenth-century ideology that I have analyzed. Contrary to popular belief, history does not repeat itself; but ideology does. In the first of these advertisements, the sacramental fire of the "castle" hearth is displaced outdoors and transformed into the "suburban" barbecue. The second advertisement is more complex and more interesting for us as a latter-day version of the ideology of "To Penshurst." Its verbal component plays upon social distinctions in a way that both maintains a hierarchy and yet neutralizes any sense of opposition between classes. It is composed of two illustrations, involving two moments in time and space that are implicitly related by the photographic overlap. The important element here is, of course, the vinyl floor tile: it provides "patrician beauty" at a "plebeian price"; and, as the model's smile and the time-lapse photography of the lower illustration suggest, it is easy to install (the lady of the house can do the job herself with no difficulty whatsoever—in other words, like the walls at Penshurst, the job is accomplished with no one's labor and no one's groan). But it is the upper illustration that dominates the page. It displays the floor. And its imagery carries the principal message, to the effect that such flooring is suitable for the consecrated domestic setting of a home: The hearth is ablaze. Beside it stands an empty chair which, by the representational conventions invoked in this tableau, must be the chair of the paterfamilias. His physical absence suggests a certain ineffability and, perhaps, a power that is institutional rather than personal. This power, represented by the empty chair beside the fire, does not quite displace the floor from the center of the picture; but it is what validates the floor symbolically. To the right, in an adjacent room stands a massive, baronial piece of furniture, atop of which is a sculpture of a lance-bearing knight on horseback. The figure does not appear to be an occidental knight. Still, it furnishes a visual equivalent of the copywriter's phrase "noblesse oblige." In addition to this piece of sculpture there are other signs of cultivation and refinement, including the books that fill the shelves to the left of the fireplace.

But the most striking visual element in this advertisement has yet to be mentioned. It is a painting; not, as one might expect, the portrait of a family member, but a huge representation of a melon from which a piece has been cut. The connotations of this image, both in its shape and in its placement like a trophy above the mantle, are not difficult to surmise. They are connotations of female sexuality and fertility in a tradition of symbolism that we have already seen in Martial and in Jonson's "ripe daughters . . . whose baskets beare / An embleme of themselves, in plum, or peare." Moreover, in the original color advertisement the most intense hue is green, the brightest green areas being the melon, the brick framing the hearth, and the blouse of the woman in the lower illustration. Because of this color scheme, the viewer's eye is likely to be drawn first to the image of the melon, then to the hearth, past the empty chair which is set off by the light beneath and to the right of it, across the floor to the female figure who is kneeling and working below; or the eye may scan the advertisement in reverse, from the kneeling woman to the painting. In either case, the order in which the viewer is led to perceive the objects in the tableau reinforces a sense of order in the home. Thus, in addition to the copywriter's wordplay ("to the manor born") on the theme of social stratification, there is, in the visual portion of this advertisement, an allegory at work concerning domesticity, the ownership of property, and the proper hierarchy of positions and roles in the management of a home.

NOTES

Unless otherwise indicated, citations from Jonson's works refer to *Ben Jonson*, ed. C. H. Herford, Percy Simpson, and Evelyn Simpson, 11 vols. (Oxford: Clarendon Press, 1925–52), hereafter cited as *H & S*. I have modernized spelling and punctuation in places.

Chapter 1. Introduction: Transformations of House and Home

1 On the notion of "semantic field" in the semiotics of culture, see Umberto Eco, *A Theory of Semiotics* (Bloomington: Indiana University Press, 1976), pp. 75–81. Eco's conception of semantics is inclusive of rhetorical and pragmatic aspects of communication. He criticizes Jerrold J. Katz, *Semantic Theory* (New York: Harper and Row, 1972), for maintaining a division between a "theory of grammar" and a "theory of rhetorical forms." Eco insists "that it is impossible to consider the rhetorical component independent of the semantic one; they are rather to be viewed as two sides of the same semiotic problem" (p. 311). Given the present state of knowledge in the study of communication and cognition, it may be premature of Eco to claim that he has produced an integrated theory of the kind he advocates. Nevertheless, I find heartening his insistence on the unity of grammar and rhetoric; although his viewpoint may not be shared by most linguists, it is likely to appeal to those trained in the study of literature and the arts and, perhaps, to cultural anthropologists as well. On the other hand, I find less attractive Eco's desire to subsume "pragmatics" under "semantics" (see p. 4); for a different view of the pragmatic basis to a semiotics of culture see Milton Singer, "For a Semiotic Anthropology," in *Sight, Sound and Sense*, ed. Thomas A. Sebeok (Bloomington: Indiana University Press, 1977), pp. 202–231.

2 Claude Lévi-Strauss, "The Structural Study of Myth," *Structural Anthropology* (Garden City, N.Y.: Anchor Books, 1967), p. 226.

3 During the past decade, the issue of what constitutes the nature of a "work" or "text" has been complicated immeasurably in the writing of the French post-structuralists and, on the domestic literary scene, in the work of Stanley Fish. I am well aware that a number of the notions I employ here—such as "representation," "function," "purpose," and "context"—are placed in question by Jacques Derrida's critique of the metaphysics of

presence in Western thought. The scope of this book will not allow for a theoretical defense of my willful persistence in this condition of metaphysical blindness. Suffice it to say here that in the absence of an alternative to a language which may embody in its very syntax and lexicon many of the assumptions we seek to interrogate—a dilemma acknowledged by Derrida himself—those of us who engage in cultural criticism must grope toward understanding in our respective ways, using the only language we have at our disposal. There is, however, a difference between Derrida's contestation of the metaphysical postulates implicit in the discourses of philosophy and criticism, and the accommodation of deconstruction to a traditional American insistence on textual autonomy inherited from the New Criticism; on this problem, see Don E. Wayne, "*Gnosis* without *Praxis*: On the Dissemination of European Criticism and Theory in the United States," *Helios*, N.S. 7, No. 2 (1979–80), 1–26.

Fish's objections to notions of the text that take meaning to be immanent are quite different from the problems raised by Derrida and his followers. Fish acknowledges a dynamic institutional and social context in which texts are *produced* by an interpretive community (though he does not attempt to contextualize further—in a manner that would be consistent with his own argument—by considering the wider social and historical ground of such literary production). In *Is There a Text in This Class? The Authority of Interpretive Communities* (Cambridge, Mass.: Harvard University Press, 1980), Fish responds to Meyer Abrams's criticism of his approach with the assertion that communication always occurs "*from within* a set of interests and concerns" (pp. 303–304). Following up on his earlier critique of the doctrine of the "affective fallacy," Fish implies here a rejection of the esthetic tradition of "disinterestedness" which, in either its Kantian or Arnoldian version, informs much of twentieth-century literary criticism. The recognition that interpretation is always a function of "interests and concerns" makes it difficult to ignore institutional, social, and historical constraints on what we may imagine to be "in" the text. As the subtitle of Fish's book suggests, not only the possible meanings of a text but its very status as an object is determined by "the authority of interpretive communities."

4 The traditional view of art in terms of harmony and order is challenged in a number of twentieth-century esthetic theories. Some of these are identified below in the notes to Chapter 6.

5 See Fredric Jameson, *The Political Unconscious* (Ithaca: Cornell University Press, 1981), chap. 6.

6 See the discussions of More's *Utopia* in Harry Berger, Jr., "The Renaissance Imagination: Second World and Green World," *Centennial Review*,

9, No. 1 (Winter 1965), 36–78; Louis Marin, *Utopiques: jeux d'espaces* (Paris: Éd. de Minuit, 1973); and Stephen Greenblatt, *Renaissance Self-Fashioning: From More to Shakespeare* (Chicago: University of Chicago Press, 1980), chap. 1. For a recent reapppraisal of Sidney's text, see Margaret W. Ferguson, "Sidney's *A Defence of Poetry*: A Retrial," *Boundary 2*, 7, No. 2, (Winter 1979), 61–95.

7 The major overviews of the literary genre include G. R. Hibbard's well-known article "The Country House Poem of the Seventeenth Century," *Journal of the Warburg and Courtauld Institutes*, 19 (1956), 159–174; Charles Molesworth, "Property and Virtue: The Genre of the Country-House Poem in the Seventeenth Century," *Genre*, 1, No. 2 (April 1968), 141–157; and William A. McClung's recent study of the genre and its architectural contexts, *The Country House in English Renaissance Poetry* (Berkeley: University of California Press, 1977). Raymond Williams, *The Country and the City* (New York: Oxford University Press, 1973), contains important and fresh comments on a few of these poems; Isabel Rivers, *The Poetry of Conservatism, 1600–1745* (Cambridge: Rivers Press, 1973), includes some illuminating remarks on the genre; James Turner's *The Politics of Landscape* (Oxford: Basil Blackwell, 1979), a study of *topographia* or rural poetry from 1630 to 1660, provides interesting commentary on some of the country-house poems. In the area of architectural history, I am indebted to Sir John Summerson, *Architecture in Britain 1530–1830*, 5th ed. (Harmondsworth: Penguin Books, 1969), and to the works by Marcus Binney, Mark Girouard, Gérard Labrot, Eric Mercer, and Sir Nikolaus Pevsner cited below.

8 Erwin Panofsky, *Gothic Architecture and Scholasticism* (1951; rpt. Meridian Books: Cleveland, 1957). On the sociological implications of Panofsky's study, see Pierre Bourdieu's postface to the French translation, *Architecture gothique et pensée scolastique* (Paris: Éd. de Minuit, 1970), pp. 135–167.

9 According to Lawrence Stone, in a lecture entitled "The Sociology of the English Country House" (Pomona College, 8 September 1978), the country house flourished as a peculiarly English institution for nearly four hundred years from approximately 1520 to 1914. Its decline was rapid during the period between the two world wars, and it was virtually moribund by 1939. Stone attributes the demise of the country house as an important institution to the changing structure of English society in the twentieth century and, especially, to the loss of cheap labor which was essential to the upkeep of such large households.

10 Harold Garfinkel, "Studies of the Routine Grounds of Everyday Activities," *Social Problems*, 11 (1964), 226, 229; cf. Aaron V. Cicourel, *The*

Social Organization of Juvenile Justice (London: Heinemann, 1976), chap. 1 and passim; on "naturalization" in literature, see Jonathan Culler, *Structuralist Poetics* (Ithaca: Cornell University Press, 1975), chap. 7.

11 Until recently, theoretical issues concerning ideology were largely omitted from the discourse of Anglo-American literary criticism. I have discussed this situation in the essay cited previously (note 3). Among social theorists the concept of ideology has been the subject of extensive discussion and debate. Yet no single definition of ideology has emerged as adequate to the varied and complex phenomena alluded to in the different usages of those who employ the term. Fredric Jameson, "The Symbolic Inference; or, Kenneth Burke and Ideological Analysis," *Critical Inquiry*, 4, No. 3 (Spring 1978), 510–511, suggests that the value of the term *ideology* in current critical debate lies precisely in its capacity to exacerbate the unsolved problem of which it is the sign, and thereby to "reproblematize" our habits of thought concerning the relationship between culture and society. Certainly the readmission of this once-taboo term into the lexicon of literary criticism has been long overdue.

12 Paul Frankl, *Principles of Architectural History: The Four Phases of Architectural Style, 1420–1900*, trans. and ed. James F. O'Gorman (1914; trans. Cambridge, Mass.: M.I.T. Press, 1968), p. 1. See also chap. 4, entitled "Purposive Intention."

13 Ibid., pp. 159–160.

14 Perhaps the emphasis is understandable given the fact that in this particular study Frankl is concerned mainly with architecture since the Renaissance, consequently with buildings conceived and erected from the perspective of a single design and designer. The idea that a building should be the expression of a uniform conceptual scheme, the embodiment of an individual's "purposive intention" fully determined and consciously set forth in the building's design, is epitomized in the classical style. The pervasiveness of this notion in the seventeenth century is strikingly evident in the architectural metaphor employed by Descartes to justify his philosophical method: "One of the first of the considerations that occurred to me was that there is very often less perfection in works composed of several portions, and carried out by the hands of various masters, than in those on which one individual alone has worked. Thus we see that buildings planned and carried out by one architect alone are usually more beautiful and better proportioned than those which many have tried to put in order and improve, making use of old walls which were built with other ends in view"; from the *Discourse on Method* (1637), in *The Philosophical Works of Descartes*, ed. E. S. Haldane and G. R. T. Ross (Cambridge: Cambridge University Press, 1967), I, 87.

15 See Mark Girouard, *Robert Smythson and the Architecture of the*

Elizabethan Era (London: Country Life, 1966), pp. 169–172.

16 For examples of the latter, see the texts by Randolph Churchill and Lord David Cecil cited as epigraphs to chapters that follow. A rather different twentieth-century view of life in the stately homes of the aristocracy is sketched by Virginia Woolf in her essay "Lady Dorothy Nevill," *The Common Reader* (New York: Harcourt, Brace, 1925), pp. 274–280.

17 Mark Girouard, *Life in the English Country House: A Social and Architectural History* (New Haven: Yale University Press, 1978), describes the birth of *Country Life* in the late 1890s. The magazine, devoted primarily to articles on country houses, "was extensively bought . . . by romantic businessmen, in Britain, America and the dominions. They read it with yearning and resolved that when they had made their pile they, too, would acquire a country house" (p. 303).

18 "Penshurst Place: 600 Years of History," British Library X700/15513. This is an earlier visitor's guide to the estate; the text is undated but it bears an aerial photograph of the house taken in 1950. For further analysis of the language of such guides, see Appendix A.

19 To employ such a distinction does not mean reverting to the sort of dichotomy put forth by Lévy-Bruhl between "pre-logical" and "logical" mentalities. It does mean acknowledging that historical thinking is the product of a particular social and existential situation, one involving intensified economic, technological, and cultural change, a situation that has characterized Western societies since the Renaissance. Certainly there are problematic aspects to the Enlightenment conception of history as "progress." Yet it is possible to recognize these difficulties and still maintain an analytic distinction between mythic and historical representations of the past; such recognition is itself the manifestation of a critical, self-conscious historiography. An eloquent treatment of these questions is Max Horkheimer and Theodor W. Adorno's *Dialectic of Enlightenment*, trans. John Cumming (1944; trans. New York: Herder and Herder, 1972). Jack Goody, *The Domestication of the Savage Mind* (Cambridge: Cambridge University Press, 1977), maintains a distinction between mythic and historical representation, relating the latter to the introduction of alphabetic writing, while at the same time refusing the value-laden cultural dichotomies of Lévy-Bruhl, Cassirer, and others. I elaborate on the implications of Goody's views for literary studies in Chapter 6 below.

20 Williams, *Country and the City*, p. 30. In contrast to Williams, McClung (*Country House in English Renaissance Poetry*, pp. 20–23) relies on evidence from conservative historians of the period in cautioning against reading the country-house poems as commentaries on or reflections of an incipient agrarian capitalism. He is right to call our attention to the terms in which the texts themselves speak: "If Jonson recognized the supposed

effects of capitalistic land policies, he is silent about the causes, preferring a moral and individual to an economic diagnosis of the disease." But McClung overstates his case in suggesting that we "discount economic history as a tool in the analysis of estate poems."

21 Williams, *Country and the City*, p. 28.

22 George Parfitt, *Ben Jonson: Public Poet and Private Man* (London: J. M. Dent and Sons, 1976), p. 161.

23 Geoffrey Walton, "The Tone of Ben Jonson's Poetry," in *Metaphysical to Augustan: Studies in Tone and Sensibility in the Seventeenth Century* (London: Bowes and Bowes, 1955), pp. 23–44; rpt. in *Seventeenth Century English Poetry*, ed. William R. Keast (New York: Oxford University Press, 1962), pp. 201–203.

24 See J. H. Hexter, "The Myth of the Middle Class in Tudor England," in his *Reappraisals in History* (New York: Harper Torchbooks, 1963), pp. 71–116, and Lawrence Stone, *The Crisis of the Aristocracy, 1558–1641* (Oxford: Clarendon Press, 1965), chap. 7.

25 In *The Return from Parnassus*, performed at Cambridge some time between 1601 and 1602, there is a satiric description of Jonson which combines reference to his comic realism with a defensive and condescending joke on his class origins: "A meere Empyrick, one that getts what he hath by observation, and makes onely nature privy to what he endites, so slow an Inventor, that he were better betake himselfe to his old trade of Bricklaying, a bould whorson, as confident now in making of a booke, as he was in times past in laying of a brick" *H & S*, XI, 364; cf. *H & S*, I, 164 (note to Conversations with Drummond, line 241).

26 Jean-Paul Sartre, *What is Literature?* trans. Bernard Frechtman (New York: Harper and Row, 1965), p. 95.

27 Christopher Hill, *Change and Continuity in Seventeenth-Century England* (Cambridge, Mass.: Harvard University Press, 1975), p. 282.

28 Walton, "Tone of Ben Jonson's Poetry," p. 213.

29 Williams, *Country and the City*, p. 28.

Chapter 2. The Mapping of an Ideological Domain

1 An interesting example is provided in Emile Benveniste's *Indo-European Language and Society*, trans. Elizabeth Palmer (Coral Gables, Fla.: University of Miami Press, 1973). Benveniste contends that etymological dictionaries have erred in deriving Greek *domos* and Latin *domus* from the same root. He argues that changes in the signification of the Greek terms for house (*domos* and later *oikos*) express transformations in the social institutions to which the vocabulary refers, the shift being from the

equivalent of "house" as an institutionalized form of social relations (i.e., the extended, patriarchal family of Homeric society) to "house" *qua* construction or edifice. With the breakdown of the prehistoric "great family" into smaller units identified with individual parcels of property, terms which had formerly denoted relationships amongst a group of people with a common origin were transferred to a material object enclosing a space that defined a new basis of social organization. "The old genealogical words become emptied of their institutional and social contact and become terminology of territorial divisions" (p. 254). By contrast, Latin *domus* always denotes "house" as a social and moral construct which is closer to the English "home."

2 With regard to changes in the structure of the family beginning in the sixteenth century, see Philippe Ariès, *Centuries of Childhood: A Social History of Family Life*, trans. Robert Baldick (New York: Knopf, 1962); Edward Shorter, *The Making of the Modern Family* (New York: Basic Books, 1975); Lawrence Stone, *The Family, Sex and Marriage in England 1500–1800* (New York: Harper and Row, 1977). Shorter argues that England and colonial America were ahead of the rest of Europe in the development of a "kinless conjugal family" unit and of a household structure that permitted sexual privacy and emotional intimacy (chap. 1). Stone describes three overlapping stages in the evolution of the family: the "Open Lineage Family" which predominated from about 1450 to 1630, the "Restricted Patriarchal Nuclear Family" which first appeared around 1530, flourished from about 1580 to 1640, and lasted at least until 1700, and the "Closed Domesticated Nuclear Family" which emerged around 1620 and was predominant among the upper and middle classes by the mid-eighteenth century. The family celebrated in Jonson's "To Penshurst" would be of Stone's second type, a "restricted patriarchal nuclear family." (The poem can be dated before the death of Prince Henry who is mentioned in line 77, which would place it not long prior to 1612.) Yet I would argue that there are already signs in this poem of values and behavior which Stone identifies with the "closed domesticated nuclear family." These include an emphasis on strong affective ties, attention to the upbringing and the education of children, and even a certain loosening of patriarchal authority to the degree that the role of the wife, while still subordinate, assumes a certain importance in its own right (see Stone, pp. 4–9, and pp. 652–666).

3 See, e.g., the *OED* entry for the word *conscience*, and my comments in Chap. 6 below; John R. Wikse, *About Possession: The Self as Private Property* (University Park: Pennsylvania State University Press, 1977), pp. 16–17, 26–29, discusses the etymology of the word *behavior* as evidence of

a possessive component to the logic of reflexivity in modern Western thought and language; on the positioning of the subject in the individual see Martin Heidegger, "The Age of the World Picture," in *The Question concerning Technology and Other Essays*, trans. William Lovitt (New York: Harper Colophon Books, 1977), pp. 115–154.

4 Walter J. Ong, S.J., *Ramus: Method, and the Decay of Dialogue, from the Art of Discourse to the Art of Reason* (Cambridge, Mass.: Harvard University Press, 1958); see, however, the objections of Rosalie L. Colie, "Literature and History," in *Relations of Literary Study*, ed. James Thorpe (New York: Modern Language Association of America, 1967), p. 21, and the qualification of Ong's views by Frances A. Yates, *The Art of Memory* (Chicago: University of Chicago Press, 1966), pp. 231 ff.

5 C. B. Macpherson, *The Political Theory of Possessive Individualism: Hobbes to Locke* (Oxford: Oxford University Press, 1964).

6 C. B. Macpherson, "A Political Theory of Property," in his *Democratic Theory: Essays in Retrieval* (Oxford: Clarendon Press, 1973), pp. 127–128. Macpherson's analysis of this change in the sense of the term is confirmed by the *OED* which notes "comparatively few examples before the seventeenth century" of *property* denoting a "thing" or "things."

7 Thomas Hobbes, *Leviathan* [1651], ed. C. B. Macpherson (Harmondsworth, Middlesex: Pelican Books, 1968), pp 382–383.

8 John Locke, *Second Treatise*, secs. 27 and 44, in *Two Treatises of Government*, ed. Peter Laslett (1960; rev. ed. New York: Mentor, 1965), pp. 328–329, 340–341. C. B. Macpherson writes that "to Hobbes not only was labour a commodity but life itself was in effect reduced to a commodity; to Locke life was still sacred and inalienable, though labour, and one's 'person' regarded as one's capacity to labour, was a commodity . . . [Locke's] confusion about the definition of property, sometimes including life and liberty and sometimes not, may be ascribed to the confusion in his mind between the remnant of traditional values and the new bourgeois values. It is this, no doubt, which makes his theory more agreeable to the modern reader than the uncompromising doctrine of Hobbes. Locke did not care to recognize that the continual alienation of labour for a bare subsistence wage, which he asserts to be the necessary condition of wage-labourers throughout their lives, is in effect an alienation of life and liberty" (*Political Theory of Possessive Individualism*, pp. 219–220).

9 The stages in the development and eventual collapse of the Tudor machinery of government are traced in Conrad Russell's *The Crisis of the Parliaments: English History 1509–1660* (London: Oxford University Press, 1971). The idea of a Tudor "administrative revolution" has received much criticism; see, e.g., Russell, pp. 110–111, and Lawrence Stone, *The*

Causes of the English Revolution, 1529–1642 (New York: Harper Torchbooks, 1972), pp. 61–63. But Stone also acknowledges the ideological importance of the growth in an administrative structure, however limited it may have been: "The landed élite was desperately seeking some new moral justification for its privileged existence, to replace the chivalric ideal of a warrior aristocracy, and the ideal of public service in administration was sanctified by the Puritan concept of the calling" (p. 99); also see Mervyn James, *English Politics and the Concept of Honor, 1485–1642*, Past and Present Supplement 3 (Oxford: Past and Present Society, 1978).

10 Christopher Hill, *Society and Puritanism in Pre-Revolutionary England* (New York: Schocken Books, 1964), p. 223.

11 Needless to say, the latter version predominated. See Roy Harvey Pearce, *The Savages of America: A Study of the Indian and the Idea of Civilization* (Baltimore: Johns Hopkins Press, 1953); also, Gary B. Nash, "The Image of the Indian in the Southern Colonial Mind," in *The Wild Man Within: An Image in Western Thought from the Renaissance to Romanticism*, ed. Edward Dudley and Maximillian E. Novak (Pittsburgh: University of Pittsburgh Press, 1972), pp. 55–86; and Stephen Greenblatt's discussion of Spenserean allegory and Renaissance colonialism, *Renaissance Self-Fashioning*, chap. 4.

12 Claude Lévi-Strauss, "The Structural Study of Myth," pp. 202–228.

13 Claudio Guillén, *Literature as System: Essays toward the Theory of Literary History* (Princeton: Princeton University Press, 1971), pp. 120–121.

14 Although antecedents can be located for the country-house poem, it is not until "To Penshurst" that the genre is fully inaugurated. In *The Poetry of Conservatism, 1600–1745*, Rivers argues that "the country house poem is a form which has no real Latin analogues, largely because the way of life it reflects has no real counterpart in Roman society" (p. 17). Among the poems which follow "To Penshurst" in the English country-house genre are Carew's "To Saxham," and "To my Friend G. N. from Wrest," Herrick's "A Panegerick to Sir Lewis Pemberton," and Marvell's "Upon Appleton House." Related poems include Jonson's own "To Sir Robert Wroth," Herrick's "A Country Life: To His Brother, Mr. Thomas Herrick," Pope's "Epistle to Burlington," and longer topographical poems such as Denham's "Cooper's Hill" and Pope's "Windsor Forest."

15 The origins of the country-house poem lie in the myths of the Golden Age and in Latin poems on related themes by Horace, Martial, and Juvenal. Since these classical sources have been discussed elsewhere, I shall not rehearse them here. McClung, *Country House in English Renaissance Poetry*, chap. 1, provides the most thorough survey of specific classical

antecedents; on the literature of the Golden Age, see Harry Levin, *The Myth of the Golden Age in the Renaissance* (Bloomington: Indiana University Press, 1969), and Robert C. Elliott, *The Shape of Utopia* (Chicago: University of Chicago Press, 1970), chap. 1; cf. Isabel River's remarks in her *The Poetry of Conservatism*, cited above; the genre may also be related to medieval accounts of the Terrestrial Paradise, a possibility I discuss below.

16 Molesworth, "Property and Virtue," pp. 145–146. Cf. Kenneth Burke, "Four Master Tropes," in *A Grammar of Motives* (New York: Prentice-Hall, 1945), pp. 503–517. In stressing the importance of the concept of "use," Molesworth relies on Hibbard, "Country House Poem of the Seventeenth Century," who writes of how these poems reflect "what the seventeenth century understood by 'nature' and . . . the whole concept of 'use' as the accepted basis for a civilized human existence."

17 Roman Jakobson, "Two Aspects of Language and Two Types of Aphasic Disturbances," in Jakobson and Morris Halle's *Fundamentals of Language* (The Hague: Mouton, 1956), p. 90.

18 Jonson, *Discoveries*, lines 1905–6 and 1930–31, in *H & S*, VIII, 621–622.

19 Jonson, Pref., *The English Grammar*, lines 10–18, in *H & S*, VIII, 465.

20 Francis Bacon, *Novum Organum* (I, lix–lx), in *The Works of Francis Bacon*, ed. and trans. James Spedding, Robert Leslie Ellis, and Douglas Denon Heath, 14 vols. (London: Longman, 1857–74), IV, 60–62.

21 Michel Foucault, *The Order of Things: An Archaeology of the Human Sciences*, trans. (New York: Vintage Books, 1973), pp. 46–77; Karl R. Wallace, *Francis Bacon on the Nature of Man* (Urbana: University of Illinois Press, 1967), pp. 118–119; Louis Marin, Intro. to A. Arnauld and P. Nicole, *La logique ou l'art de penser* (Paris: Flammarion, 1970), pp. 7–23.

22 Thus, for example, in his well-known essay on Jonson, T. S. Eliot writes: "Whereas in Shakespeare the effect is due to the way in which the characters *act upon* one another, in Jonson it is given by the way in which characters *fit in* with each other. The artistic result of *Volpone* is not due to any effect that Volpone, Mosca, Corvino, Corbaccio, Voltore have upon each other, but simply to their *combination* into a whole. And these figures are not personifications of passions; separately, they have not even that reality, they are *constituents*" (some of the emphasis is mine); see Eliot, "Ben Jonson," in *Ben Jonson: A Collection of Critical Essays*, ed. Jonas A. Barish (Englewood Cliffs, N.J.: Prentice-Hall, 1963), p. 18. In her introduction to *Every Man in His Humor* (New Haven: Yale University Press, 1969), Gabriele Bernhard Jackson writes that "Jonsonian comedy is the comedy of non-interaction . . . we remember individual

characters and confrontations, as though the story were a means to achieve certain juxtapositions. These moments of intersection constitute characteristic Jonsonian comedy; the design is not organic but geometric" (pp. 1–2). She speaks of "the characteristic additive technique of Jonson's comedy" (p. 15), and of relationships among characters as "collisions": "Seen from without, a moment of collision is a point at which two (or more) consciousnesses, like billiard balls of different colors, touch surfaces with a perceptible click and part" (p. 27).

23 Jonas A. Barish, *Ben Jonson and the Language of Prose Comedy* (1960; rpt. New York: Norton, 1970), p. 2.

24 Wesley Trimpi, *Ben Jonson's Poems: A Study of the Plain Style* (Stanford: Stanford University Press, 1962), pp. 126, 236.

25 Francis Bacon, Pref. to *Novum Organum*, in *The Works of Francis Bacon*, IV, 40.

26 See Kenneth Burke, *A Rhetoric of Motives* (New York: Prentice-Hall, 1950), pp. 133–134; and, the Frankfurt Institute for Social Research, *Aspects of Sociology*, trans. John Viertel (Boston: Beacon Press, 1972), pp. 182–185.

27 Barish, *Ben Jonson and the Language of Prose Comedy*, pp. 278–279.

28 Jonson, *Discoveries*, lines 1976–80, *H & S*, VIII, 623.

29 Paul M. Cubeta, "A Jonsonian Ideal: 'To Penshurst,'" *Philological Quarterly*, 42, No. 1 (January 1963), 15.

30 Williams, *Country and the City*, p. 28. A complexity of a very different sort from that focused on here is revealed in the chapter on "To Penshurst" in Alastair Fowler's *Conceitful Thought: The Interpretation of English Renaissance Poems* (Edinburgh: Edinburgh University Press, 1975), pp. 114–134.

31 Erich Auerbach, *Mimesis*, trans. Willard R. Trask (1953; rpt. Princeton: Princeton University Press, 1968), p. 39.

32 Ibid., pp. 70–71.

33 George Williamson, *The Senecan Amble: A Study in Prose Form from Bacon to Collier* (1951; rpt. Chicago: University of Chicago Press, 1966), p. 208; Trimpi, *Ben Jonson's Poems*, p. 62.

34 For classification of the verse genres in which Jonson chose to write, see Trimpi, *Ben Jonson's Poems*, chaps. 7–8.

35 Barish, *Ben Jonson and the Language of Prose Comedy*, pp. 56–57.

36 Ibid., pp. 87–89.

37 Ibid., p. 86. On the relationship between language and personality in Jonson, see too, Parfitt, *Ben Jonson*, pp. 30–35, 94–103.

38 Burke, *A Grammar of Motives*, p. 507.

39 Marin, Intro. to *La logique ou l'art de penser*, p. 13.

40 My thinking here draws on Fish's probing analysis of the epistemological conflict underlying the polarities of seventeenth-century prose style, in his *Self-Consuming Artifacts: The Experience of Seventeenth-Century Literature* (Berkeley: University of California Press, 1972), pp. 377–378.

41 Williams, *Country and the City*, p. 28.

42 The text can be found in *Historical Poems of the XIVth and XVth Centuries*, ed. Rossell Hope Robbins (New York: Columbia University Press, 1959), pp. 121–127; or see the version in modern English by A. L. Morton in the appendix to his *The English Utopia* (London: Lawrence and Wishart, 1952).

43 Elliott, *Shape of Utopia*, pp. 5–6.

44 In the context of the poem's argument opposing Nature to Culture, the concept of the "humanly natural" is somewhat paradoxical. I shall discuss this in detail later; for the moment, it may be worthwhile to note that the family's wisdom and virtue are represented as the signs that it follows Nature, while at the same time "Nature" is defined according to a normative, culturally determined conception of what constitute wisdom and virtue.

45 This argues against seeing the poem simply as an evocation of the Golden Age; rather, it may reflect the doctrine of plenitude as opposed to the idea of retrogression in Nature, a doctrine which Jonson followed Bacon and others in supporting. Compare for example, Gabriel Harvey: "You suppose the first age was the goulde age. It is nothinge soe. Bodin defendith the goulde age to flourishe nowe, and our first grandfathers to have rubbid thorowghe in the iron and brasen age at the beginninge when all thinges were rude and unperfitt in comparison of the exquisite finesse and delicacye, that we ar growen unto at these days." *Letter-Book of Gabriel Harvey, A.D. 1573–1580*, ed. Edward J. L. Scott, Camden Society, N.S., 33 (1884; rpt. New York: Johnson Reprint Corp., 1965), p. 86.

46 The only apparent negative construction in the section which inventories Nature at Penshurst is "never failes" in line 20, and this can be shown by semantic analysis to be a form of double negation for the purpose of making an emphatic affirmative statement. Moreover, "never failes" refers primarily to a temporal continuum (the abundance is *always* present) rather than to the presence or absence of the objects themselves.

47 Cf. Chap. 5, n. 19 below.

48 Williams, *Country and the City*, pp. 28–34; L. C. Knights, *Drama and Society in the Age of Jonson* (London: Chatto and Windus, 1937); for a fuller discussion of the limitations of Knights's classic study, see Don E. Wayne, "*Drama and Society in the Age of Jonson*: An Alternative View," *Renaissance Drama*, N.S. 13 (1982), 103–129.

Chapter 3. The Poem

1 Roman Jakobson, "Closing Statement: Linguistics and Poetics," in *Style in Language*, ed. Thomas A. Sebeok (Cambridge, Mass.: M.I.T. Press, 1966), pp. 350–377.

2 In employing the distinction between Nature and Culture I do not allude to the early work of Lévi-Strauss, where the attempt to "trace the line of demarcation between the two orders guided by the presence or absence of articulated speech" produced vexed questions which Lévi-Strauss himself acknowledges in the preface to the second edition of his *The Elementary Structures of Kinship*, trans. J. H. Bell, J. R. Von Sturmer, and R. Needham (Boston: Beacon Press, 1969). Nor do I mean to imply that this distinction is a universal category of human thought. I do think that a historically and culturally specific form of the antithesis between Nature and Culture is an evident strain of late-Renaissance and Enlightenment ideology; in this regard, see Lester G. Crocker, *Nature and Culture: Ethical Thought in the French Enlightenment* (Baltimore: Johns Hopkins Press, 1963), pp. 3–17. On naturalization as a fundamental ideological operation, see Chap. 1 above.

3 Sir Henry Wotton, *Elements of Architecture* (1624), in *Somers Tracts*, ed. Walter Scott, 2d ed. (London, 1810; rpt. New York: AMS Press, 1965), III, 602–3; Sidney implies a similar order of priorities in the *Arcadia*, in *The Prose Works of Sir Philip Sidney*, ed. Albert Feuillerat (1912; rpt. Cambridge: Cambridge University Press, 1963), I, 15, when he describes the shepherds' and Musidorus's approach to Kalander's house "about which they might see (with fitte consideration both of the ayre, the prospect, and the nature of the ground) all such necessarie additions to a great house."

4 Angus Fletcher, *Allegory: The Theory of a Symbolic Mode* (Ithaca, N.Y.: Cornell University Press, 1964), p.128.

5 Gérard Labrot, *Le palais Farnese de Caprarola: essai de lecture*, Collection Le Signe de L'Art, dir. Pierre Francastel, No. 5 (Paris: Klincksieck, 1970), pp. 16–17.

6 Sigmund Freud, "Negation" (1925), trans. Joan Riviere, in *General Psychological Theory: Papers on Metapsychology*, ed. Philip Rieff (New York: Collier Books, 1963), pp. 213–217.

7 Trimpi, *Ben Jonson's Poems*, p. 197.

8 These are, of course, conventional pastoral images. But their appearance here, in association with the historical references that follow immediately, and not elsewhere in the section, is significant.

9 A case in point is a letter of Sir William Browne, who was in the service of Sir Robert Sidney, to the latter, 7 July 1602, *Letters and Memorials of*

State, ed. Arthur Collins (London, 1746), II, 257. Browne is preoccupied throughout the letter in locating himself precisely in time and space. From its opening: "On Thursday Night late, about Nine or Ten of the Clock I arryved at Margett, and the next Morning early took Horse towards London, stayed two Howers att Canterbury, where, in your Lordships Name. . . [etc.]," to an absurdly conscientious attempt at the close to mark the exact moment of the letter's posting: "I am now putting Foot in Sturrop this present Saturday Morning at Four of the Clock, the 7th of July, 1602," this piece of correspondence is an extreme form of metonymy throughout. The meaning of Browne's letter is comprehensible only in terms of the context and the relationship to which the metonymy refers: a servant of rank writing to a master of higher rank and presenting an accounting of service rendered in a form that anticipates the punching in and punching out of a time card in a modern factory. On the emergence of the Work = Time = Money concept in the early stages of capitalist development, and the consequent significance of literary references to clock time, see E. P. Thompson, "Time, Work-Discipline, and Industrial Capitalism," *Past and Present*, 38 (Dec. 1967), 56–97.

10 Cf. *Discoveries* (lines 1306–8), where Jonson writes: "The great theeves of a State are lightly the officers of the Crowne; they hang the lesse still; play the Pikes in the Pond; eate whom they list" (*H & S*, VIII, 603).

11 Martial, *Epigrams*, ed. and trans. Walter C. A. Ker (London: Heinemann, 1919), I, 198–199.

12 Sir Walter Ralegh to Sir Edward Stradling, 26 September 1584, Letter 16, *Stradling Correspondence*, ed. J. M. Traherne (London: 1840), pp. 22–23.

13 Charles, Lord Howard of Effingham to Stradling, 21 September and 26 September 1584, Letters 3 and 4, ibid., pp. 3–6.

14 Sir James Croft to Stradling, 15 December 1583 and 17 September 1584, Letters 32 and 34, ibid., pp. 39–42.

15 Sir Francis Walsingham to Stradling, 20 September, 21 September, and 27 September 1584, Letters 21, 22, and 23, ibid., pp. 27–30; see also Sir Henry Sidney to Stradling, 29 September and 20 October 1584, Letters 14 and 15, pp. 20–22.

16 Ibid., p. xii; cf. Lord Howard of Effingham to Stradling, February 1586, Letter 6, pp. 9–11.

17 Julia Cartwright, *Sacharissa: Some Account of Dorothy Sidney, Countess of Sunderland, Her Family and Friends 1617–1684*, 2d ed. (London: Seeley and Co., 1893), notes that "the eldest daughter, Lady Mary, married Sir Robert Wroth; the second, Lady Katherine, became the wife of Sir Louis Mansel; the fourth, named Philipp after her lamented uncle

[Sir Philip Sidney; she married Sir John Hobart]; and the seventh, Barbara, was married in 1622 to Sir Thomas Smythe, soon afterwards created Viscount Strangford, and one of the richest owners in Kent [his grandfather, of the same name, was a merchant who became one of the most powerful financiers of Elizabeth's reign; he was made sheriff of London in 1599, took part in the management of the Virginia Company after being knighted by James I on his accession, and, in 1606, was elected Governor of the East India Company]" (p. 10; cf. pp. 131–132).

18 Sir Robert Sidney to Lady Barbara Sidney, 20 April 1597, *Letters and Memorials of State*, ed. Collins, II, 43–44; J. C. A. Rathmell, "Jonson, Lord Lisle, and Penshurst," *English Literary Renaissance*, 1, No. 3 (Autumn 1971), 250–260, provides additional evidence of Lady Barbara's affection for her children, and cites Robert Sidney's frequent praise of his wife's skill in managing the household during his long absences from Penshurst. She seems even to have had a hand in overseeing some of the building projects on the estate, as is suggested by a letter of May 1594 in which Robert writes to her: "I need not send to know how my buildings goe forward, for I ame sure you are so good a housewyfe you may be trusted with them" (quoted in Rathmell, p. 252).

19 Rowland Whyte to Sir Robert Sidney, 22 December 1599, *Letters and Memorials of State*, ed. Collins, II, 153.

20 Ariès, *Centuries of Childhood*, pp. 348–350.

21 See Nancy Chodorow, *The Reproduction of Mothering: Psychoanalysis and the Sociology of Gender* (Berkeley: University of California Press, 1978), pp. 208–209.

22 Marcel Mauss, *The Gift: Forms and Functions of Exchange in Archaic Societies*, trans. Ian Cunnison (1925; trans. New York: Norton, 1967), p. 1.

23 Jonson apparently experienced such humiliation personally. Drummond gave the following account of a dinner to which Jonson had been invited by Lord Salisbury (Robert Cecil): "Being at ye end of my Lord Salisburie's table with Inigo Jones & demanded by my Lord, why he was not glad, 'My Lord,' said he [Jonson] 'you promised I should dine with yow, bot I doe not,' for he had none of his meate, he esteamed only yt his meate which was of his owne dish" ("Conversations with Drummond," *H & S*, I, 141. I have modernized punctuation for the sake of clarity). A further indication of Jonson's dislike for Cecil occurs several lines later in Drummond's record: "Salisburie never cared for any man longer nor he could make use of him" (I, 142). *H. & S.* note a similar judgment of the Cecils by Francis Bacon: "For in the time of the Cecils, the father and the son, able men were by design and of purpose suppressed" (I, 167; from a letter to Buckingham

dated August 12, 1616). It is not unlikely that Jonson had the Cecils in mind among others when he wrote disparagingly in "To Penshurst" of "other lords" and their houses.

24 Cubeta, "Jonsonian Ideal," p. 23.

25 Concerning this passage, William E. Cain argues, in a fine essay, "The Place of the Poet in Jonson's 'To Penshurst' and 'To My Muse,' " *Criticism*, 21, No. 1 (1979), 34–48, that "even as Jonson indicates the closing of certain distinctions, he struggles against his knowledge that these all too clearly remain. His phrase 'there's nothing I can wish' bypasses—and as a result draws our notice to—the elements of fantasy and wish-fulfillment in this passage, which moves forward as a prolonged 'as if' (line 74). Jonson's praise of his Lord is wonderfully generous, but perhaps not wholly sanguine in its implications for the poet himself" (p. 40).

26 See the dedication, to the earl of Pembroke, of Jonson's *Epigrammes* (lines 17–21), *H & S*, VIII, 25–26.

27 See Marin, *Utopiques*, pp. 257 ff.

Chapter 4. The House

1 For a discussion of the decline of the great hall in country-house architecture and its sociological significance, see Eric Mercer, "The Houses of the Gentry," *Past and Present*, 5, No. 2 (1954), 11–31. Mercer's article is an outstanding example of an analysis of architectural forms in terms of their significance for broader questions of economic, social, and cultural history. In this case the emphasis is on floor plans and the changes in such plans from the mid-sixteenth century to the Restoration, as an index of the social transformation of England during that period.

2 Roger Howell, *Sir Philip Sidney: The Shepherd Knight* (Boston: Little, Brown, 1968), pp. 7–8; see, too, Frances A. Yates, "Elizabethan Chivalry: The Romance of the Accession Day Tilts," in *Astraea: The Imperial Theme in the Sixteenth Century* (London: Routledge and Kegan Paul, 1975), pp. 88–111.

3 Eric Mercer, *English Art, 1553–1625*, Vol. 7 of *The Oxford History of English Art* (Oxford: Clarendon Press, 1962), pp. 3–5.

4 "The circle of Protestant humanists of which Burghley became the leader may have been accustomed in their youth to make fun of Gothic barbarity and the romances. But as they grew older tradition became more important to them: governments tend to grow more conservative and in addition they realised that romantic impulses could be harnessed to the service of the state. As a result one finds, for instance, Burghley's own houses growing more, rather than less, Gothic as the years went on." Girouard, *Robert Smythson and the Architecture of the Elizabethan Era*, p. 46; see

also, Girouard, "Elizabethan Architecture and the Gothic Tradition," *Architectural History*, 6 (1963), 23–39.

5 Mercer, *English Art, 1553–1625*, p. 33.

6 *Prose Works of Sir Philip Sidney*, I, 15.

7 Bacon, "Of Building," *Essays or Counsels Civil and Moral* (1625) in *Works of Francis Bacon*, VI, 481.

8 Complaining of his countrymen's lack of respect for lastingness in building, Robert Reyce wrote in 1618: "And first of their buildings, among which sort I reckon their castles so often mentioned in the days of our forefathers, the ruins whereof are yet in many places extant, so that at this day here is in Suffolk no castle fully standing, or at leastwise none fortified or defensible. Such is the state and policy of this land at this day, and so far differing from former times, and the present administration of other countries, who think that the security of a commonwealth is impaired when such buildings are ruinated. . . .

"The next sort of buildings are their mansions and dwelling houses, which by the traces of antiquity yet remaining, I find to be far differing from them of the former times, who used in the situation of their houses to regard profit more than pleasure, and safety more than wholesomeness of the air. . . . These [ancient] houses were always built low not with many rooms or above one or two stories, but these more in length than in largeness. Thick were their walls, of squared or rough stone, brick or strong timber, their windows small, their chimneys large, or instead of them to have round hearths in the midst of their great halls or rooms [as at Penshurst], with round holes or louvres aloft in the roof, which carried away the smoke never offending; whereas our building at this day is chiefly to place the houses where they may be furthest seen, have best prospect, sweetest air and greatest pleasure, their walls thin . . . their lights large, all for outward show, their rooms square, raised high commonly with three and often with four stories, their chimneys as many but small, their roofs square, and so slender that they are enforced often to repair." Robert Reyce, *Breviary of Suffolk* (1618), as quoted in Lawrence Stone, *Social Change and Revolution in England, 1540–1640* (London: Longman, 1965), pp. 127–128.

9 Cf. Howell, *Sir Philip Sidney*, pp. 80, 93–95, 247. Lawrence Stone points out that Henry Sidney was a partner in one of the earliest projects to manufacture steel in England. But this venture, on which Sir Henry embarked in 1565, was ruined by competition from Baltic imports. By 1583, Sir Henry had to order the sale of some of his lands in order to be delivered "out of that miserable thraldome of usurye" (*Crisis of the Aristocracy, 1558–1641*, pp. 351, 540). A final irony concerning the Sidneys' financial indebtedness toward the end of the century is the fact

that although Sir Philip died at Sutphen on October 17, 1586, the spectacular funeral procession, recorded in a famous engraving designed by Thomas Lant, did not occur until almost four months later on February 6, 1587. The reason for the delay was the necessity of paying Sir Philip's enormous debts and the selling of more Sidney lands to cover these as well as the funeral costs. Sir Philip's father-in-law, Sir Frances Walsingham, who was in charge of arrangements for the funeral and who paid much of the expense himself, told Leicester: "[It] doth greatly afflict me that a gentleman that hath lived so unspotted a reputation, and had so great a care to see all men satisfied, should be so exposed to the outcry of his creditors. His goods will not suffice to answer a third part of his debts already known." Quoted in Frederick S. Boas, *Sir Philip Sidney, Representative Elizabethan: His Life and Writings* (London: Staples Press, 1955), p. 190.

10 Mercer, *English Art, 1553–1625*, pp. 10–11, 57–58.

11 Ibid., pp. 85–86.

12 Nikolaus Pevsner, *The Englishness of English Art* (New York: Praeger, 1956), pp. 187–188.

13 Ibid., p. 187; cf. pp. 96, 113.

14 Ibid., p. 113. Similarly, in his book *The Tudors* (1955; rpt. London: Fontana/Collins, 1972), p. 47, Christopher Morris cites the Pulteneys, who built the manor house at Penshurst, as the example of businessmen who founded noble houses in the fourteenth century by financing the wars of Edward III. The history of the ennobling of merchants and the consequent *embourgeoisement* of aristocratic culture is a long and complex one.

15 Nigel Nicolson, *Great Houses of the Western World* (New York: Putnam, 1968), p. 25; the most thorough consideration of the problem of dating the various stages of the house's construction is Marcus Binney, "Penshurst Place, Kent: The Seat of Viscount De L'Isle, VC, KG," in four parts, *Country Life*, 151 (9 and 16 March, 27 April, 4 May 1972), 554–558, 618–621, 994–998, 1090–1093; see also "The Architectural Development of Penshurst Place," text by Marcus Binney and Anthony Emery, plans by Myrna White and Peter Willis (Oldhill, Dunstable, Bedfordshire: ABC Historic Publications, 1975). There is some discrepancy among these texts concerning the dating of the Long Gallery. I am obliged to Viscount De L'Isle for confirming that it was probably added by Robert Sidney between 1599 and 1607 for his wife, Barbara, whose coat of arms is carved over one of the doorways (Letter received from Viscount De L'Isle, 22 August 1983).

16 Mercer, "The Houses of the Gentry," p. 13.

17 Nicolson, *Great Houses of the Western World*, p. 25.

18 H. Avray Tipping, *English Homes: Period I*, Vol. 1: *Norman and Plantagenet, 1066–1485* (London: Offices of Country Life, 1921), p. 168.

19 Margaret Wood, *The English Medieval House* (London: Phoenix House, 1965), p. 52.

20 "The very newness of . . . [the Sidneys'] status is best confirmed by the passion with which they attempted to conceal it. If one were to trust the genealogies of the family as they were prepared for Sir Henry Sidney he would find the family descended from respectably old stock. According to these documents, the founder of the Sidney family in England was one William de Sidne, a knight who is represented as having been in the service of Henry II before he became King. There is, in fact, no real evidence that William de Sidne ever existed. When Sir Henry Sidney, anxious to provide his family with a suitably elevated heritage, paid £6 in 1568 to 'the Heralds at London for my Lord's Petigrewe' he received ample for his expenditure in the form of a spurious genealogy and forged documents to support it. The deception was eminently successful; although Sir Henry was doubtless aware of the nature of the documents, Philip believed firmly in the truth of his French ancestry" (Howell, *Sir Philip Sidney*, p. 18).

21 William H. Hale, Intro. to *The Domesday of St. Paul's of the Year 1222*, Camden Society, O.S. 69 (1858; rpt. New York, London: AMS Press, 1968), p. xxxii.

22 Hill, *Society and Puritanism in Pre-Revolutionary England*, chaps. 12, 13.

23 John Bossy, "The Character of Elizabethan Catholicism," in *Crisis in Europe, 1560–1660*, ed. Trevor Aston (Garden City, N.Y.: Anchor Books, 1967), pp. 237–238.

24 Bacon, "Of Gardens," *Essays or Counsels Civil and Moral* (1625), in *Works of Francis Bacon*, VI, 485.

25 In his letters to his wife, Robert Sidney shows at least as much concern for the garden as he does for his building projects. On 26 October 1594, he writes from Richmond: "I pray you send me word if my buildings be finished and how my garden goes forwards"; on 25 September 1595: "Sweethart. I pray you remember to send to Jaques, the gardner, to come to Penshurst against Alhalowtyde, and to bring yellow peaches, apricots, cherry and plum trees to set along the wall towards the church"; and, from Flushing on 2 October 1596: "I ame glad to heare my garden goes so wel forward: and as much for your sake is yt as mine own that I bestow the charge. I wil send over some trees from hence" (*Historical Manuscripts Commission, 77: Report on the Manuscripts of Lord De L'Isle and Dudley Preserved at Penshurst Place, Kent*, 6 vols. [London:

HMSO, 1925–1966], II, 157, 164, 226). An entry in John Evelyn's Diary for 9 July 1652 suggests that the garden at Penshurst enjoyed a considerable reputation during the late sixteenth and early seventeenth centuries: "We went to see Penshurst . . . famous once for its gardens and excellent fruit" (*Diary of John Evelyn*, ed. William Bray [Washington and London: Dunne, 1901], I, 278).

26 Roy Strong, *The Renaissance Garden in England* (London: Thames and Hudson, 1979), p. 20.

27 *Prose Works of Sir Philip Sidney*, I, 17–18.

28 Elizabeth Burton, *The Elizabethans at Home* (London: Secker and Warburg, 1958), pp. 213–214.

29 Sir Walter Ralegh, Preface, *History of the World* (London, 1614), sig. B6[r]. See also Christopher Hill, *Intellectual Origins of the English Revolution* (Oxford: Clarendon Press, 1965), pp. 182–183.

30 The beginnings of historiographical change in England can be traced even further back than the Reformation, to the reign of Henry VII. In a well-known discussion, E. M. W. Tillyard, *Shakespeare's History Plays* (1944; rpt. New York: Collier Books, 1962), pp. 40–42, 74, analyzes how the chroniclers justified the accession of Henry Tudor as the providential restoration of a line purportedly descending directly from the ancient British kings. Despite this emphasis on divine providence, the "Tudor myth" depended in part on a type of naturalism concerning human character. Thus, the standard Tudor chronicle represented Henry V as innately good and Richard III as innately evil.

31 See Eleanor Rosenberg, *Leicester, Patron of Letters* (New York: Columbia University Press, 1955), p. 61.

32 On the relationship between law and the history of historiography in the period, see J. G. A. Pocock, *The Ancient Constitution and the Feudal Law* (Cambridge: Cambridge University Press, 1957); Hill, *Intellectual Origins*, chap. 4; Peter Burke, *The Renaissance Sense of the Past* (New York: St. Martins Press, 1970), pp. 32–38. There are, of course, a number of conflicting ideas of history among Renaissance writers. Herbert Weisinger, "Ideas of History during the Renaissance," in *Renaissance Essays from the Journal of the History of Ideas*, ed. Paul Oskar Kristeller and Philip P. Wiener (New York: Harper and Row, 1968), pp. 74–94, sorts these into six categories: "the idea of progress, the theory of the plenitude of nature, the climate theory, the cyclical theory of history, the doctrine of uniformitarianism, and the idea of decline" (p. 75). It is significant that, regardless of their differences, all six notions involve a primary concern with the nature of Nature.

33 Jean Bodin, *Method for the Easy Comprehension of History* (1566), trans.

Beatrice Reynolds (1945; rpt. New York: Norton, 1969), pp. 15–17.

34 Ibid., pp. 85–86.

35 Julian H. Franklin, *Jean Bodin and the Sixteenth-Century Revolution in the Methodology of Law and History* (New York: Columbia University Press, 1963), pp. 77–79; see, too, J. W. Allen, *A History of Political Thought in the Sixteenth Century* (1928; rpt. with rev. bibliography, London: Methuen, 1961), pp. 394–444; and Preston King, *The Ideology of Order: A Comparative Analysis of Jean Bodin and Thomas Hobbes* (London: Allen and Unwin, 1974).

36 Jean Bodin, *The Six Bookes of a Commonweale* (1606), trans. Richard Knolles, facsimile rpt. ed. Kenneth Douglas McRae (Cambridge, Mass.: Harvard University Press, 1962), I, ii, 8.

37 Bodin, *The Six Bookes of a Commonweale*, III, vii, 361.

38 See King, *Ideology of Order*, pp. 85–95, and passim.

39 Bodin, *The Six Bookes of a Commonweale*, I, iv, 20.

40 Ibid., IV, iv, 476.

41 Rosenberg, *Leicester*, pp. 85 ff.

42 Howell, *Sir Philip Sidney*, pp. 218–219. Buchanan spent much of his adult life in France and was influenced by, and may have had some influence on, French thought concerning politics and history. On the naturalistic elements in Buchanan's political writings, see Allen, *History of Political Thought*, pp. 340–342.

43 To Robert Sidney, 18 October 1580, Letter 42, *Prose Works of Sir Philip Sidney*, III, 130.

44 Howell, *Sir Philip Sidney*, p. 220.

45 To Robert Sidney, *Prose Works of Sir Philip Sidney*, III, 130–131.

46 Ibid., pp. 131–132.

47 Hill, *Intellectual Origins*, pp. 162, 181.

48 Thus, for example, Arthur O. Lovejoy argues that a number of writers, including "the two most eminent English spokesmen of neo-classical aesthetic doctrine [Pope and Dr. Johnson] may be seen in the act of giving away the key to the classicists' position, by shifting the aesthetic connotation of 'conformity to nature' from simplicity to complexity and from regularity to irregularity," that is, from the classical to the Gothic. Lovejoy sees this "Gothic revival" as a result of the "transfer of the aesthetic *principle of irregularity*—as a newly discovered implication of the rule of 'imitating Nature'—from the art in which it had first manifested itself on a great scale—that of laying out gardens—to architecture." A. O. Lovejoy, "The First Gothic Revival and the Return to Nature," in *Essays in the History of Ideas* (Baltimore: Johns Hopkins Press, 1948), pp. 155, 160 and passim. I am not disputing Lovejoy's analysis, but only suggesting that his

description of a "Gothic revival" rationalized by the neoclassical doctrine of "imitating Nature" is a particular though probably a more generalized occurrence of a connection that had already been drawn much earlier in the history of English architecture. What Lovejoy is referring to is a *theoretical formulation* according to rational and naturalistic principles of a shift away from regularity in architecture which occurred during the eighteenth century. In practical terms, however, and in some writings during the late sixteenth and early seventeenth centuries, resistance to classical regularity and the persistence of the Gothic style were already identified with a conception of Nature.

49 Printed by Robert Wyer, n.d. (*Short-Title Catalogue*, 3373). This text appears to be an earlier version of the first eight chapters of *A Dyetary of Health* (ca. 1542), which is reprinted in Andrew Boorde, *Introduction and Dyetary, with Barnes in the Defence of the Berde*, ed. F. J. Furnivall, Early English Text Society, E.S., No. 10 (London: 1870; rpt. Millwoood, N.Y.: Krauss Reprint Co., 1975), pp. 223–304.

50 Ian Watt, *The Rise of the Novel* (1957; rpt. Harmondsworth, Middlesex: Penguin, 1963), pp. 144–45.

51 See above, Chap. 2, n. 2. Also Hill, *Society and Puritanism*, chap. 13; Stone, *Crisis of the Aristocracy*, pp. 593, 610–611; and Louis B. Wright, *Middle-Class Culture in Elizabethan England* (1935; rpt. Ithaca: Cornell University Press, 1958), chap. 7. The ideological complexities of seventeenth-century attitudes toward childhood are traced by Leah Sinanoglou Marcus, *Childhood and Cultural Despair* (Pittsburgh: University of Pittsburgh Press, 1978).

Chapter 5. The Home

1 Wotton, *Elements of Architecture*, in *Somers Tracts*, III, 627.

2 Cf. Lovejoy, *Essays in the History of Ideas*, Essays VII and VIII, pp. 99–165; Pevsner, *Englishness of English Art*, p. 164. This is the ideal for a garden expressed in well-known poems by Marvell ("The Garden" and "The Mower against Gardens") and by Pope ("Epistle to Burlington"). The functions of allegory and rhetoric in the design of such apparently "natural" gardens are analyzed by Ronald Paulson in his *Emblem and Expression: Meaning in English Art of the Eighteenth Century* (Cambridge, Mass.: Harvard University Press, 1975), pp. 19–34.

3 See Earl Miner, *The Cavalier Mode from Jonson to Cotton* (Princeton: Princeton University Press, 1971), p. 7.

4 Rathmell, "Jonson, Lord Lisle, and Penshurst," pp. 250–260.

5 On the Sidneys' financial difficulties, see Chap. 4, n. 9, above; the family's

somewhat improved financial situation after Robert Sidney's succession was due in part to his marriage to the Welsh heiress Barbara Gamage.

6 Knights, *Drama and Society in the Age of Jonson*, chap. 7; cf. Wayne, "*Drama and Society in the Age of Jonson*: An Alternative View," pp. 103–129.

7 Cubeta, "Jonsonian Ideal," p. 15.

8 Fletcher, *Allegory*, p. 136; see Fletcher's earlier discussion, pp. 108 ff., of the ancient meaning of *kosmos* and its traditional allegorical function.

9 Ibid., pp. 118–120.

10 Ibid., pp. 294–295.

11 The negation of Culture can thus be partly read as an unconscious strategy to allow an image of the goods to enter the consciousness of the speaker or of those for whom he is speaking while denying their desire for such goods and for what they represent. Here, again, the negative constructions may be interpreted as negation in Freud's sense (*Verneinung*), that is, "a repudiation, by means of projection" (see Chap. 3, n. 6, above). The negation of Culture at the beginning of "To Penshurst" may then be understood not simply as repudiation, but also as the projection of a desire for the power identified with ornament, power which the Sidneys, perhaps, and the poet, certainly, lacked.

12 See Karl Marx, *Capital* (New York: International Publishers, 1967), III, 795–796.

13 Williams, *Country and the City*, p. 32.

14 Here I draw a sociopolitical implication from the Derridean axiom that "coherence in contradiction expresses the force of a desire"; see Jacques Derrida, "Structure, Sign, and Play in the Discourse of the Human Sciences," in *The Structuralist Controversy*, ed. Richard Macksey and Eugenio Donato (Baltimore: Johns Hopkins Press, 1972), p. 248.

15 Sir Philip Sidney, *An Apology for Poetry*, ed. Forrest G. Robinson (Indianapolis: Bobbs–Merrill, 1970), pp. 37, 57.

16 Hibbard, "Country House Poem of the Seventeenth Century," p. 165.

17 Cubeta, "Jonsonian Ideal," p. 15.

18 Hugh Maclean, "Ben Jonson: Notes on the Ordered Society," in *Essays in English Literature from the Renaissance to the Victorian Age, Presented to A. S. P. Woodhouse*, ed. Millar Maclure and F. W. Watt (Toronto: University of Toronto Press, 1964), pp. 42–68.

19 In fact "To Penshurst" is an exact illustration of one type of ideological distortion described by Karl Mannheim in his *Ideology and Utopia: An Introduction to the Sociology of Knowledge*, trans. Louis Wirth and Edward Shils (1936; rpt. New York: Harvest Books, 1964): "An example of the third type of ideological distortion may be seen when this ideology as a

form of knowledge is no longer adequate for comprehending the actual world. This may be exemplified by a landed proprietor, whose estate has already become a capitalistic undertaking, but who still attempts to explain his relations to his labourers and his own function in the undertaking by means of categories reminiscent of the patriarchal order" (p. 96).

Chapter 6. Beyond the Ideology of the Text: The Rhetorical Strategy of Jonson's Classicism

1 The concept of esthetic *potentiality* is useful, though we need not accept uncritically the distinction between "abstract" and "concrete" potentiality on the basis of which Lukács rejects literary modernism in favor of realism; see Georg Lukács, "The Ideology of Modernism," in *Realism in Our Time* (New York: Harper Torchbooks, 1971), pp. 21 ff. Bloch's conception of "Utopian fulfillment" is described by Fredric Jameson in *Marxism and Form* (Princeton: Princeton University Press, 1971), p. 146, as "the 'tendency' and the 'latency,' respectively, of things in the present: dynamic possibilities of historical development on the one hand, and the more perceptual or aesthetic potentialities of the same objects on the other. [These two aspects of Utopian fulfillment] . . . correspond to dramatic and lyrical modes of the presentation of not-yet-being." For Barthes, in his later writings, "jouissance" stands in opposition to all forms of ideological analysis (including his own earlier work); in *The Pleasure of the Text*, trans. Richard Miller (New York: Hill and Wang, 1975), he writes: "All socio-ideological analyses agree on the *deceptive* nature of literature (which deprives them of a certain pertinence): the work is finally always written by a socially disappointed or powerless group, beyond the battle because of its historical, economic, political situation; literature is the expression of this disappointment. These analyses forget (which is only normal, since they are hermeneutics based on the exclusive search for the signified) the formidable underside of writing: bliss [*jouissance*]: bliss which can erupt, across the centuries, out of certain texts that were nonetheless written to the glory of the dreariest, of the most sinister philosophy" (p. 39). His point, though perhaps overstated for polemical reasons, serves to remind us of the libidinal aspects of the acts of writing and reading. As I have indicated in my text, I take this as a necessary and complementary qualification rather than a repudiation of notions of potentiality that stress cognitive and critical activities enabled by the literary text.

2 See Mikhail Bakhtin, *Rabelais and His World*, trans. Hélène Iswolsky (Cambridge, Mass.: M.I.T. Press, 1968). Bakhtin analyzes the oppositional relationship in Rabelais between the pluralistic discourse of marketplace and carnival on the one hand, and the official language and culture of the

Middle Ages on the other. Although he tends to see Renaissance literature as a special case here, having to do with historical and linguistic transformations in this period (see pp. 273–277, 465 ff.), the concept of communication as "dialogic" or "polyphonic" is a general principle of his thought; with regard to the latter, see the essays by Bakhtin collected in *The Dialogic Imagination*, ed. Michael Holquist, trans. Caryl Emerson and Michael Holquist (Austin: University of Texas Press, 1981), and Michael Holquist, "The Politics of Representation," in *Allegory and Representation: Selected Papers from the English Institute*, 1979–80, ed. Stephen J. Greenblatt (Baltimore: Johns Hopkins Press, 1981), pp. 163–183; also see Ju. M. Lotman, "The Sign Mechanism of Culture," trans. Ann Shukman, *Semiotica*, 12 (1974), 301–305.

3 Earlier, we saw that the ideological function of the architectural organization of space and of architectural decoration is more immediately evident (and, therefore, more difficult for critics to ignore) than the textual coding and decoding of ideology in a poem. By the same token, the pleasure and the cognitive uses of the architectural are in certain quite tangible ways more immediate and concrete, and therefore easier to locate, than the more abstract pleasure and knowledge afforded by the poetic. I speak in a relative sense here, of course, for certainly there are abstract aspects to the architectural and concrete aspects to the poetic. The latter is described by Elizabeth Sewell in a lovely phrase as the "sound-look" of the poem, in *The Structure of Poetry* (London: Routledge and Kegan Paul, 1951), pp. 47 ff. It is probably the immediate, concrete presence of the structure in architecture, coupled with the fact that a building is not simply an object but an organization of social space into and through which one moves, that has led poets to employ architectural metaphors in describing the pleasures of the poetic; for a deeply sympathetic study of this tradition, see Ellen Eve Frank, *Literary Architecture* (Berkeley and Los Angeles: University of California Press, 1979). These qualities are also no doubt responsible for the long philosophical tradition of employing architecture as a model for memory traced by Yates, *Art of Memory*. And Hegel, despite his overschematic representation of the ontology of esthetic forms, with their final subordination to philosophy as the ultimate human expression of the "self-cognition" of absolute spirit, was perhaps right in viewing architecture as the most primary concrete form of the beautiful; see the selections from Hegel's *Vorlesungen über die Ästhetik*, in *Hegel: On the Arts*, ed. and trans. Henry Paolucci (New York: Frederick Ungar, 1979).

4 Goody, *Domestication of the Savage Mind*, p. 37.

5 The literary potential of this kind of tension is realized in the later Middle Ages and the Renaissance when Latin literacy and control over the alphabet by a "craft-elite" gives way to the vernacular and to a broader social

literacy: see Eric A. Havelock, *Origins of Western Literacy* (Toronto: Ontario Institute for Studies in Education, 1976), pp. 76–77; and Bakhtin, *Rabelais and His World*, pp. 465–473.

6 In religion, the mystical writings of the sixteenth and seventeenth centuries are especially interesting in this regard. Steven E. Ozment, *Mysticism and Dissent: Religious Ideology and Social Protest in the Sixteenth Century* (New Haven: Yale University Press, 1973), concludes his study of six magisterial dissenters of the sixteenth century by identifying a fundamental conflict in their writings: "The impulse to reform competes with a desire to abandon society altogether—truly to die to the world. It is not too much to say that in such dissent the seeds of social disintegration are as prominent as those of individual liberation" (p. 247). Michel de Certeau, in "L'énonciation mystique," *Recherches de Science Religieuse*, 64, No. 2 (April–June 1976), 183–215, focuses on mystical discourse within the Roman Catholic Church between the time of Teresa of Avila (1515–1582) and Angelus Silesius (1624–1677). Such literature "has its origin in an unstable society, where Tradition has become what is distant and past. It responds to a need to restore a dialogue" (p. 183); its emphasis is therefore on the "subjective" mode of enunciation, rather than on the "objective" organization of what is enunciated by the text (pp. 194–200). On the social and psychological aspects of autobiographical writing in this period, see Paul Delany, *British Autobiography in the Seventeenth Century* (London: Routledge and Kegan Paul, 1969), especially chap. 2: "The Renaissance and the Rise of Autobiography." On poetry in this context, see Louis L. Martz's "The Action of the Self: Devotional Poetry in the Seventeenth Century," in *Metaphysical Poetry*, ed. Malcolm Bradbury and David Palmer (Bloomington: Indiana University Press, 1971), pp. 101–121, as well as Martz's major study *The Poetry of Meditation*, 2d ed. (New Haven: Yale University Press, 1962).

7 See H. Stuart Hughes, *Consciousness and Society: The Reorientation of European Social Thought, 1890–1930* (New York: Vintage Books, 1961), p.8.

8 There are a number of letters that corroborate this view, though they also suggest that written expressions of sentiment were the prerogative of the husband in the relationship. An early one, written from London in September 1588, while Robert was returning from a trip to Scotland, is brief but ardent: "Sweet wenche, I will not write you any other thing at this time but that I came yester night very [*sic*] to this towne and will make all hast to come to you . . ." (*Historical Manuscripts Commission, 77, De L'Isle and Dudley MSS*, II, 102). Another, written during one of his absences as governor of Flushing, shows considerable warmth and tenderness for Barbara at the time of her approaching confinement: "My dear Barbara,

Thinck not long I pray you of mine absence, for I ame well and love you, but go in company with his Excellency. . . . Assure your self I wil not live if I be not with you before you bee brought to bed, for nothing in the word [*sic*] shall stay mee but God from being with you. . . . I wish myself with you, and every day our troops draw neerer and neerer unto you . . ." (Ibid., II, 112–113). In a letter written in 1600 to Sir John Harington, Robert Sidney refers with affection to the comfort and companionship provided by his wife during a recent illness: "My malady is much abated; my wife hath been my doctor, my nurse, my friend, and my sovereign cure" (Sir John Harington, *Nugae Antiquae*, ed. Henry Harington [1779; rpt. Hildesheim: Georg Olms, 1968], II, 254–255). Rathmell discusses aspects of Robert Sidney's correspondence that bear on Jonson's poem in his "Jonson, Lord Lisle, and Penshurst."

9 L. C. Knights, "Ben Jonson: Public Attitudes and Social Poetry," in *A Celebration of Ben Jonson*, ed. William Blissett, Julian Patrick, and R. W. Fossen (Toronto: University of Toronto Press, 1973), p. 187. Knights is referring to the essay by J. C. A. Rathmell cited above.

10 Kent Co. Arch., U 1500 P1. This bird's-eye map, showing the house, park, and village, bears the title "A Survey of Penshurst Place Park in ye parish of Leigh Bidburrough and Penshurst in the County of Kent: Belonging to the heirs of ye Right Honourable Robert Earl of Leicester," and is signed William Burgess. It appears to have been dated in the lower-right-hand corner but the writing there has been obscured. The archive dates it from about 1740. The large area surveyed by the map, its poor though quaint draftsmanship, and its somewhat deteriorated condition make it difficult to reproduce here.

11 Richard S. Peterson, *Imitation and Praise in the Poems of Ben Jonson* (New Haven: Yale University Press, 1981); Thomas M. Greene, *The Light in Troy: Imitation and Discovery in Renaissance Poetry*, Elizabethan Club Series, 7 (New Haven: Yale University Press, 1982).

12 Greene, *Light in Troy*, pp. 40–47; also see Paolo Rossi, "The New Science and the Symbol of Prometheus," in his *Philosophy, Technology, and the Arts in the Early Modern Era*, trans. Salvator Attanasio, ed. Benjamin Nelson (New York: Harper and Row, 1970), pp. 176–177; and Paul Alpers's judicious comment on "intertextuality" in his "What is Pastoral?" *Critical Inquiry*, 8, No. 3 (Spring 1982), 440.

13 I intend here an elaboration, to larger discursive units than phrases or sentences, of the distinction between *constative* and *performative* utterances first postulated by J. L. Austin and developed, with some criticism of Austin, by Emile Benveniste. We saw one manifestation of such tension in the introduction of the authorial "I," beginning at line 65 of "To Penshurst" (Chap. 3, above). At this point in the poem, description gives

way to narration and to a more specifically historical perspective. There is also a shift in rhetorical strategy toward a type of utterance that refers to itself as authenticator and, therefore, to a degree, as producer of the image conveyed by the poem as a whole. This kind of utterance exhibits precisely what Benveniste describes as the "peculiar quality" of the performative: "that of being self-referential, of referring to a reality that it itself constitutes by the fact that it is actually uttered in conditions that make it an act" (*Problems in General Linguistics*, trans. Mary Elizabeth Meek [Coral Gables, Fla.: University of Miami Press, 1971], p. 236). Benveniste gives the example of the word "hereby" in phrases such as "The King hereby decrees that . . ." where "hereby" is an indicator of the authority that authenticates an utterance as an *act*. Moreover, the "hereby" may be implicit as well as explicit. I would argue that its equivalent can be found in Jonson's dedication of his book of epigrams to the earl of Pembroke, where he writes, "In thanks whereof I returne you the honor of leading forth so many good and great names (as my verses mention on the better part) to their remembrance with posteritie . . . ," and that it is implied throughout "To Penshurst." For a somewhat different but related perspective on this self-referential aspect of Jonson's verse, see Don E. Wayne, "Poetry and Power in Ben Jonson's *Epigrammes*: The Naming of 'Facts' or the Figuring of Social Relations?" *Renaissance and Modern Studies*, 23 (1979), 79–103.

14 A number of models already exist that point in such a direction. One thinks immediately of the Russian Formalists' notion of art as defamiliarization, a "making strange" (*ostranenie*), and of Brecht's similar though more politicized concept of the "estrangement effect" (*Verfremdungseffekt*). The work of Bakhtin, cited earlier, provides another possible approach, as does the more recent semiotic theory of Lotman with its stress on the diversity of codes at the level of direct communication and on the necessary function of "noise" in the exchange of information (see the article by Lotman cited above). A similar concept of the necessity of "noise" for communication and cultural innovation is evident in Morse Peckham's *Man's Rage for Chaos: Biology, Behavior, and the Arts* (New York: Schocken Books, 1967), p. 10. Yet another nontraditional approach to the esthetic is the Althusserian idea of art as a dislocation or deformation of ideology developed in Pierre Macherey's *A Theory of Literary Production* (1966; trans. London: Routledge and Kegan Paul, 1978); see Terry Eagleton, "Pierre Macherey and the Theory of Literary Production," *Minnesota Review*, N.S., No. 5 (Fall 1975), 134–144, and Eagleton's *Criticism and Ideology* (London: NLB, 1976). The broader implications of a theory of "noise" in culture and history are considered by Anthony Wilden, *System and Structure*, 2d ed. (London: Tavistock, 1980), chap. 13.

15 Louis Althusser, "A Letter on Art in Reply to André Daspre," in *Lenin and Philosophy and Other Essays*, trans. Ben Brewster (New York: Monthly Review Press, 1971), pp. 222–223.

16 See Heidegger, "Age of the World Picture." Heidegger's description of what he calls the "modern" lacks an empirical foundation, and, compared with others, such as Marx and Weber, he makes little attempt to explain the social mediations of the historical phenomena he describes. But his essay does offer a succinct yet full descriptive and interpretive synthesis of the way in which the individual becomes the "subject," and in certain respects he penetrates more deeply to the metaphysical and psychological aspects of the "modern" than do writers who are more directly concerned with the relationship between ideas and social praxis. In Heidegger's conception, because the emergence of man as subject is itself the index of a historical differentiation, terms like "world view" or "viewpoint" have little meaning in connection with earlier periods: "The world picture does not change from an earlier medieval one into a modern one, but rather the fact that the world becomes picture at all is what distinguishes the essence of the modern age [*Neuzeit*]" (p. 130). Heidegger acknowledges the roots of this conception of the world as picture in Plato's metaphysics. But it is the instrumentality of the idea that distinguishes the modern. Hence, Heidegger asserts axiomatically that "machine technology remains up to now the most visible outgrowth of the essence of modern technology, which is identical with the essence of modern metaphysics" (p. 116).

17 Erwin Panofsky, *Meaning in the Visual Arts* (Garden City, N.Y.: Doubleday Anchor Books, 1955), p. 278.

18 Orgel and Strong compare the use of perspective devices in Inigo Jones's settings for the Stuart masques, which are oriented toward a single point of view, that of the king, with a stage design involving multiple perspectives created by Palladio and Scamozzi for the Teatro Olimpico at Vicenza. In the masque, the perspective served to reinforce the sense of hierarchy at court and provided a complement to the absolutist political doctrine of the divine right of kings. By contrast, in the Teatro Olimpico, designed for an academy of social equals, a variety of perspectives reinforced the idea of a plurality of separate but equal viewpoints. Common to both systems is the notion of the *uniqueness* of point of view, represented by the single focal point from which the illusion created by a perspective setting is realized in the theater. See Stephen Orgel and Roy Strong, *Inigo Jones: The Theatre of the Stuart Court* (London and Berkeley: Sotheby Parke Bernet, University of California Press, 1973), p. 7 and passim; Orgel, *The Illusion of Power: Political Theatre in the English Renaissance* (Berkeley: University of California Press, 1975), pp. 10–16; also Strong, *Renaissance Garden in England*, pp. 118, 203.

19 O. B. Hardison, Jr., "The Two Voices of Sidney's *Apology for Poetry*," *English Literary Renaissance*, 2, No. 1 (1972), 94, detects in Sidney's discussion of the existing state of English poetry a different attitude from the earlier parts of the *Apology*, a shift from "the Platonizing, idealizing tradition of humanist poetics to the critical and rationalistic poetic of neoclassicism." Cf. Ferguson, "Sidney's *A Defence of Poetry*," p. 74.

20 For an account of these experiments in quantitative verse, see William A. Ringler, Jr.'s, commentary in his edition of *The Poems of Sir Philip Sidney* (Oxford: Clarendon Press, 1962), p. xxxiii–xxxiv, 389–393. All subsequent citations from Sidney's poems refer to this edition.

21 Girouard, *Robert Smythson and the Architecture of the Elizabethan Era*, pp. 169–172; Mercer, *English Art, 1553–1625*, pp. 86, 150; Yates, "Elizabethan Chivalry: The Romance of the Accession Day Tilts," p. 180.

22 David Kalstone, *Sidney's Poetry: Contexts and Interpretations* (Cambridge, Mass.: Harvard University Press, 1967), p. 180.

23 Prometheus is invoked here primarily as a figure of heroic suffering; but Sidney is probably alluding also to Renaissance typologies in which Prometheus is thought of as the heroic prototype of an active human intellect, and in which the celestial fire of the pagan myth is sometimes associated with the Christian notion of divine inspiration. See Erasmus, *The Antibarbari* (1520), trans. Margaret Mann Phillips, in *Collected Works of Erasmus*, vol. 23, ed. Craig R. Thompson (Toronto: University of Toronto Press, 1978), p. 117; Ralegh, *History of the World*, Bk. II, chap. vi, sec. 4, p. 266; Spenser, *Faerie Queene*, II, x, 70; Bacon, *Wisdom of the Ancients*, in *Works of Francis Bacon*, VI, 745–753. Sidney's *An Apology for Poetry* (1595) contains no mention of Prometheus; but in his Christian-Platonist notion that "the skill of the artificer standeth in that *Idea* or fore-conceit of the work, and not in the work itself" (p. 16), in his comparison of the poet to the Christian god, "the heavenly Maker of that maker" (p. 17), and in his observation that "both Roman and Greek gave divine names unto it [poetry], the one of prophesying, the other of making" (p. 50), Sidney may imply the figure of Prometheus, the arch-maker, whose name (Gk., "forethought") is Latinized and Christianized as "Providence" by some Renaissance authors (see, e.g., Bacon, loc. cit.); cf. Rossi, "New Science and the Symbol of Prometheus," pp. 174–186, and Don Cameron Allen, *Mysteriously Meant: The Rediscovery of Pagan Symbolism and Allegorical Interpretation in the Renaissance* (Baltimore: Johns Hopkins Press, 1970), pp. 175–176, 193, and passim.

24 Eduard Wechssler, quoted in C. S. Lewis, *The Allegory of Love* (Oxford: Oxford University Press, 1938), p. 2; Mark Rose, *Heroic Love* (Cambridge, Mass.: Harvard University Press, 1968), observes that "the glamor of love melancholy was in part the result of a curious semantic confusion. Early

Latin translators of Greek manuscripts connected the Greek word *eros* with the Latin words *herus* and *heros*, and consequently believed that their authors meant to associate love with heroism and magnanimity" (pp. 11–12).

25 Ernst Cassirer, *The Individual and the Cosmos in Renaissance Philosophy*, trans. Mario Domandi (Philadelphia: University of Pennsylvania Press, 1972), pp. 132, 134.

26 Richard C. McCoy, *Sir Philip Sidney: Rebellion in Arcadia* (New Brunswick: Rutgers University Press, 1979), chap. 3.

27 Such anxiety is more openly expressed in Sidney's *Defence of the Earl of Leicester*, in *Miscellaneous Prose of Sir Philip Sidney*, ed. Katherine Duncan-Jones and Jan Van Dorsten (Oxford: Clarendon Press, 1973), pp. 129–141, which is both a reply to an anonymous libel of his uncle that appeared in 1584, and a calculated defense of Sidney's own hereditary status. The latter function is hardly concealed by the rather awkward disclaimer that "[I] truly am glad to have cause to set forth the nobility of that blood whereof I am descended, which, but upon so just cause, without vainglory could not have been uttered" (p. 134).

28 Jerome Mazzaro, *Transformations in the Renaissance Lyric* (Ithaca: Cornell University Press, 1970), p. 145.

29 Kalstone, *Sidney's Poetry*, p. 150.

30 See McCoy, *Sir Philip Sidney: Rebellion in Arcadia*, passim; Arthur Marotti, " 'Love Is Not Love': Elizabethan Sonnet Sequences and the Social Order," *English Literary History*, 49 (1982), 396–428; I have benefited, too, from an unpublished paper by Ann Rosalind Jones and Peter Stallybrass, "Courtship and Courtiership: The Politics of *Astrophil and Stella*"; also relevant here, though not focusing primarily on *Astrophil and Stella*, are Louis Adrian Montrose, "Celebration and Insinuation: Sir Philip Sidney and the Motives of Elizabethan Courtship," *Renaissance Drama*, N.S. 8 (1977), 3–35, and Ferguson, "Sidney's *A Defense of Poetry*," pp. 84–85.

31 Ralph Cohen, "Innovation and Variation: Literary Change and Georgic Poetry," in *Literature and History*, Clark Library Papers by Cohen and Murray Krieger (Los Angeles: William Andrews Clark Memorial Library, 1974), p. 6, argues that the first criterion that distinguishes innovation from imitation (as variation) "is that the poets, and, subsequently, the contemporaneous critics that comment upon them *identify* the innovations." Jonson's reference, as early as 1600, to "my strange poems," discussed below, is a case in point.

32 "Spencer, in affecting the Ancients, writ no language: Yet I would have him read for his matter; but as Vergil read Ennius" (*Discoveries*, lines 1806–8).

33 Stephen Toulmin and June Goodfield, *The Discovery of Time* (New York: Harper and Row, 1965), p. 74. On Jonson's "bias against change," see Jonas Barish, *The Antitheatrical Prejudice* (Berkeley: University of California Press, 1981), pp. 143–146.

34 Auerbach, *Mimesis*, pp. 321, 389–390; Arthur O. Lovejoy. "The Parallel of Deism and Classicism," in his *Essays in the History of Ideas* (Baltimore: Johns Hopkins Press, 1948), pp. 79–98. Cf. Bakhtin, *Dialogic Imagination*, p. 325; Sartre, *What Is Literature?* pp. 85–86; and the sections on classical discourse in Roland Barthes's *Writing Degree Zero*, trans. Annette Lavers and Colin Smith (1953; trans. London: Cape, 1967). In an earlier version of the present discussion, Don E. Wayne, "Mediation and Contestation: English Classicism from Sidney to Jonson," *Criticism*, 25, No. 3 (1983), 211–237, I focus more emphatically on the limitations of these and other negative appraisals of classicism.

35 Jonson's ability to lay claim to such status owed much to the example of Sidney whose *Apology* or *Defence of Poetry* "is also a defense of the speaking subject" (Ferguson, "Sidney's *A Defence of Poetry*," p. 62).

36 Sartre, *What Is Literature?* pp. 75–76.

37 This distinction occurs frequently in Jonson. The last quoted phrase is from the dedication "To the Reader" which followed upon the failure in the theater of *The New Inn* (1629); see *H & S*, VI, 397. For a related discussion, see Barish, *Antitheatrical Prejudice*, pp. 132–154.

38 On the tendency, from the eleventh century onward, of the feudal aristocracy to lay more emphasis on hereditary dignity of birth, and on the Church's role in the development of ritual ceremonies that gave rise to the concept of "chivalry," see John B. Morrall, *The Medieval Imprint* (Harmondsworth: Penguin Books, 1970), pp. 107–114.

39 For a sociological analysis of the concurrence of elitist and egalitarian elements in the writings of Shakespeare and his contemporaries, see Arnold Hauser, *The Social History of Art* (1951; rpt. New York: Vintage Books, n.d.), II, 150 ff. Hauser sketches in broad strokes; but, on the whole, his discussion is balanced and informative, and some of his points are applicable to Jonson as well as Shakespeare.

40 *The Forrest*, XI, lines 21–30; cf. *Every Man in His Humor* (Quarto, 1601), II, ii, lines 1–34, and *Discoveries*, lines 30–32.

41 See *Mercury Vindicated from the Alchemists at Court* (1616), lines 176–215, in *Ben Jonson: The Complete Masques*, ed. Stephen Orgel (New Haven: Yale University Press, 1969), pp. 221–223.

42 Marotti, " 'Love Is Not Love,' " p. 418, cites earlier manifestations of the idea, in Spenser's commendatory sonnet to the translation of Nenna's *Nennio*, and as far back in English literature as Chaucer's Wife of Bath's Tale. See, too, the adages collected under the category of "Nobilitie" in Sir Thomas Elyot's *The Bankette of Sapience* (1534), facsimile rpt. in Elyot,

Four Political Treatises (Gainesville: Scholar's Facsimiles and Reprints, 1967), pp. 176–177. My point is not that the idea of nobility based on "merit" originates with Jonson, but that his manner of expressing it in the poem to Jephson is more direct and more personally contentious than the earlier instances which either dramatize the principle (as in the story told by Chaucer's Wife of Bath, or in the speeches of Marlowe's Tamburlaine) or present it in a more abstract, aphoristic mode (as in the abovementioned texts by Elyot and Spenser).

43 In Sidney's *Arcadia* (Bk. I, chap. 2), Kalander asserts: "I am no herald to enquire of mens pedegrees, it sufficeth me if I know their vertues . . ." (*Prose Works of Sir Philip Sidney*, I, 15). Both Curtis Brown Watson, *Shakespeare and the Renaissance Concept of Honor* (Princeton: Princeton University Press, 1960), p. 77, and James, *English Politics and the Concept of Honor, 1485–1642*, p. 64, take this statement too literally as an expression of Sidney's personal viewpoint; neither acknowledges the fictive context in which the assertion appears. In other respects, James's study is an exemplary account of how the concept of honor was modified under the Tudors to give "parity, or even priority, to virtue over lineage, learning over arms, and 'nobility dative' conferred by the state over hereditary nobility," a development in which the circle of Sir Philip Sidney played an important part (p. 59). But if Sidney did assert the priority of virtue over lineage, it was probably more a token of his didactic espousal of humanist ideas than a sign of indifference to the matter of ancestry (Watson, p. 78). William Harrison, a man of lower birth than Sidney but of apparently more conservative views, registers the same shift in values in his account of contemporary notions of gentility: "Gentlemen be those whom their race and blood, *or at the least their virtues*, do make noble and known" (my emphasis); see Harrison's *Description of England* (1587), ed. George Edelen (Ithaca: Cornell University Press, 1968), p. 113. It is significant that Harrison connects "virtues" to "race and blood" not by the inclusive conjunction *and* but by the mark of an alternative *or*, and that he adds the further qualifying phrase "at the least." The necessary connection of "virtues" with "race and blood" is thus attenuated by suggesting "virtues" as an alternative qualification for the title of gentleman. In comparison with Jonson's poem to Jephson, Sidney's pronouncement—if indeed it can be taken as an unqualified principle of Sidney's—is patronizing and in keeping with his position; and Harrison's statement has a peculiarly grudging tone that is explained, perhaps, by his ensuing description in sardonic and somewhat exaggerated terms of how a man of means might "for money have a coat of arms bestowed upon him by the heralds" (p. 114).

44 See James, *English Politics and The Concept of Honor, 1485–1642*, pp. 58–72.

45 Such conflict, and the revival of chivalry in which it was played out, would

seem to have little in common with the sort of competition we think of in connection with business and trade. But the English Renaissance court, unlike its medieval predecessors, was the sovereign machinery of an emerging nation-state in which the struggle for power among aristocratic factions was itself an aspect of early capitalist development. For an analysis of this situation, see Immanuel Wallerstein, *The Modern World System* (New York: Academic Press, 1974), pp. 256 ff.; also see Montrose, "Celebration and Insinuation," pp. 5–6, and Frank Whigham, "The Rhetoric of Elizabethan Suitors' Letters," *PMLA*, 96, No. 5 (1981), 864–882.

46 Edmund Wilson, "Morose Ben Jonson" (1948), rpt. in *Ben Jonson: A Collection of Critical Essays*, ed. Jonas A. Barish (Englewood Cliffs, N.J.: Prentice-Hall, 1963), pp. 60–74. A more balanced psychological assessment is that of E. Pearlman, "Ben Jonson: An Anatomy," *English Literary Renaissance*, 9, No. 3 (Autumn 1979), 364–394.

47 Sir Philip Sidney to Robert Sidney, 18 October 1580, Letter 42, *Prose Works of Sir Philip Sidney*, III, 132; *An Apology for Poetry*, p. 87; *Astrophil and Stella*, Sonnet 18.

48 With regard to the above remarks on Spenser, see Rosenberg, *Leicester, Patron of Letters*, p. 348; Daniel Javitch, *Poetry and Courtliness in Renaissance England* (Princeton: Princeton University Press, 1978), pp. 160–161; Richard Helgerson, "The Elizabethan Laureate: Self-Presentation and the Literary System," *English Literary History*, 46 (1979), 193–220. Puttenham writes: "Then forasmuch as [the poets] were the first observers of all naturall causes and effects in the things generable and corruptible, and from thence mounted up to search after the celestiall courses and influences, and yet penetrated further to know the divine essences and substances separate, as is said before, they were the first Astronomers and Philosophists and Metaphysics," in his *The Arte of English Poesie* (1589; facsimile rpt. Kent, Ohio: Kent State University Press, 1970), p. 25.

49 Hauser, *Social History of Art*, pp. 70–71.

50 On plagiarists and "poet-apes," see, e.g., *Epigrammes* LIII and LVI, and "To my worthy and honour'd Friend, Mr. George Chapman, on his Translation of Hesiod's Works, & Dayes," *Ungathered Verse* XXIII. I have discussed ambiguities in Jonson's praise of Donne and Beaumont in "Poetry and Power in Ben Jonson's *Epigrammes*," pp. 92–94.

51 In a similar fashion, Bacon writes in his essay "Of Ceremonies and Respects," *Essays or Counsels Civil and Moral* (1625): "But if a man mark it well, it is in praise and commendation of men as in gettings and gains: for the proverb is true, *That light gains make heavy purses*; for light gains come thick, whereas great come but now and then" (*Works*, VI, 500).

52 *OED* entries for "the Exchange" and "the Burse" indicate that the terms were first employed in this sense after the opening of the Royal Exchange in London, built by Sir Thomas Gresham in 1566.

53 *Ben Jonson: The Complete Poems*, ed. George Parfitt (Harmondsworth, Middlesex: Penguin Books, 1975), p. 554.

54 William Empson, "*Volpone*," *Hudson Review*, 21, No. 4 (Winter 1968–69), 654.

55 Sir Philip Sidney, *An Apology for Poetry*, p. 37.

56 Stone, *Crisis of the Aristocracy, 1558–1641*, p. 128.

57 Gervase Holles, *Memorials of the Holles Family 1493–1656*, ed. A. C. Wood, Camden Soc., 3d ser., 55 (London: Camden Society, 1937), p. 99.

58 Hobbes, *Leviathan* (1651), pp. 139, 151. On literary manifestations of the shift from status to contract as the basis of political obligation in England, see Wayne, "*Drama and Society in the Age of Jonson*: An Alternative View," pp. 103–129.

59 On the tensions inherent in Sidney's attitude toward the chivalric code of honor, see Hiram Haydn, *The Counter-Renaissance* (1950; rpt. New York: Grove Press, 1960), chap. 9; James, *English Politics and the Concept of Honor, 1485–1642*, pp. 68–72; McCoy, *Sir Philip Sidney*, pp. 182-183.

60 The *OED* entry for *conscience* is prefixed by the following note: "The word is etymologically, as its form shows, a noun of condition or function, like *science*, *prescience*, *intelligence*, *prudence*, etc., and as such originally had no plural: a man or a people had *more* or *less* conscience. But in sense 4 [i.e., the moral sense] it came gradually to be thought of as an individual entity, a member or organ of the mental system, of which each man possessed *one*, and thus it took *a* and *plural*. So *my conscience*, *your conscience*, was understood to mean no longer our respective shares or amounts of the common quality *conscience*, but to be two distinct individual *consciences*, mine and yours."

61 See, e.g., the analysis of Bacon's essay "Of Simulation and Dissimulation" (1625) in Fish, *Self-Consuming Artifacts*, pp. 101–108; as Fish has ably demonstrated, Bacon's essay is far more ambiguous than its confident opening indictment of dissimulation would suggest.

62 See the long passage beginning "*Language* most shewes a man: speake that I may see thee . . . ," in the *Discoveries*, lines 2031–2160, *H & S*, VIII, 625–629.

63 The point is made, though perhaps too forcefully, by Daniel C. Boughner, *The Devil's Disciple: Ben Jonson's Debt to Machiavelli* (New York: Philosophical Library, 1968), p. 148, who argues that "a strong tincture of Machiavellianism colors Jonson's anti-Machiavellian treatise" (p. 151).

64 Georg Lukács, *The Theory of the Novel*, trans. Anna Bostock (1920; trans. Cambridge, Mass.: M.I.T. Press, 1971), p. 29; Martin Heidegger, "Remembrance of the Poet," and "Hölderlin and the Essence of Poetry," both trans. by Douglas Scott and included in *Existence and Being*, 2d ed. (London: Vision Press, 1956), pp. 251–290, 293–315; John Crowe Ransom, "The Concrete Universal: Observations on the Understanding of Poetry," in his *Poems and Essays* (New York: Vintage Books, 1955), p. 170.

65 What Robert C. Elliott has said in *The Power of Satire: Magic, Ritual, Art* (Princeton: Princeton University Press, 1960), concerning the satirist's relation to society, can stand as a description of the underside to Jonson's work in general: "The pressure of his art works directly against the ostensibly conservative function which it is said to serve. . . .

"Society has doubtless been wise, in its old pragmatic way, to suspect the satirist. Whether he is an enchanter wielding the ambiguous power of magic, or whether he is a 'mere' poet, his relation to society will necessarily be problematic. He is of society in the sense that his art must be grounded in his experience as social man; but he must also be apart, as he struggles to achieve aesthetic distance. His practice is often sanative, as he proclaims; but it may be revolutionary in ways that society cannot possibly approve, and in ways that may not be clear even to the satirist" (pp. 274–275).

Appendix A: A Note on Deixis *in Descriptions of Penshurst*

1 On the concept of *deixis* in linguistic theory, see John Lyons, *Introduction to Theoretical Linguistics* (Cambridge: Cambridge University Press, 1968), pp. 275–281 and 413. In Aristotle's rhetoric, what is usually translated as the "demonstrative enthymeme" (an argument that "draws conclusions from admitted premises") is actually called by Aristotle *deiktikon enthumema*; see *The "Art" of Rhetoric*, trans. John Henry Freese (Cambridge, Mass.: Harvard University Press, 1959), pp. 294–295; cf. Kenneth Burke's discussion of "demonstrative" or "epideictic" rhetoric in his *A Rhetoric of Motives* (1950; rpt. in a single volume with *A Grammar of Motives*, Cleveland: Meridian Books, 1962), pp. 594–596.

2 Eco, *A Theory of Semiotics*, p. 116.

3 "Penshurst Place: 600 Years of History." (See Chap. 1, n. 18 above.)

INDEX

Numbers in italics refer to pages on which illustrations appear.

DESIGNED BY BRUCE GORE
COMPOSED BY PIED TYPER
LINCOLN, NEBRASKA
MANUFACTURED BY CUSHING-MALLOY, INC.
ANN ARBOR, MICHIGAN
TEXT IS SET IN CALEDONIA, DISPLAY LINES IN TIMES ROMAN

Library of Congress Cataloging in Publication Data

Wayne, Don E., 1941–
Penshurst: the semiotics of place and the poetics of history.

Includes bibliographical references and index.
1. Jonson, Ben, 1573?–1637. To Penshurst. 2. Penshurst Place (Kent) 3. Semiotics and literature. I. Title.
PR2625.T63W39 1984 821′.3 83-40273
ISBN 0-299-09770-6